Knowledge, Innovation and Economy

To
Halina,
Jakub, and Mateusz

Knowledge, Innovation and Economy

An Evolutionary Exploration

Witold Kwaśnicki

Technical University of Wrocław
Wrocław, Poland

Edward Elgar
Cheltenham, UK • Brookfield, US

© Witold Kwaśnicki, 1996

Published by
Edward Elgar Publishing Limited
8 Landsdown Place
Cheltenham
Glos GL50 2HU
UK

Edward Elgar Publishing Company
Old Post Road
Brookfield
Vermont 05036
US

British Library Cataloguing in Publication Data
Kwasnicki, Witold
  Knowledge, Innovation and Economy:
  Evolutionary Exploration
  I. Title
  330.1

Library of Congress Cataloguing in Publication Data
Kwasnicki, Witold, 1952–
    Knowledge, innovation and economy: an evolutionary exploration /
Witold Kwasnicki
    Includes bibliographical references and index.
    1. Evolutionary economics. I. Title
HB97.3.K93   1996
330—dc20   95–31938
                                                            CIP

ISBN 1 85898 349 5

Printed and bound in Great Britain by
Hartnolls Limited, Bodmin, Cornwall

Contents

List of Tables   vii
List of Figures   viii

Preface   xi

Part I
Knowledge and Evolution

1. Conventionalism in Socio-economic Analysis   3
   Methodology of Research of Contemporary Physics   5
   Conventionalism in Economics – Methodological Proposition   13

2. Knowledge Development as an Evolutionary Process   16
   Development of Knowledge and Biological Evolution   17
   Structure of the Hereditary Information   23
   Mode of Development   24
   Mechanisms of Fulguration of Archetypes   25

3. Taxonomy of Knowledge   30
   Epigenetic Paragons   33
   Image of the World   35
   Image of the Society   44
   Image of the Economy   46
   Epistechne   51
   Paradigm   67

Part II
Economics and Evolution

4. Neoclassical and Evolutionary Perspectives in Economics   71
   Optimization and Equilibrium   76
   Knowledge   77
   Concept of Competing Firms   78
   Perception of Time   80
   Random Factors   81

5. The Evolutionary Model of Industry Development   83
   Firms' Decisions   86
   Firms' Entry   93

Competition of Products in the Market   94

6. Economic Analysis and the Model   101
   How are Prices Set?   102
   Long- and Short-term Objectives in the Decision-making Process   110
   Concentration of Industry   115
   The Cost of Production and the Productivity of Capital   122
   Economies of Scale   127
   Demand Function   135
   Economy is a Dynamic System   141
   Bounded Rationality and Fluctuations in Industry Development   147

7. Innovation and Economic Development   162
   Search Process   165
   Differentiation and Competition of Products   168
   Innovation – Groping in the Dark   171
   Innovation Regimes   180
   Entry and the Industry Structure   188

8. Chance and Necessity in Economic Development   195

Appendix
Basic Values of the Model Parameters   203

Bibliography   207

Index   217

Tables

3.1. Waves of development; the Western hemisphere   33

6.1. Long- and short-term objectives (inflexible strategy);
characteristics in the years 20–100   113

6.2. Flexible strategies in the decision-making process;
characteristics in the years 20–100   114

6.3. Industry concentration; global characteristics at the equilibrium
state   117

6.4. Concentration of the market. Non-uniform firms' size
distribution   120

6.5. The cost ratio; constant market size, uniform firms' size
distribution   123

6.6. The cost ratio ($\gamma = 1\%$)   125

6.7. Economies of scale – equilibrium values ($a = 5$, $b = 0$)   129

6.8. Computability and average profit (in the period 60–100)   154

6.9. The basic Fourier periods (in years)   157

7.1. The innovation strategies   172

7.2. Price and industry structure in different innovation regimes   181

7.3. The 'no entry–free entry' experiment   191

Figures

2.1. Diagram of evolution – biology   21
2.2. Diagram of evolution – knowledge development coupled with biological evolution   22
5.1. General structure of the evolutionary industrial model   84
5.2. Causal relationships in the evolutionary industrial model   85
6.1. Neoclassical supply and demand functions   101
6.2. Coordinates of the parameters for the largest firms; the markup PSP ((a) and (c)), the O_1 PSP ((b) and (d))   106
6.3. Price to cost ratio for the O_1 and the markup PSPs, and for two values of the unit cost of production   107
6.4. Profit to capital ((a), (c), (e)) and the global production ((b), (d), (f)); the O_1 and the markup PSPs   109
6.5. Profit to capital ratio for different relative importance of long- and short-term firms' objectives   111
6.6. Investment to capital ratio for different relative importance of long- and short-term firms' objectives   112
6.7. Fluctuations of the profit to capital ratio – perfect competition, small ρ and δ 119
6.8. Free entry and the penetration time   121
6.9. The cost ratio   124
6.10. Profit to sales ratio for expanding market   125
6.11. Economies of scale – six modes of development   128
6.12. Economies of scale and the industry concentration   130
6.13. Profit/capital ratio for different modes of economies of scale   132
6.14. Economies of scale – price, price margin and unit costs of production   133
6.15. Economies of scale – global production, firm's production and profit to capital ratio   134
6.16. Growth of the market size   137
6.17. Wave-like development for negative growth rate and small industry concentration   138
6.18. Demand function; price elasticity (β)   139
6.19. Long-run development and the disruptive unit cost of production   143
6.20. Long-run profit and random fluctuations of the unit cost of production   144
6.21. Long-run profit and random fluctuations of the market size   145
6.22. Long-run profit and innovation   147

6.23. Profit to capital ratio; SV and Π strategies and two levels of computability: λ = 6 and λ = 10 (*L* = 10)   151
6.24. Profit to capital ratio for the selected values of firms' computability   152
6.25. Investment to capital ratio for diversified firms' computability   153
6.26. Investment to capital ratio for small deviations of the firms' computability   155
6.27. Spectral density of profit/capital (a), and investment/capital ratios (b)   156
6.28. Profit/capital and investment/capital ratios; diversified firms' computability; pure competition   158
6.29. Profit/capital and investment/capital ratios; diversified firms' computability; oligopoly   159
7.1. Trajectories of development for different modes of the search process   173
7.2. Technical competitiveness in the two runs: mutation and imitation (left), and mutation, imitation and recrudescence (right)   178
7.3. Price and its diversity in two runs: mutation and imitation (left), and mutation, imitation and recrudescence (right)   179
7.4. Innovation regimes: variable cost of production (a), technical competitiveness (b) and productivity of capital (c)   182
7.5. Price for different innovation regimes: cost (a), technical performance (b) and productivity (c)   182
7.6. Variable cost of production (a), technical competitiveness (b) and productivity of capital (c) in the 'complex' regime   186
7.7. The supply/demand ratio for different innovation regimes   187
7.8. Cost of production (a), technical competitiveness (b) and productivity of capital (c) in the 'no entry–free entry' experiment   189
7.9. Number of firms in the 'no entry–free entry' experiment (upper and lower charts respectively)   190
7.10. Market shares of the eight largest firms in the 'no entry–free entry' experiment   192
7.11. Supply to demand ratio in the 'no entry–free entry' experiment (upper and lower charts respectively)   193
7.12. Price in the 'no entry –free entry' experiment (left and right charts respectively)   194
8.1. Trajectories of development and path-dependence   200

Preface

The evolutionary perspective in economic analysis has been gaining significance since at least the early 1950s. Many new books and papers in journals devoted to this not essentially new, but much refreshed view of economic analysis appeared in the last decades. The evolutionary perspective opposes in many aspects the neoclassical view of orthodox economics, but there are some indications that both mainstreams of economic analysis co-evolve and each pertains to the best of the antagonist.

I embarked on the research in evolutionary economics at the end of the 1980s. In the previous years, at the end of the 1970s and the beginning of the 1980s, I was engaged in general research on evolutionary processes, and particularly in developing the models of biological evolution of asexual, sexual-haploid and sexual-diploid populations. Some results were published but most of them are still unpublished, mainly due to my fascination with evolutionary perspective in economic analysis and preoccupation in that field in the last years. In February 1988 I was invited by Luc Soete and Gerald Silverberg to participate in the opening workshop of a new institute – Maastricht Economic Research Institute on Innovation and Technology, MERIT. I presented the paper on the role of diversity in evolutionary processes; the economic problems tackled in the workshop's papers were essentially new to me. These few days are marked in my memories as my great personal economic education. My trip back to Poland, lasting over 15 hours, allowed me to think the whole matter over. I was waiting for the train in Köln for about two hours, and at that time the first, very unclear, idea on the possibility of applying my biological model to the analysis of economic problems came to me. During the long trip on the train from Köln to Wrocław I worked out the details of the model, and within the next year I programmed the model and made the first, very promising computer simulations. After my return to Wrocław I read very carefully the book by Richard Nelson and Sidney Winter on *An Evolutionary Theory of Economic Change*, which I had just got from Richard Nelson. No doubt that work of Nelson and Winter essentially shaped my stream of thoughts and helped me to see the junction between evolutionary ideas in economic analysis and my earlier research on general properties of evolutionary processes. Discussion with Gerald Silverberg in the next year, when I visited MERIT in November, encouraged me to continue my efforts and further develop the model. In the next two years I was engaged in making 'cosmetic' improvements of the model to make its behaviour more closely reflect reality and to investigate the behaviour of the model under extreme simulation conditions. In 1992, I decided to publish the first results of the simulation of the model, as I considered them promising and interesting (Kwaśnicki and Kwaśnicka, 1992). As I understood my work, it is still far from being complete, but I think the present book constitutes a whole and may contribute to the ongoing discussion on evolutionary economics. The model of industry behaviour and its simulation results, presented in the second part of the book, form the main body of the text. But economy and economic analysis are parts of the wider socio-cultural process, so I consider it necessary to place the model in a wider perspective. The first part of the book is devoted to more general problems (methodology, knowledge development, and a general view on cultural and social evolution) and readers not interested in those matters may go directly to the second part, which is devoted to industrial dynamics problems. To make the book as short, and as comprehensive, as possible, all the chapters tackle only the most important aspects of the related subjects. In fact, some chapters demand more detailed and wider consideration. I hope that I will do this in the future, but I am convinced that at the present stage of the model's development it is enough to mark only the main thesis and general problems. Physics is frequently considered as the ideal and normative pattern of science. On the basis of this supposition many economists use the matured mathematical tools of physics and apply them almost directly in their description of the behaviour of social and economic systems. But social systems have their own peculiarities and it seems unjustifiable to make a direct application of the formal apparatus of physics to describe such diversified entities of human processes. I believe that economists may learn a lot from physicists, not through applying directly their formal apparatus but by applying their matured methodology of research to the study of social phenomena. So, in the first chapter I present a short description of conventionalism, which is in my opinion the prevailing methodology of research of contemporary physics and which seems to me to be very useful for economists and other social scientists. At the end of the chapter, I make a plea for the proper application of biological metaphor in evolutionary economics and the achievements of contemporary physics. Physics is the most developed of all contemporary sciences, especially if we think about the elaborated methodology of research, philosophical background and mathematics used. The other truth is that proper use of biological metaphors may be intellectually very fruitful. It seems that future development of theoretical economics should be based on a balanced application of current achievements of physics and biology, with concurrent efforts by economists to work out proper mathematical tools applicable to the description of economic phenomena.

I believe that all evolutionary processes, starting from biological evolution, through cultural, social and technological evolutions, and ending in the development of our personal knowledge, have common, general properties. Knowledge is the basis for any human action and the evolution of ideas may be considered as the essence of human evolution. We may discuss much about the material evolution related to, for example, evolution of tools, technological evolution, and so on. But all material, tangible evolutions are based first of all on the evolution of ideas, that is, on our personal knowledge. In the second chapter, I present my personal view on knowledge development as an evolutionary process. Parallels, similarities and discrepancies between the knowledge development and the biological evolution are presented in this chapter.

Economy and economic analysis are parts of the general process of knowledge development and the evolution of ideas. Cultural and social evolutions influence the development of economy as well as the development of economics, both being significant elements in social sciences. Therefore in the next chapter, I present a view on modes of knowledge development and I propose the so-called taxonomy of knowledge. I see the development of a human system as a set of waves of different frequencies. I am far from any deterministic vision of historical development and I greatly oppose the view that 'history repeats' itself. Development of any part of human activity is a unique, historical process, but it seems possible to point out a number of problems and questions faced by, and to be solved and answered by, any civilization and any society. The fundamental problems and questions have remained constant in a few thousand years' history of human civilizations but the solutions and answers differ. In this chapter, a list of some categories of problems and questions related to cultural, social, economic and research spheres of human activity are stated. I do not pretend that the proposed categories exhaust all the questions which are troubling human beings, but I think that they are the most important ones. Human beings are conservative in their nature, and all the time they try to cling on to prevailing explanations, but they also have free will and an internal force impelling them to search for alternative answers if problems arise. If faced by obstacles, which are not possible to overcome on the basis of an existing set of answers and currently used routines, we try to modify the answers to reach our ends. It is much easier to modify the answers related to our almost everyday problems than those related to, for example, our worldview, or ideology. This is one of the reasons for diversified waves of development related to different spheres of human activity. The longest waves are related to cultural development (or civilization, as some historians call them); within each cultural cycle we observe a few cycles related to the social (political) system, and within a social cycle a few cycles related to economic organization, and so on up to the modes of research (paradigms). The proposition put forward in this chapter needs further separate and thorough elaboration; here I present it mainly to point out that even if we discuss some specific economic problem, for example, industry organization, all the time we ought to keep in mind that this specific problem is a part of the more general evolutionary process.

To understand the proposition of the evolutionary view of industrial dynamics it seems profitable to consider the main differences between the two main perspectives in economic thinking which prevailed and competed in economic analysis in the last decade. So the second part starts with the chapter in which a short characterization of neoclassical and evolutionary perspectives in economic analysis is presented. To make the arguments of both perspectives more distinguishable the characteristics of both attitudes are greatly stylized. What is interesting is a kind of co-evolution of these two approaches which has been observed in recent years – neoclassical economists try to incorporate some evolutionary ideas into their theories, and vice versa some neoclassical ideas are included in evolutionary models.

The next four chapters deal with the proposed model of industrial evolution. There is close interrelationship between the model of industrial evolution and the general model of knowledge development presented in the first part of the book. In fact most ideas presented in the first part are adjusted to the specific circumstances of industrial development and are expressed in the more formal, mathematical way. What ought to be stressed is that, as usual in scientific research, the development of any model is not a linear process; on the contrary it is a highly iterative process going back and forth: from an idea, or hypothesis, expressed in a verbal form, next put in the form of an equation (or equations) and incorporated into the model, and finally back to the initial idea to modify (or to exclude) it. Frequently it occurs that a verbally expressed idea, which at first glance looked quite reasonable and very promising, when incorporated into the model turns out to be wrong – in the sense that the mathematical model which was satisfactory before the incorporation of that idea, generates quite unreasonable results after its inclusion. During the model's development it was frequently necessary to modify the initial idea or even to throw it away. So in fact the verbal model of evolution presented in the first part of the work and the simulation model of industrial evolution presented in the second part were developed in parallel, reciprocally influencing each other. Not going into details, I would like briefly to express my personal approach to the research – we may have a lot of nice looking ideas, which when written down give the impression of being very reasonable and quite coherent, but to check that coherence we ought to try to express those ideas in more or less qualitative, mathematical (or simulation) models and next, through investigation of the dynamics of the model, study whether all those hypotheses incorporated into the model give reasonable results. If so, we are reassured that our thinking is going in the right direction.

The basic model, presented in Chapter 5, embraces only an 'economic' part of industrial process, that is, without a research process causing the emergence of innovation. A simulation study of the basic model, presented in the succeeding chapter, aims to show similarities and dissimilarities between the model's behaviour and the classical, well-known modes of development of real processes. As Nicholas Kaldor (1961) writes:

Any theory must necessary be based on abstraction; but the type of abstraction chosen cannot be decided in a vacuum: it must be appropriate to characteristic features of economic process as recorded by experience. Hence the theorist, in choosing a particular theoretical approach, ought to start off with a summary of facts which he regards as relevant to his problem. Since facts, as recorded by statisticians, are always subject to numerous snags and qualifications, and for that reason are incapable of being accurately summarized, the theorist, in my view, should be free to start off with a 'stylised' view of facts – i.e. concentrate on broad tendencies, ignoring individual details, and proceed on the 'as if' method, i.e. construct a hypothesis that could account for these 'stylised facts' without necessary committing himself to the historical accuracy, or sufficiency, of the facts or tendencies this summarized.

Following his proposition I start off with seven important 'stylised facts', namely:

- for a given market, the margin of price and firms' profit increase with the concentration of industry (for example, from perfect competition, through oligopoly, duopoly, and ending with monopoly);
- there is a specific relationship between economies of scale and an industry concentration, namely the larger the economies of scale the greater industry concentration;
- 'the capital/labour ratio is rising more or less in proportion to productivity, and it is highest amongst the richest nations and lowest among the poorest, the capital/output ratio is much the same as between poor and rich countries – it is no higher in America ... than it is in India'(Kaldor, 1985, p. 67). Kaldor calls it 'one of the best established "stylised facts" of capitalist development';
- in the presence of innovation, there is no uniform price for all products sold on the market but the great diversity of price is observed;
- emergence of innovation leads to temporal monopoly of the pioneer firm; at the first phase after innovation introduction the monopoly firm gains extra profit that disappears in time, when competitors imitate the innovation;
- skewed distributions of business firms' size and their long-term stability is the well established 'stylised facts' of industrial demography; size distributions of firms of real industries are very similar ('look like') to Pareto, Yule, or log normal distributions;
- industrial development is a unique historical process in which path-dependence and cumulative causation play an important role.

Some new insights into industrial development are also provided in chapter 4, for example, (1) the invariability of industry behaviour for a constant value of the factor equal to multiplication of unit cost of production and productivity of capital (so-called cost ratio), (2) the roles of long-term and short-term objectives of a firm, or (3) observations on the emergence of fluctuations in industrial development.

An evolutionary part of the model related to the search process for innovation is included in the basic model and presented in Chapter 7. Mechanisms of search for innovation seem to be the common property of all evolutionary processes, and in fact this part of the industrial model is 'borrowed' from my former model of biological evolution. It is reflected also in the nomenclature used, such as mutation, recombination, and so on, so well known in biological models. Presented in this chapter, the results of the simulation of the model with an embedded search process expose the impact of the innovations on the modes of industry development.

The intriguing problems of contemporary economics related to cumulative causation and path-dependence are shortly discussed in the last chapter. The title of this chapter 'Chance and necessity ...' is clearly borrowed from the famous book of Jacques Monod.

According to the conventional principle of 'idealization and stepwise concretization' presented in Chapter 1, the model presented in the second part of the book may not be considered as the final entity. I treat the model as the first step to its further development.

Acknowledgements

I would like to express my thanks to my colleagues and co-workers of the Futures Research Center (where I started to work on this book) and of the Institute of Engineering Cybernetics of the Technical University of Wrocław (where I finished it) for creating a friendly and very stimulating atmosphere. Of many people to whom I am very grateful I would like especially to mention two names: Karol I. Pelc, whose advice and encouragement helped me to overcome problems and continue my work, and Wojciech Wróblewski, with whom I held long discussions, when still working at FRC, and whose many critical comments were extremely valuable to me.

PART I

Knowledge and Evolution

1. Conventionalism in Socio-economic Analysis

Since at least the end of the 19th century the principal aim of mainstream economics was to make economic analysis a 'hard science', similar to that of the natural sciences. It is not the aim of this short chapter to discuss the problem of the deficiencies of the mechanistic metaphor of classical physics and its extension into economics. The problem has been discussed thoroughly by many authors, for example, Georgescu-Roegen, 1971; Hodgson, 1993; Mirowski, 1989. I would like only to point out that instead of directly applying the formal apparatus of physics in economic analysis it is much more fruitful to apply the matured methodology of research worked out by physicists during the past hundreds of years, and combine that methodology with the evolutionary view of natural and social processes worked out by biologists and social scientists. Physics, the most spectacular of the natural sciences in the last four centuries, has frequently been considered as the most advanced of all natural sciences and as the ideal pattern for such 'hard science'. The general strategy to reach that goal in economics, and to a slightly lesser degree in other social sciences, was to apply a similar formal approach (that is, to use mathematical devices like those applied by physicists to describe the natural processes of material reality) to socio-economic sphere of human life. Economic processes have been described in terms of difference and differential equations. In accordance with the Newtonian paradigm underlying neoclassical theories, economic analysis was based on the pattern worked out in classical mechanics, by analogy to the mechanistic system (a planetary system, a machine, a clockwork device), that is, 'a closed autonomous system ruled by endogenous factors of a highly selective nature, self-regulating and moving to a determinate, predictable point of equilibrium' (Weisskopf, 1983).

But all the time, albeit in a minority, some economists tried to find alternative ways of development for economic analysis. The research efforts for such an alternative were intensified in the 1950s, when the first fissures appeared in the foundations of the neoclassical building. Herbert Simon (1959a) wrote straightforwardly: 'The social sciences have been accustomed to look for models in the most spectacular of the natural sciences. In economics, it has been common enough to admire Newtonian mechanics ... and to search for the economic equivalent of the laws of motion. But this is not the only model for science, and it seems, indeed, not to be the right one for our purposes.' The research programme based on the Walrasian approach declined, the difference–differential models have become more and more unrealistic. Defenders of the neoclassical programme claimed that discrepancies between the behaviour of models and the development of real processes are due to the wrong initial assumptions (axioms) on the basis of which the models are built.

There are some fundamental differences between the natural processes of material (physical) world and the social processes, so that the direct applications of formal approaches of physicists to describe the processes of social tissue would be impossible and irrelevant. The main differences relate to:

- Judgements of value and free will of human beings which lead to conscious and subconscious processes of choice. Decision-making processes observed only in the social sphere of life are made on the basis of our expectations, and our scale of values.
- In contrast to the situation of physicists, students of social processes are not able to make repetitive experiments (for example, in laboratories) of consciously created initial social conditions. The only source of information for social researchers are records of real processes of socio-economic development.[1]
- Since the times of Galileo and Kepler until the end of the 19th century the main axiom of physics was to deal only with measurable variables. All variables presented in the model should be well defined (so-called operationally defined) to make the quantitative measurement of each variable possible. This postulate seems to be impossible to fulfil in social sciences in general, and in economics in particular. At least up to now, we have not been able to make analogous physical devices to measure some essential variables describing the social phenomena. Our decisions are based on some qualitative evaluations of the past development and actual state of the art of our socio-economic environment. Therefore the models of socio-economic processes are a mixture of qualitative and quantitative variables as well as recurrent and non-recurrent events (Kwaśnicka and Kwaśnicki, 1984; Lendaris, 1980).

What I propose is to base economic analysis not on the formal achievements of physics, and on almost direct applications of the mathematical apparatus of physics to economics, but to base the

---

[1] Someone may say that natural scientists, for example, astronomers and cosmologists, are in a very similar situation in that they are also not able to make experiments, and that their main sources of information are unique observations of natural processes. It is only partly true; in fact their ability to make laboratory experiments in which they simulate conditions which, as they expect, occur or have occurred in natural processes in the Universe is much greater (for example, some nuclear processes of fusion expected to occur inside stars may be simulated in physicists' laboratories).

methodology of research of economic analysis on the matured methodology of physics – developed in the last 300 years and considerably modified by Einstein, Planck, Heisenberg, and many others in the first half of the 20th century. To do so it is necessary to discard a significant part of the formal apparatus of contemporary physics not directly applicable to economics and to work out a specific formal apparatus, more relevant to socio-economic processes. As Kenneth Boulding writes:

> one of the great opportunities ... for the next few decades is the development of a mathematics which is suitable to social systems, which the sort of 18th-century mathematics which we mostly use is not. The world is topological rather than numerical. We need non-Cartesian algebra as we need non-Euclidean geometry, where minus minus is not always plus, and where the bottom line is often an illusion. So there is a great deal to be done. (Boulding, 1991)

The computer simulation approach may be considered as one such alternative way to develop a more specific apparatus of economic analysis.[2] Discontinuities of development are natural phenomena observed in socio-economic processes, and in a sense, these discontinuities form the essence of socio-economic systems. To make the difference equations approach applicable in economic analysis, the assumption of continuity is frequently made. But the differential calculus breaks down if one tries to apply it to describe discontinuities of development, for example, in the opinion of Prigogine (1989) classical dynamics of stable dynamical systems is not suitable for models of human systems: 'The dynamics of unstable systems comes closer to the basic properties of socio-economic systems.' The search for alternative approaches of economic analysis goes in different directions, for example, applications of chaos theory, fuzzy sets theory, catastrophe theory and game theory, to name only a few.

The model should reflect reality as far as possible but should also be as simple as possible, mainly to enable its easy handling and quick comprehension.

METHODOLOGY OF RESEARCH OF CONTEMPORARY PHYSICS

John Stuart Mill, the leading theoretician of 19th-century inductionism, acknowledged that in some situations scientific laws are discovered not by

---

[2] Application of the computer simulation approach may be misused; it is very easy to make a simulation model so complicated that nobody except the builder of the model is able to comprehend and use it in the research. New formal apparatus should be very carefully designed and should be a rational combination of 'old' mathematics developed in physics and a pure simulation approach, frequently based on a far-reaching analogy of real mechanisms of development and the model.

using the method of induction but by the method of asserting hypotheses.
He wrote:

> An hypothesis is any suspicion which we make (either without actual evidence, or on
> evidence avowedly insufficient) in order to endeavour to deduce from it conclusions
> in accordance with facts which we know to be real, under the idea that, if the
> conclusions to which the hypothesis leads are known truths, the hypothesis itself either
> must be, or at least, is likely to be, true. ... An hypothesis being a mere suspicion, there
> are no other limits to hypotheses than those of human imagination. ... When Newton
> said, 'Hypotheses non fingo', he did not mean that he deprived himself of the facilities
> of investigation afforded by assuming in the first instance what he hoped ultimately to
> be able to prove. Without such assumptions, science could never have attained its
> present state; they are necessary steps in the progress to something more certain; and
> nearly everything which is now theory was once hypothesis. (Mill, 1950, pp. 261,
> 264–5)

In spite of the frequently expressed opinion, especially by philosophers
and researchers in former ages, no law of physics is an inductive
generalization of observed facts. Inductionism, as well as anti-inductionism,
assumes that each law of nature is a statement which can be evaluated as
true or false. But there is no such law which could be considered in
isolation; each law is part of a given theory. It is much more convenient to
assume that laws of nature are neither true nor false, but are inferred from
some conventions of using words. Different sets of laws represent different
modes of description of the experienced world. The crucial problem is not
the logic values of the laws but in what circumstances given sets of laws
(theories) represent the most efficient, fertile, didactic and instructive way
of describing the reality. From this point of view experiments are not the
only sources of data (information) on the basis of which laws are
formulated, and no single law is tested in them. If we choose between
alternative theories we do not evaluate any single assumption, law, or
conclusion which are parts of each theory. We try to build sub-criteria and
try to evaluate each alternative theory applying these sub-criteria. In the next
step of our evaluation process, subjective weights are attached to each
sub-criterion and on the basis of the general index thus constructed the
whole theory is evaluated. This general index helps us to find a final answer
to the general question: which theory do we prefer?[3] It seems that the most
important and the most popular sub-criteria are:

---

[3] This way of evaluation is not specific to science. Let us think about any evaluation, for
example, of some products just bought or given to us for testing; we do not evaluate any single
characteristic of the product or any detail of its construction, instead, besides the price, we take into
account such characteristics as: reliability, availability of service, efficiency and the exploitation
costs, convenience of use, aesthetic values, and so on, and on the basis of these partial criteria a
general index of performance is constructed.

1. *correctness*, that is, consequences of the theory ought to be very close to the results of experiments and/or observations;
2. *consistency* – the theory ought to be consistent not only internally but also with other commonly accepted theories used to describe similar or related phenomena;
3. *universality* – consequences of the theory ought not to be confined to individual cases, as intended at the initial stages of the theory development;
4. *simplicity* – the theory ought to create order in the formerly isolated phenomena; some evaluations based on individual feelings of harmony and beauty are also taken into account in this partial evaluation;
5. *fecundity* – the theory ought to throw new light on well-known phenomena; it ought to be the generator of new discoveries. This criterion is especially important for active scientists who at some stages of their development accept a theory with poor evaluations based on any other criteria but see great opportunities for further development of the approach, or the possibility of applying the theory to particular research problems;
6. *usefulness* – this practical criterion dominates frequently in sciences, being very close to engineering and industry.

It does not mean that the list is complete, some individuals may apply different criteria, but as was said, the above six criteria are historically justifiable. They have been frequently mentioned by researchers since the times of ancient Greece, although weights (importance) ascribed to each criterion were different in different historical periods, and even are different for different scientific communities.

The essential aim of making an experiment is to illustrate the power of a given theory. If an experiment gives positive results the only statement drawn from it is that of confirmation of the usefulness of a given set of hypotheses, laws, ideas and concepts to a proper description of a given part of reality. The negative result of an experiment proves only that the proposed way of describing the reality is somewhat wrong but is not sufficient to refute this theory. In most cases the negative result of an experiment is an incentive to make modifications to the assumed hypotheses. The opinion that no single, isolated law is tested in experiments, but rather the whole theory is evaluated, was expressed by Duhem (1914; see also Quine, 1953). Results of experiments do not indicate clearly which part of the theory should be changed or refuted, and which should stay unchanged. The necessary changes are made by the researcher on the basis of his (or her) intuition and experience, and therefore frequently the changes are also unsatisfactory in the succeeding experiments. The process of fitting the theory to the experimental results and observations is, to a great degree, an interactive process. Frequently, during some stages of the development of a model (theory), the researcher does not consider some empirical fact and makes some arbitrary decisions on the shape of the theory; the only constraints are logical ones, for example, the statements of the theory must not be contradictory.

At the end of the last century, Pierre Duhem (1894) published some results from his observations of research processes in physics. His main theses are still valid, even reinforced by the history of ideas in the 20th century. The main theses of Duhem may be summarized as follows:

1. Experiments made by physicists are never systematic and scrupulous observations of phenomena; they are their theoretical interpretations. Contrary to common understanding, practical facts (for example, an indication of experimental instrument) are immediately translated into a language of theoretical facts. The researcher plays an active role in the process of collecting and verifying the facts. A classification of facts is the personal activity of each researcher, and the prospect of finding analogies and proper relations between different facts essentially depends on the personal skills of the researcher.

2. Research experiments (in contrast to didactic experiments and experiments related to the practical applications of physics) are always induced (provoked) by existing problems, formulated within the relevant theories. Therefore theories are ahead of experiments and observations. Observations and experiments do not lead consciously to discoveries and theories, but rather are the tools of their verification. Any experiment is always an interpretation of a given phenomenon, but also the results of experiments allow correction and improvement of theoretical interpretations of that phenomenon.

3. Laws of physics are never true or false, they are always only approximations. 'Physics does not know absolute truths' (Duhem, 1894, p. 228).

4. Physics has to use mathematical apparatus to bring order to 'numerous and intertwined facts, and within abundant laws composing intricate chaos' (Duhem, 1894, p. 184), but in essence it is an experimental science. Physicists verify whole theories, not single statements (Duhem, 1894, pp. 187–8).

5. There is no possibility of making *experimentum crucis*, that is, there is no possibility of stating on the basis of experimental results that a hypothesis is the absolute truth; there is no possibility of alleging that all possible hypotheses related to some group of phenomena have been exhausted (Duhem, 1894, p. 194).

In 1891 Poincaré proposed the term 'convention' as the name for a specific kind of demarcation statement, namely 'disguised definitions'. In his opinion: 'Axioms of geometry are neither synthetic statements *a priori*, nor synthetic empirical statements, they are disguised definitions [*les définitions déguisées*] – or conventions' (Poincaré, 1891).

Conventions are in a sense rigorously true statements (*rigoureusements vrais*). Decisions concerning terminology are the sources of their truth. Convention does not say anything about the real world. Convention is 'neither truth, nor untruth, it is convenient' (Poincaré, 1935, p. 239). Relevant conventions are chosen not entirely arbitrarily; they are controlled mainly by the results of ongoing experiments.[4]

Different formulations of the laws of classical mechanics are in reality definitions and not empirical statements, for example, the second law of Newton in the form proposed by Kirchhoff that 'a force is proportional to a mass multiplied by an acceleration' is not in fact empirical but became a convention. The certainty of this law flows from our will, we treat it as an agreement – a convention (Poincaré, 1925, p. 122).

Formulation of any law, even the most exact one, is always incomplete. Complete formulation should contain the enumeration of all antecedents followed by the consequent. Fulfilment of this requirement is not possible in practice. It is not possible to exclude the fact that all parts of the universe influence, more or less, the phenomenon under consideration. But even if it were possible to enumerate all antecedents, the number of these conditions appears to be so large that it would be almost impossible to fulfil them at any moment (Poincaré, 1925, p. 249). All laws are a kind of approximation or idealization of reality. Has anybody made the experiment in which no force acts on the mass? If not, then why do we consider such a case in one of Newton's laws?

Theory in physics, in Duhem's understanding, is 'a system of mathematical statements deduced from a relatively small number of principles, the main aim of which is to represent (symbolize) – as simple, and complete and exact, as possible – some set of empirical regularities [*les lois expérimentales*]' (Duhem, 1883, p. 24). Each theory constitutes a system, that is, it is a set of all statements containing all logical consequences. Duhem was aware that this set also comprises statements which had not yet been formulated. 'It is possible to deduce frequently from a physical theory an expression which is not an observed regularity [*une loi observé*] but observable regularity [*une loi observable*]' (Duhem, 1914, p. 450). Duhem did not use Poincaré's term, convention; instead he used to speak about principles, or axioms, or sometimes he called them hypotheses. 'Principles may be called hypotheses in an etymological sense because they are the true foundations of the theory' (Duhem, 1914, p. 25).

---

[4] 'What's in a name? that which we call a rose; By any other name would smell as sweet' William Shakespeare (1564–1616) *Romeo and Juliet*, a. II, 2. 'Name is a guest of reality' Zhuang-zi (Czuang Tsy), (369–286 BC).

In the opinion of Duhem, as for Poincaré, hypotheses or even whole theories may be constructed quite arbitrarily. During the process of a theory construction a physicist may not consider some empirical facts – he is allowed 'to choose a way which suits him' (Duhem, 1883, p. 313). But he is not allowed to build the theory on a foundation of contradictory hypotheses (Duhem, 1914, pp. 25 and 355).

A theory in the process of construction has to be immediately confronted with empirical facts (results of experiments and observations). Only on the basis of such a confrontation may theory reach a physical (empirical) sense (Duhem, 1914, p. 314). The agreement of the theory with experimental results is the only criterion of truth (Duhem, 1914, p. 26). It is worth mentioning once more that no single hypothesis should be verified alone, outside the system to which it belongs. But whole theories, perceived as a system, are empirically verified (Duhem, 1914, p. 327).

Expressions, abstract and symbolic terms are related to real, directly observable objects, but theoretical properties or some relations between the objects are not related to directly observable relationships between these objects. Symbolic terms relate solely to properties and relations of fictional objects. Fictional objects constitute some idealization of reality, an idealization of concrete objects; they were referred to by Duhem as 'schemes', or 'mental entities' (*éstre de raison*, Duhem, 1914, pp. 263–9). All physical laws expressed as statements with abstract-symbolic terms are called by Duhem symbolic relations (*une relation symbolique*). 'Physical law is a symbolic relation the application of which to concrete reality [*à la réalité concrète*] requires knowledge and acceptance of the whole theory' (Duhem, 1914, p. 254).

Schemes, or mental entities are constructed to represent real objects. Carrying out research on properties of gases, physicists do not deal directly with concrete gas, but with some 'scheme of gas' (Duhem, 1914, p. 266). Considering some properties of a specific gas, e.g., oxygen, on the basis of the general scheme of gas, the particular scheme of the gas is constructed. Oxygen may be treated as an ideal liquid, studied by scientists, with a certain density, temperature, and pressure. The relation between these three properties is established and expressed by some well-understood equation. For some period of time this 'scheme of oxygen' was considered to be adequate to describing the properties of real gas. But later this scheme was considered as 'too simple and incomplete to depict properties of real gas'. The old scheme was replaced by a new one with the inclusion of its dielectric properties (Duhem, 1914, p. 264). It also happens that in some situations the new scheme, or mental entity, is still inadequate and it is necessary to replace it by a more complicated and more complete scheme. In general, no scheme, no mental entity can be, and is, perfect. Physicists cannot use any decisive schemes mainly because all real objects, even the simplest one, may be characterized in manifold, diversified ways. So, the construction of any scheme should be treated as an attempt to extract specific properties of a given object which, from the point of view of research, are considered as especially important. Physicists focus their attention on real, concrete objects, but to do so it is necessary to make some idealizations. Real objects are examined indirectly through the examination of some schemes or mental entities. To make such an examination physicists use specific mathematical, formal apparatus.

Abstract-symbolic terms, such as mass, temperature and pressure, refer to some real and concrete objects, but not only to them. They also refer to idealized properties of these objects, that is, to schemes or mental entities constructed to represent relevant objects of the material world.

Such theoretical terms contain abstract meanings similar to spontaneous abstraction observed in common parlance, such as 'horse', 'tree', or 'white', 'colourful'. But in contrast to words used in common parlance, the terms of schemes are not only abstract but also symbolic (i.e. theoretical). The meaning of such symbolic terms is given by relevant theory. The same word used to express some physical law changes its meaning, so the law may be accepted by a physicist accepting one theory and rejected by physicists accepting another theory (Duhem, 1914, p. 252). Some symbolic terms – such as 'ideal gas' or 'absolute temperature' – have no counterpart in concrete, real objects. They refer solely to the idealization of real objects and have only symbolic (i.e. theoretical) meaning. In this sense the physicists (not only of the 20th century but almost all renowned physicists of the last 400 years, beginning with Galileo, Descartes, Kepler and Newton) are very close to the basic assumptions of Plato's ontology. Werner Heisenberg (1979, p. 209), during the symposium in Athens in 1964, expressed the opinion that contemporary physics proclaimed itself in favour of Plato. Simplest units of matter are in essence not physical objects in the common understanding of this term. They are forms, ideas which may be unequivocally expressed only in the language of mathematics. A very similar opinion was expressed at the end of the 19th century by Heinrich Rudolf Hertz, whose methodological attitude was much closer to mechanicism than to Platonism. Looking at the 'history' of famous expressions (physical laws), one gets the impression that since their formulation they live their own life. They are more 'intelligent' than their creators and followers, in the sense that the expressions' consequences, as observed in their further development and application, are much larger than it was assumed and expected at the beginning.

Meanings of common parlance terms are cultivated and moulded unconsciously, in a spontaneous way; in contrast, meanings of theoretical terms (symbols, and abstract-symbolic terms) are worked out a during much more conscious, hard and long formation process closely connected with constructed physical theories. As an example Duhem (1914) uses a genesis and development of the theory of gravitation. He writes that to understand the essence of Newton's theory it is necessary to be aware of the slow transformations of the concept of gravitation over the centuries, starting from Greek science. A very similar opinion, but related to development of the theory of syphilis, may be found in the book by Ludwik Fleck (1980) on *Emergence and development of scientific fact.*[5] On the basis of the development of the concept (scientific fact) of syphilis since the end of the 15th century to the modern concept of the Wassermann reaction, Fleck analysed the historical and social context of 'every act of cognition'.

It may be said that Poincaré and, especially, Duhem, in their descriptions of the axiomatic and deductive system of theoretical physics proposed some specific method of research in physics, which may be called the method of *idealization, through abstraction, and stepwise concretization.* Physics, making efforts to construct a mathematical system to describe well-defined parts of the real world, meets different categories of phenomena (for example, friction between material bodies, resistance of air during the motion of a material body, electrical phenomena on the surface of a material body, and so on). Construction of a theory which includes all such phenomena is very complicated and in fact 'exceeds the limits of the human mind'. So to tackle such a complicated set of phenomena it is necessary to choose some easy-to-tackle method of endeavour. Thus the first step is to simplify the basic problem (for example, to discard all friction, resistance of movement) and to prepare a theoretical representation of such simplified reality, that is, to construct an outline, a framework. In the next stages of development the theory will be more and more 'complicated', more complex, through the sequential addition of all consciously discarded phenomena, but also through the addition of those phenomena which in fact have been discarded unconsciously but the existence of which has been recognized in the succeeding phases of the theory's development – as a result of new facts, new observations, development of related theories, or simply as a result of researchers' rethinking and reflections. The theory is also changed through the continuously ongoing process of confrontation of the theory and the results of numerous experiments.

A process of theory concretization through its succeeding modifications may be called the process of theory improvement, and it is an evolutionary process (Kwaśnicka and Kwaśnicki, 1986a, Kwaśnicki and Kwaśnicka, 1989). The more 'cultivated' and more correct the theory is, the more

---

[5] Nearly all epistemological considerations of development of science are based on the development of physics and astronomy (H. Poincaré, P. Duhem, K. Popper, Th.S. Kuhn, P.K. Fayerabend, A. Koyré, E. Nagel, I. Lakatos and W.V.O. Quine, to name only a few). Fleck's work departs from this general trend. First publication of Fleck's book was in 1935. He was an immunologist and biologist, and had drawn his epistemological conclusions on the basis of the development of medicine (history of a disease) and, what is interesting, many of his findings are very similar to those of Duhem, Kuhn, and others.

convinced we are that the logical order embedded in the theory reflects the ontological order of reality. Proper development of the theory allows us also to believe that relations between observable facts, as stated by the theory, reflect, closer and closer, the factual relations between real objects.

Conventionalism proposes a specific conception of scientific development. It does not postulate gradual development through the simple adding of actual results to the old 'truths', but it also does not postulate the radical replacement of old theories by the new one without acknowledging the possibility of incorporating earlier theories and knowledge into the ongoing advances in research.

There are two main aims of building a theory; first, it is a classification entity of observed phenomena and, related to this, leads to a better understanding of the mechanisms of development, and second, through the logical application of axioms and discovered laws the theory enables the prediction of non-observable, up to now, phenomena, or the clarification of some phenomena which previously have escaped our attention.

CONVENTIONALISM IN ECONOMICS – METHODOLOGICAL PROPOSITION

As we have already noted, the research efforts of economists since the end of the 19th century have been focused on making the economy a 'hard science', mainly through applying sophisticated mathematical apparatus similar to that used by classical physics. We do not deny great achievements of this research programme in understanding the mechanisms and processes of economic development, but the last few decades show that this programme has reached its limits. Many researchers emphasize the inefficiencies of this approach, even some kind of reaction against using a formal approach to describe economic development is observed and in many cases verbal models are preferred. It seems that economy as a science is in a period of transition from the domination of one research programme to the ensuing one – from mechanistic paradigm to, let us call it, evolutionary paradigm. Changes are going on in both 'camps' – neoclassical economists approve of some evolutionary ideas and try to incorporate them into their neoclassical models, but also evolutionary economists intensify their efforts to work out more adequate models and borrow some ideas from classical and neoclassical theories.

My proposition is closely related to the research tradition of evolutionary economists, that is, those who see economy as a historical process and seek an inspiration in the analogy of economic development to organic evolution. But it would not be good for theoretical economics to rely only on the biological metaphors and disregard efforts to be also the 'theoretical physics of social sciences'. Physics is the most mature of all contemporary sciences, especially if we think about the worked-out methodology of research, philosophical background, and mathematics used, but the other truth is that properly applied biological metaphor may be intellectually very fruitful, and may enhance the creative process. It seems that modern economic analysis ought to be based on balanced applications of current achievements of physics and biology, with concurrent efforts by economists to work out proper mathematical tools applicable to the description of economic phenomena.

Neither do I propose to utterly reject neoclassical economics; on the contrary, in the formal treatment of economic process and attempts to build formal (mathematical) models of economic development, all achievements of classical or neoclassical models ought to be adapted, but it is proposed that instead of making efforts to apply directly the formal apparatus of modern physics to economic analysis (even the most advanced one related to, for example, chaos theory, dissipative structures, game theory, nonlinear dynamics and unstable systems) economists should use as their base the methodology of research applied in physics, similar to that sketched out in the previous section. First of all the behaviour of economic models should be compared frequently with real development processes. A model can be some kind of normative device only after a thorough confrontation of the model with the reality.

What we observe in the modelling efforts of economic phenomena is the domination of relatively simple models whose function is to describe a single phenomenon (such as cyclical development, emergence of a specific structure of the market, chaotic development of market stock); only rarely are attempts made to describe a whole set of phenomena observed within a well-defined part of economic activity (such as industry and the stock market). There is no such tradition in orthodox economic analysis to cut off and isolate a fraction of reality and then to try to work out a succession of models of the realm using the above-mentioned approach based on the conventionalist principle of *idealization and stepwise concretization.*[6]

When constructing a model we should try to reflect in it some general mechanisms of economic development (the representation of real mechanisms in a model is not one to one, the projection is made in some more or less idealized form) and some properties observed in the real development should be the result of the co-working of the mechanisms built into the model. We may say that some well-known properties (for example, cyclical development, specific structure of the market) ought to be a kind of

---

[6] Although some individual efforts in this direction may be pointed out, for example, the work of Richard Nelson and Sidney Winter on their evolutionary model in the 1960s and 1970s (completed by Nelson and Winter, 1982), and, initiated in the middle of the 1970s, the work of Gunnar Eliasson and his team (for example, Eliasson, 1985) on the micro-to-macro model of the Swedish Economic System (MOSES).

by-product of our modelling efforts. Virtues of this approach are twofold. On the one hand, if we observe such (say, *classical*) properties in our model's behaviour we are confident that we are on the right track to imitate real mechanisms of development, and on the other hand, this confirmation suggests the particular conditions of the emergence of such properties, and enables us to understand better the real mechanisms of economic development. In the end we are able to evaluate the circumstances of emergence (or not) of some particular properties for different conditions of cooperation of the same general mechanisms of development. It is also possible to create some artificial conditions of cooperation of the built-in mechanisms, never (or rarely) observed in reality, and to notice how the economy would behave if such conditions were imposed (it is a situation similar to that of physicists who create some well-defined, sometimes artificial, conditions in their laboratory experiments).

My postulate is that we should think primarily about mechanisms of development and about the cooperation of these mechanisms, and not about the possibilities of describing some particular properties of economic development in a single or a relatively small number of differential or difference equations.

I believe that such a roughly outlined research programme in economic analysis, based on principles of conventionalism, and itself containing an evolutionary perspective, will lead to a more accurate description of economic reality and finally, as in physics, economic theory will consist of (1) experimental domain, (2) mathematical domain, and (3) conventional interpretation.

2. Knowledge Development as an Evolutionary Process

To understand the development of human systems, and economic development in particular, we should primarily try to understand the creative processes of human being, that is, the processes of the development of human knowledge on a personal level and the development of human knowledge as a historical process.

I propose to use biological analogy to build a model of knowledge development (Kwaśnicki, 1987; and Kwaśnicka and Kwaśnicki, 1986b, Kwaśnicki and Kwaśnicka, 1989a). The concept presented in this chapter constitutes the foundation for the evolutionary model of industry development presented in the following chapters.

The idea that the development of human knowledge is similar to biological evolution is not new; at the end of the 19th century Ludwig Boltzmann (Boda, 1955, pp. 106–7) wrote that thinking emerges and evolves in a similar way to biological organs. The analogy is seen by many contemporary researchers, for example, Lorenz (1977, p. 372) and Popper (1979), to mention only two. Karl Popper (1979, p. 261) writes that 'the growth of our knowledge is the result of a process resembling what Darwin called "natural selection"; that is, *the natural selection of hypotheses*: Our knowledge consists, at every moment, of those hypotheses which have shown their (comparative) fitness by surviving so far in their struggle for existence; a competitive struggle which eliminates those hypotheses which are unfit.'

The main aim of this chapter is to propose a far-reaching isomorphism between the individual knowledge of a man and a genome (genotype) of biological organism. Recognition of such isomorphism may be helpful in a better understanding of the mechanisms of knowledge development.

The emergence of radical innovations (breakthroughs, turning-points, whatever they may be called), such as new paradigms in knowledge development or new biological species, is one of the most interesting, and considered as fundamental for both processes (that is, knowledge development and biological evolution). The process of substituting one scientific theory for another is called by Motycka (1990) situation $T_1 - T_2$; T_1 and T_2 are two competing theories. Situation $T_1 - T_2$ is considered by Motycka as one of the most essential epistemological problems. Mechanisms of the emergence of such radical innovations are still unclear and some explanations are very controversial. I hope that the proposed isomorphism may shed a new light on this problem, and may suggest some common mechanisms of the emergence of such breakthroughs in human systems and in biological evolution.

The well-known expressions used to describe the process of emergence of radical novelty, such as *progress, development, evolution, genesis, heredity*, and so on, do not grasp the exact meaning of the true act of creation, that is, the emergence of a new system's properties which are not observed until the moment of creation and are not possible to predict in advance. Following Konrad Lorenz (1977), I propose to name this act of emergence of new, nonpredictable properties *fulguration*. To fulgurate conveys the sense of to flash, to glint, or to fulminate. The etymology of this word comes from the Latin *fulgur*, which means a flash of lightning, or a thunderbolt, and *fulguritus*, to strike by thunderbolt. Medieval theists and mystics coined the word *fulguratio* to name the act of creating something new, something that had never existed before. By using this word they probably intended to express the direct influence of the heavens. I use the term fulguration to designate the act of origin of a radical novelty in evolutionary processes, such as a new species or a new paradigm.

As has already been mentioned, the basis of development in every sphere of human activity is human knowledge, but the core of the development of human knowledge is the creative uneasiness of man, the inventor. What are the mechanisms of fulguration, mechanisms of inspiration, which lead to breakthroughs in science and technology? What are the factors, in the process of the development of science and technology, which accelerate the rate of cultural, economic and technological development?

DEVELOPMENT OF KNOWLEDGE AND BIOLOGICAL EVOLUTION

In our understanding, evolution is the specific process of a search for better solutions (types, ideas) by means of trial and error. A special, and distinguishing, feature of this process is the existence of two mechanisms – the generation of new types (ideas) and the selection of types. There is no doubt that the basic unit of evolution is an individual, for example, a technician or scientist – with his, or her, knowledge – as in biological evolution, where the basic unit is an organism with its genes (genotype).[1]

---

[1] Sometimes in order to make an analysis of the specific properties of evolutionary processes it is more convenient to assume other units of evolution, for example, products or firms, as in the approach of Nelson and Winter (1982), and Kwaśnicki and Kwaśnicka (1989a, 1992); some biologists postulate also that natural selection acts on species – to some extent it is justifiable if biological evolution is considered in a very long, palaeontological, perspective. Even if we do such aggregations, all the time we ought to keep in mind that they are 'unnatural' abstractions at the root of which rest more fundamental natural processes, inherently attributed to the individual (in human evolution) and the organism (in biological processes).

Many students of human invention processes point out that 'sources of invention' should be sought in the individual efforts of independent individuals but many others suggest that the times for individual inventors have already passed and attribute inventions to group efforts, especially in big corporations. Confusion is probably caused by a different understanding of the meaning of the adjective 'individual'. There is no 'social' or 'group' mind, all human minds act independently, and every new idea must arise in one's mind, so in the end every inventor is an individual inventor and emergence of every invention is the result of individual efforts. The only distinguishable meaning of the adjective 'individual' may relate to the conditions of research under which an inventor does his (her) work:

> whether he is self-employed or works as an employee under contract for some other individual or institution; whether he is free to do what he wishes or is under agreement to think and work within prescribed lines; whether he works in a large team or a small one; whether within the team, he is one of many subject to the control of others or is the head of a group following his instruction and providing his ancillary services. (Jewkes et al., 1969, p. 81)

The majority of inventions being studied by Jewkes et al. (1969), can be classified as individual inventions in the sense that the pioneering idea and the foundation work was carried through by men (women) who were working on their own behalf. Even if in some cases the backing of research institutions may be identified it may still be said that individuals were autonomous and free to follow their own ideas without impediment.[2]

A great part of the knowledge of an individual consists of *paragons*[3] – of perception, cognition, behaviour, understanding, and so on. Paragons play a role analogous to genes in biology and determine, in some way, the behaviour of an individual in some well-defined life situations. Examples of paragons are: ritual action (conditioned by genes or culture), systems of law, technological standards, statements and theorems of scientific theories, successive steps of algorithms applied in solving standard (normal) scientific and technical problems and everyday duties to be fulfilled during the working day. The set of paragons of an individual is called his *individuality*, in contrast to *personality* which, in our understanding, is the social image of the individual described in terms of his comportment, roles, and mettle. The etymology of individuality and personality suggests their usage. Individuality comes from the Latin *individuum* – an integral whole; *individuus* – indivisible, inseparable. The hereditary information – genes of

---

[2] For support of the individualistic view of the sources of inventions see also the personal opinions of outstanding inventors presented for example, in Kenneth A. Brown (1988).

[3] I use the term paragon to underline the ideal type of patterns of behaviour. A paragon in this context means a pattern of excellence or perfection. The Ten Commandments (the Laws of Moses) are such paragons at the cultural level. The term paragon comes from the Italian *paragone* which means comparison, probation, and the Greek *parakonan*, that is, to sharpen.

an organism and paragons of an individual – are indivisible, cohesive entities, structures (Kwaśnicki, 1987). The Latin *persona* probably comes from an Etruscan word meaning *mask*. In primitive societies a mask (or costume) was put on a man to symbolize his place and function in the society. Personality in this context means the social roles and attitudes of an individual. There is close parallelism between individuality and genotype, and between personality and phenotype. The fitness of an organism depends directly on its phenotype and a phenotype is a product of a genotype and an epigenetic environment. The process is similar to that of knowledge development – evaluation of an individual's activity depends directly on his personality, and personality is some product of individuality and educational environment. So, in evolutionary processes, we may distinguish two spaces: (1) discrete space of individualities (genotypes), and (2) continuous space of personalities (phenotypes); and two transformations: (1) from individuality (genotype) into personality (phenotype), and (2) from personality (phenotype) into an index of evaluation of an individual (fitness of organism in biology).

The results of a simulation of our model of evolutionary processes confirm the hypothesis that the existence of the two spaces, and associated with these spaces two transformations, play an essential role in the fulguration process. I also postulate that mechanisms of the generation of new sets of paragons – i.e. new individualities – are analogous to biological mechanisms of mutation and the recombination of genes.

Two main areas of an individual's subjective knowledge are distinguished:

1. Paragons of individuality (the so-called *active* paragons), and *latent* (redundant) paragons which are stored by an individual but do not belong to the individuality, that is, these latent paragons do not affect personality, but at any time they may be incorporated into the set of paragons' individuality.[4]

2. Knowledge of the environments in which an individual lives; this knowledge consists of facts, events, human activities and their evaluation, and so on. This area of knowledge enables an internal, subjective evaluation of others' personalities, as well as self-personality evaluation. This element of knowledge enables the building of a personal, hypothetical adaptive landscape and a subjective evaluation of concepts, ideas, and so on, before their verbalization by an individual. This kind of knowledge also enables us to attempt so-called thought experiments and make internal evaluations.[5]

---

[4] There is some evidence that the latent type of genes exists in biological organism, for example, it has been estimated that only about 2% of human DNA is used to build the human proteins. What is the role of the remaining 98% of DNA? Part of the redundant DNA plays the role of structural genes but it seems that the main part of this DNA is not used by human organisms, being the latent DNA.

[5] On the role of thought experiments in natural sciences see, for example, Kuhn (1985), a

Most of the human paragons, either active or latent, are unconscious to each of us and exist in our minds in a nonverbal form (see, for example, Lorenz, 1977, p. 289; Schumpeter, 1960, pp. 135–6). Michael Polanyi (1962, 1967) calls this kind of knowledge 'tacit', that is, knowledge which cannot be articulated. As Polanyi writes (1967, p. 4): 'We know more than we can tell'. The quintessence of tacit knowledge is that it can be used almost freely by its holder (although in most cases unconsciously), but cannot be directly communicated to someone else. Individual skills, competence and talents are based mainly on tacit knowledge. Such organization of our knowledge is probably the outcome of the evolutionary forces (selective mechanisms) acting during the long phylogenic evolution of the human species. It is much more efficient for an individual to focus attention on a small part of individual activity and leave the other activities to unconscious processes. Anyway, our perception of the world would have to look very strange if each of us were conscious of all surrounding (external) and internal processes.

In this context it is necessary to say a few words about the problem of the transition of paragons between independent individuals; more technical problems related to the transition mechanisms will be discussed later on, here I would like only to remark that the majority of paragons are seldom verbalized or visible to others. In most real situations each individual tries to reconstruct the paragons of other individuals on the basis of observations and analysis of their behaviour; so it may be said that even if two individuals use the same term to name, as they expect, the same paragon (for example,'You shall not bear false witness against your neighbour'), the shape of this paragon, as it exists in both minds, may be quite different, such that human actions based on that paragon also differ. The degree of 'verbalization' depends on the type of paragons; some technical skills, for example, those related to ways of search for solutions in typical problem situations (e.g., preparation of scientific experiments), are much easier to describe, but some of them, for example those related to cultural background and ethics, are demonstrated mainly through personal examples of behaviour in typical life situations. Since transmission of knowledge is a highly iterative process performed in interactive mode, both instructor and 'apprentice' try to understand each other and at each step of education verify that the understanding is correct.

Two mechanisms, opposites in the sense of creation of diversity, namely the generation of new types (solutions) and the selection of types, play an essential role in evolutionary processes. The biological selection process is the result of the mutual interaction of population and the environment in which the population acts. The selection process is observed at every stage

---

chapter "A Function for Thought Experiments".

of an individual's development (i.e. during an ontogeny). At least in principle it is possible to calculate the overall probability of an individual surviving from zygote to an adult (procreation) age and bearing offspring (this probability may be a measure of the reproductive success of an individual, called fitness).

A selection process in the development of knowledge is also observed at different stages of personality development. Each man (human being) is evaluated during his (her) upbringing and educational process. Later on, at the stage of adult personality each of us is evaluated on the basis of the results of our work which are the direct results of our acquired knowledge (i.e. paragons of our personalities).

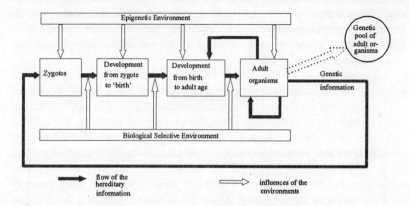

Figure 2.1.   Diagram of evolution – biology

The mechanisms of generation of new genotypes in biology are rather well understood; basic mechanisms of genotype generation are mutations and recombination (crossing-over, chromosome recombination, and so on).There is some evidence (see, for example, Popper and Eccles, 1977) that analogical mechanisms of mutations and recombination may be observed in the human mind (see the section on 'Mechanisms of fulguration of archetypes' below).

Basic phenomena observed in biological evolution and in the development of knowledge are summarized in Figure 2.1 (biology) and in Figure 2.2 (knowledge). The four essential stages of development of biological individuals (sexual organisms) are distinguished in Figure 2.1, namely the formation of zygotes, development from zygote to 'delivery', development from 'delivery' to procreation age, and development of adult organisms. An environment in which biological organisms live is partitioned into two environments (Waddington, 1974) – epigenetic and selective. The epigenetic environment shapes phenotypes of biological organisms at all stages of their development, and the selective environment acts on phenotypes and controls their survival rate (that is, passing from one stage of development to the succeeding one). In some animal species a simple extra-genetic transmission of behaviour (a social learning) is observed, which is indicated by arrows in the last two stages of development (interaction between adults and young individuals). Such extra-genetic transmission was observed for the first time in the behaviour of birds (Larousse, 1990, p. 221) in the suburbs of many English towns. It was noticed that some small birds, especially coaltits and sparrows, opened milk bottles (for example, through making holes in the metallic caps) and drank off the cream. This phenomenon was first observed in Southampton in 1921. Investigations of the dates and places indicate that this kind of behaviour emerged in some specific places and slowly spread to other neighbourhoods. Only a few birds discovered the possibility of reaching food in this way and the others did the same through imitation (learning).

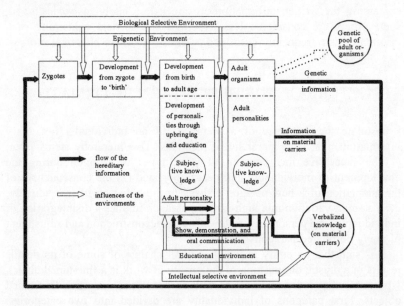

Figure 2.2. Diagram of evolution – knowledge development coupled with biological evolution

The development of personal knowledge is strongly connected with the biological evolution of man. An essential role in knowledge development is played by extra-genetic transmission of paragons (cultural and social learning). As before, from the biological point of view there exist two environments mentioned earlier – epigenetic and selective. But human beings also live in a cultural environment and from the cultural and social points of view we may distinguish two environments, namely the educational environment and the intellectual selective environment (Figure 2.2). Personality is shaped by the educational environment on the basis of written knowledge as well as on the basis of verbal communication. A very important role in social and personal learning is played by tacit ways of paragon transmission such as show, instruction, training, demonstration, exemplification, and so on. The emergence of adult personality frequently occurs before the maturation of the biological adult organism – it is indicated by the shaded arrow at the bottom of the third stage of the different phases of development. Some paragons are transmitted through the social and personal education process on the basis of written knowledge. Contents of this written knowledge (the knowledge pool of the human species) are also affected by the intellectual selective environment – some pieces of information may be considered important and the carriers containing the written information are much less likely to be destroyed; some others are considered less important and carriers containing such information are frequently destroyed or disappear in the historical process.

STRUCTURE OF THE HEREDITARY INFORMATION

I postulate the existence of a hierarchy of an individual's hereditary information, that is, a hierarchy of paragons. This hierarchy stems from: (1) the successive incorporation of some types of paragon during the development of individuality and personality, and (2) the consequences of the adaptation of a new paragon's shape to the cohesion of individuality; even a small variation in a high-ranking paragon implies a disintegration of individuality, and personality, followed by the reconstruction and adjustment of many correlated paragons.

It is said that an entity in which a small change of some of its details results in a drastic diminishing of the quality of work is a fine-tuned object. I postulate that individualities, as well as genotypes, are such fine-tuned objects. First paragons of individuality are divided into two categories: *archetypal* and *cosmetic*. Archetypal paragons remain unchanged during a relatively long period of personality development, while cosmetic paragons change frequently according to local and temporal changes in the environment in which an individual lives. The cosmetic paragons allow incremental adaptation of the personality to local, highly diversified, environments. Diversity of paragons may be used as a criterion for dividing the paragons into these two categories and building up the postulated hierarchy. The smaller the diversity of this category of paragons within a chosen society, the higher the rank of a paragon is.

I suggest that there exist six taxa of archetypal paragons, namely: (1) genetically determined paragons (epigenetic paragons), (2) the image of the world, (3) the image of the society, (4) the image of the economic system, (5) the *epistechne*, and (6) the paradigm. A description of the main categories of paragons of the above six taxa is presented in the next chapter.

The paradigm is the lowest taxon of archetype and is analogous to species in biology. The activity of an individual, formulated in terms of paragons, ranked below the paradigm belongs to the cosmetic category and is differently named by different authors, for example, Kuhn (1962) calls it 'normal science as puzzle-solving', Freeman et al. (1982) and Mensch and Schopp (1977) call it 'incremental innovations' or 'rationalizing innovations', Nelson and Winter (1982) speak about 'natural trajectories' and Dosi (1983) refers to 'technological trajectories'.

MODE OF DEVELOPMENT

A direct consequence of the existence of the hierarchy of hereditary information is a perception of the mode of development of evolutionary processes. Because of the strong cohesion of archetypal paragons, improvement of the personality (phenotype) requires simultaneous changes in a relatively large number of paragons (genes). Improvements of archetypes (fulgurations) are relatively rare events, in contrast to the frequent occurrences of small improvements in the cosmetic domain. Therefore we observe gradual changes at the cosmetic level and jumps in development at the archetype level.

In our understanding, a long-range development of evolutionary processes (among them of knowledge development at personal and social levels) is cyclical with two phases in each cycle, namely, the *substitution phase* and the *quasi-equilibrium phase*. The transition from a quasi-equilibrium phase to the ensuing, substitution phase, is connected with a fulguration of a new and better archetype. The duration of the quasi-equilibrium phase is much longer than the duration of the substitution phase. In the quasi-equilibrium phase the evolutionary system is in a near stasis state and individuals adjust to a varying environment through changes of cosmetic paragons.

Similar views concerning a rough mode of long-term development of technology and economy may be found, for example, in Schumpeter (1960); Freeman (1979); Sahal (1981, p. 33); Freeman et al. (1982). Freeman (1979) writes:

> a process of intermittent, uneven, or cyclical development is maybe more usual than a smooth incremental process. The bunching of groups of related inventions and the investment needed to bring about their widespread introduction is a more probable

pattern of development than the incrementalism associated with run-of-the-mill modifications to established technologies, responding to minor changes of the market.

The new archetype delimits the scope of possible changes in the cosmetic domain, that is, a new archetype demarcates in the cosmetic domain a new canalized pathway of change – a *chreod*, to use Waddington's terms:

> The stabilization of a progressive system acts to ensure that the system goes on altering in the same sort of way that it has been altering in the past. Whereas the process of keeping something at a stable, or stationary, value is called homeostasis, ensuring the continuation of a given type of change is called homeorhesis, a word which means preserving a flow. A phrase used to describe such systems, is to say that the pathway of change is canalized. For the pathway itself one can use the name chreod, a word derived from Greek, which means 'necessary path'. (Waddington, 1977)

Probably a new form of higher taxon demarcates analogous chreods in all lower taxa of the archetypal paragons. The personal development of man and the resulting social development of human societies are bounded by our biological constitution; sometimes it is said that we are prisoners of our biological nature. The same may be said about all other taxa: the accepted worldview (the image of the world) delimits, more or less broadly, the spectrum of our acceptable views on forms of organized society, or ways of economic order; the accepted social view delimits the spectrum of acceptable economic orders, and so on, down to the lowest taxa of human knowledge (paradigm, and cosmetic).

MECHANISMS OF FULGURATION OF ARCHETYPES

As we have already noted, evolution is the result of the interplay of two, opposite in the sense of the diversity causation, random processes, namely the generation of new types (solutions, ideas) and the selection of types. At any time each individual is characterized by two sets of paragons: (1) active, that is, paragons employed by an individual in his (her) everyday practice, and (2) latent, that is, paragons which are stored by an individual but are not actually applied. Latent paragons may be included in the active set of paragons at any moment during the individual's development. The whole set of an individual's paragons may be partitioned into separate subsets, or segments, consisting of similar paragons employed by the individual in different domains of his (her) activity. In the case of industry, or of a university researcher, examples are segments relating to methods of making experiments, collection of data, ways of presenting the results of research (for example, writing papers, participation in conferences), cooperation with other researchers, and so on. In each segment, either active or latent paragons may exist.

The set of paragons employed by an individual may evolve. The random process of their modification is governed by four basic mechanisms, namely: *mutation, recombination, transition* and *transposition*. Mutations cause the appearance of new, original shapes (forms) of a paragon. It is highly speculative to speak about the probability of discovering a new paragon through mutation (i.e. the probability of paragon mutation) but it seems that, as with biological evolution, on average, the probability is relatively small, and seemingly of the same order for each human being. The individual may also gain knowledge of other individuals by imitation (recombination) of some paragons employed by competitors or collaborators. It seems that an imitation-recombination of a whole segment is more probable than imitation of isolated paragons, that is, an individual may gain knowledge about a relatively wide domain of activity of another individual, for example, by employing a specific method of experimentation. But an individual may gain knowledge of a single paragon. In contrast to the set of paragons gained through recombination, which in principle are a well-adapted set of paragons and may be built almost directly into a set of individual paragons, the majority of such isolated paragons gained from other individuals do not fit the well-adapted set of individual paragons and could not be built directly into that set of paragons. A single paragon may be transmitted (*transition*) with some probability from individual to individual and it may be presumed that after transition a paragon belongs to a subset of latent paragons. At any time a random *transposition* of a latent paragon to a subset of active paragons may occur.

In general, the probability of transposition of a paragon for any individual is relatively small. But randomly, from time to time, the value of this probability may abruptly increase and we observe very active processes of search for a new combination of paragons. I call this phenomenon *recrudescence*.[6] Recrudescence is viewed as an intrinsic ability of an individual to innovate by employing some reckless, insane ideas. This ability is connected mainly with the personalities of the individuals. Pure random factors play an essential role in the search for innovations by recrudescence. As a rule, mutation, recombination and transposition on a normal level (that is, with low probabilities in long periods) contribute to small improvements and short periods of recrudescence contribute to the emergence of radical innovations (fulguration).

---

[6] Recrudescence comes from the Latin *recrudesco* (to break out, to open, to renew) and *recrudescere* (to become raw again). Recrudescence means a new outbreak after a period of abatement, inactivity or after a dormant period. I suggest that the mechanism of generating innovation by recrudescence is a general mechanism observed in all evolutionary processes, for example, in biological evolution, in development of knowledge, and in economic development. Results of simulations of our models of biological evolution and the model of industry development suggest that recrudescence is essential for long-term evolution and permits escape from so-called evolutionary traps (see, for example, page 176).

The mechanism of recrudescence frequently acts in subconscious states caused by dreams or illness. Scientists, artists and great reformers frequently admit that their most valuable ideas and achievements emerged from the nebulous parts of subconsciousness in the form of very raw material, which is subsequently improved in conscious processes (Dubois, 1986). Recrudescence reflects phenomena frequently observed in creative processes and described as revelation, vision, bisociation (Arthur Koestler), gestalt-switch (Karl Popper), or abduction (Charles Sanders Peirce). As Peirce (1934, p. 113) writes: 'The abductive suggestion comes to us like a flash. It is an act of *insight*, although of extremely fallible insight. It is true that the different elements of hypothesis were in our minds; but it is the idea of putting together what we had never before dreamed of putting together which flashes the new suggestion before our contemplation'. Even the intercessor of pure rationalism, René Descartes, admitted that his famous *Discours de la Méthode* was the result of subconscious inspiration during the drowsiness of an uncontrolled dream (see Ortega y Gasset, 1967, p. 82). Admissions of this type of invention are reported by many inventors and scientists, for example, Alfred R. Wallace (Wallace, 1898, pp. 139–40) confessed in his *The Wonderful Century. Its Successes and Failures* that the idea of natural selection had come to his mind when he was very ill during his stay in Ternate (Moluccas) and suffered frequent attacks of ague (malaria).[7] During one such attack of shivering he thought of the problem of the origin of the species and something made him recall Malthus's *Essay on Population*, which he had read ten years earlier. Wallace associated some of Malthus's ideas with the well-known facts from the behaviour of wild animals, and subconsciously the idea of the survival of better-adapted individuals flashed into his mind. Within two hours he worked out the main points of his theory. He worked on the essay during the next two evenings and sent it to Charles Darwin.[8]

To consider fulguration of archetypes in the historical perspective (i.e. at the social level) it is also necessary to take into account processes of rare interchanges (transitions) of knowledge between individuals with barely related archetypes (that is, between individuals with different cultural backgrounds or individuals representing different scientific disciplines). A fulguration seen at the social level is the result of a series of relatively frequent inventions occurring in a chain fashion within a group of individuals engaged in a specific research area. As a rule, the chain of changes is triggered by a random event (the recrudescence mechanism may be involved in this process). The extreme case is the fulguration of an

---

[7] Quotation from Urbanek (1984). Some other examples of revolutionary ideas sparked off by dreams may be found in Popper and Eccles (1977, pp. 496–7).

[8] As is well known, Darwin and Wallace were invited by Charles Lyell to the Linnean Society in London and published their theories on 1 July 1858.

archetype as a result of one radical invention. In part this saltationistic view of evolution is represented in economy by Kuznets (1966). He writes that an epochal innovation 'may be described as a major addition to the stock of human knowledge which provides a potential for sustained economic growth – an addition so major that its exploitation and utilization absorb the energies of human societies and dominate their growth for a period long enough to constitute an epoch in economic history'.[9]

As a rule, initial inventions in the chain leading to a radical innovation are disadvantageous, so there arises the question: how is it possible that these deviant ideas 'survive' and are not quickly eliminated from the research environment? The existence of deviant ideas would be possible in the case of a highly tolerant, liberal selective environment but in such a case the average quality of research would drop significantly and it would be very difficult to separate promising ideas from hopeless ones. In the historical process an effective way to avoid this undesirable situation has been worked out, namely a partition of the whole population of individuals into a number of semi-isolated sub-populations (schools in science, 'demes' (Wright, 1982) in biology). The structure of the partition is such that there exist a few relatively big demes ('normal science' in the words of Kuhn, 1962) with a high ratio of information interchanges and a great number of very small demes (diversified schools), consisting of a relatively small fraction of the whole population, where some deviant ideas are able to survive. The emergence of radical innovation (fulguration) is frequently observed within such small sub-populations. An important role in the long-term evolution is played by rare interchanges of hereditary information (paragons, genes) between these small sub-populations (schools in science, demes in biology). Therefore the term 'semi-isolated sub-population' seems to be the proper one to describe the essence of the structure of evolving populations.

It is my postulate that the triggering of the chain of changes which leads to the fulguration of archetypes in knowledge development is caused by mechanisms analogous to biological processes of mutation, recombination and, mainly, recrudescence of paragons and that the most effective way to penetrate distant areas of the adaptive landscapes (i.e. search for radical innovation) is through recrudescence and rarely occurring inter-deme recombination.

The main aim of this chapter was to show essential similarities and

---

[9] Quotation from Mensch and Schopp (1977). Similar views on the saltationistic mode of biological species fulguration may be found in Bateson (1984), de Vries (1901–1903), Beurlen (1937), Goldschmidt (1940, 'Hopeful monsters'), and Schindewolf (1950). A recent revival of interest in the non-gradual mode of biological evolution is observed after the publication of the theory of punctuated equilibria by Niles Eldredge and Stephen J. Gould (Gould and Eldredge, 1977; Eldredge and Gould, 1972).

differences of knowledge development and biological evolution. To sum up, the main similarities are: in the structure of hereditary information (active and latent paragons and genes, the hierarchy of hereditary information – archetypal and cosmetic); in the existence of two transformations (from the hereditary information to phenotypes, and from phenotypes to an index of evaluation); and in the mechanisms of generation of new types (mutation, recombination, transition and transposition). The main differences are in the existence of conscious decision-making processes in the development of knowledge. Biological organisms collect no information on the preferences of environment and do not predict short-term development of the population and environment. In contrast, human beings collect such information, which enables men (women) to build hypothetical, local adaptive landscapes in which they form their expectations about future development. In the end human decisions are based on such formed expectations. The next essential difference is that of the unit of evolution and the unit of selection. In biological evolution an organism is a unit of evolution as well as a unit of selection. In knowledge evolution we observe a separation of these two aspects of evolutionary processes: the unit of evolution is an individual (or, for example, a firm in the industry model) and the unit of selection is an idea, a theory (or a product, a commodity in the industry model), that is, a result of efforts of the unit of evolution. This second difference leads to a slightly different interpretation of the selection equations in the model of knowledge development (our model of industry development may be suitable as an example of that peculiar interpretation).

3. Taxonomy of Knowledge

In the preceding chapter the proposition of the evolutionary process of knowledge development was presented. The hypothesis that organization of individual knowledge is ordered in a similar way to organization of hereditary information in a genome of biological organism was suggested. In this chapter a proposition of a hierarchy of paragons divided into six taxa of knowledge is presented. I am not able to describe each taxon in terms of paragons, but I do point out some categories of paragons. The situation is similar to that in biology. Biologists describe each taxon by giving examples of organisms of a specific taxon and describe each taxon in terms of phenotypes (morphological traits) of the organism.

I propose to distinguish six taxa of individual knowledge (and in this way also taxa of 'social' knowledge): (1) epigenetic paragons (i.e. genetically determined paragons), (2) the image of the world, (3) the image of the society, (4) the image of the economy, (5) the *epistechne* and (6) the paradigm.

Research on knowledge development and the search for explanations of breakthroughs and revolutions (fulgurations) in science and technology is frequently confined to an analysis of the methods of research and an analysis of the contents of scientific theories (or an analysis of patents in the case of technology). In other words, the research on patterns of knowledge development is made on the level of the *epistechne* and paradigms. The only exception known to me is Amsterdamski (1983), who analyses the development of science at a level higher than paradigm, that is, he studies the development of science as changes of a so-called 'ideal of science'. His 'ideal of science' is partly similar to our 'image of the world'.

In my opinion, the search for explanations of breakthroughs and revolutions in science and technology should not be confined to considerations of processes within the fields of science and technology. They are created by outstanding personalities. Analyses of biographies of the reformers show how important in the creation of their achievements has been the role played by their ideas on cultural, social and economic orders. As Werner Heisenberg (1987, p. 13) writes in his scientific autobiography, written in the form of Socrates dialogues:

> Science is created by people. This fact understandable in itself is easily forgotten and reconsidering it might be helpful to diminish the, frequently criticized, gulf between two cultures, humanistic-artistic and techno-scientific. ... In these dialogues physics does not play the most important role. Frequently human, philosophical and political problems are involved and it is the author's hope that it will be clearly visible how difficult it is to separate science from those more general problems.

Examples of similar opinions are numerous. Let us quote only one of the outstanding physicists, Erwin Schrödinger (1952), who once wrote that:

> there is a tendency to forget that all science is bound up with human culture in general, and that scientific findings, even those which at the moment appear the most advanced and esoteric and difficult to grasp, are meaningless outside their cultural context. A theoretical science unaware that those of its constructs considered relevant and momentous are destined eventually to be framed in concepts and worlds that have a grip of the educated community and become part and parcel of the general world picture – a theoretical science, I say, where this is forgotten, and where the initiated continue musing to each other in terms that are, at best, understood by a small group of close fellow travellers, will necessarily be cut off from the rest of cultural mankind; in the long run it is bound to atrophy and ossify however virulently esoteric chat may continue within its joyfully isolated groups of experts.

I emphasize the importance of the taxa above *epistechne* and paradigm, namely the image of the economy, the image of the society, the image of the world, and the epigenetic paragons, for science and technology development. I see no possibility of providing a formal proof of the existence of proposed taxa but it is possible to find some corroboration of that taxonomy. One of the possible ways to search for such corroboration is by showing similarities between successive stages of the development of individual knowledge and the parallel stages of the historical development of knowledge in a given cultural realm. Such parallelism observed in the development of knowledge would be similar to that observed in biological evolution and concisely expressed in the famous statement of Ernst Haeckel (1834–1919) that 'ontogeny recapitulates phylogeny'.[1]

Partial proof that the intellectual development of a human being is, in some sense, a recapitulation of the cultural development of human civilization may be found in the work of Jean Piaget. In his opinion (Piaget, 1977, pp. 37 and 83) the solution to the most basic problems of formation of notions and analysis of the mind's operations lies in the domain of psychogenetic research. In his opinion, psychology is a kind of embryology of the mind: as the description of stages of individual development, and especially as the research on the mechanisms of this development. Psychogenesis is an integral part of embryogenesis, which does not end at the moment of a child's birth but continues until the equilibrium state of an adult is reached. The basic notions of physical space, time, speed, causality, and so on, emerged as a result of common sense far in advance of any

---

[1] First observations on this regularity were made by Karl Ernst von Baer (1792–1876), who stated that embryos of animals of different taxa look the more similar the earlier the development phase is, and that when we look at the development process of embryos, first we observe general traits of higher taxa (for example, type, group, order), next traits of the lower taxa, and in the end individual traits of the organisms.

scientific contents of these notions. The intellectual prehistory of human societies will probably remain unknown to us, therefore it is necessary to research the formation of these notions in a child; it will be some kind of mind's embryology which may give similar results and findings as research on the ontogeny of organisms did for comparative anatomy.

Study of the personal intellectual development of man may be used also as the second stream of the search for evidence of our proposition of taxonomy of knowledge. If we look closely at the personal development of human beings, records show that the forms of paragons of the higher taxa are modified less frequently than those of the lower taxa. A researcher is much more eager to change his (her) methods of research (for example, of making scientific experiments) through the adoption of more efficient methods than through a change his (her) beliefs, or moral attitudes, shaped during his (her) first, 'youthful' phases of development.

The time span of the domination of given categories of paragons within large societies may be appropriate as the third element of corroboration of the hypothesis on the taxonomy of paragons. Let us assume that it is possible to describe at any moment of historical time and within a relatively large society dominant categories of description of the reality. In the long-term development of the society we can observe significantly longer periods of the domination of paragons belonging to higher taxa than of those belonging to lower taxa. An attempt to validate this hypothesis on the basis of the evolution of the Mediterranean Culture is presented in this chapter. It has been assumed that within a relatively large society, an evolution of a given taxon is an 'outcome' of all paragons of that taxon as observed in all members of the society; and, for example, the 'outcome' of paragons of the image of the world determines what is called civilization (or culture in the narrow sense); the outcome of the image of society's paragons settles the political and social order of the society; the paragons of the methods of management determine the economic system; and the *epistechne*'s paragons determine the epistemological and technological systems of scientists and engineers in the given society.

It ought to be underlined that at any chosen period of human history different categories of paragon coexist and at any time we observe great diversity of paragons. It is possible to find a wide spectrum of opinions, a wide spectrum of thought categories within the chosen society; but it seems that at any time it is possible to distinguish the dominant categories of thought – what is frequently called the spirit of the time. What I present below is my supposition on the question of what the main stream of thought is, and what the prevailing categories of paragons are, as observed in some well-defined periods of human development.

Estimations of the duration of the substitution phase and the quasi-equilibrium phase for five taxa are presented in Table 3.1. These are subjective evaluations, made mainly to illustrate a hypothetical dynamics of evolution of different taxa. Apart from the image of the world, the estimations are made on the basis of observed historical changes in Europe and North America in the last 500 years. The four most recent changes of the image of the world were observed in European civilization:

- between the 6th and the 7th centuries BC in Greece,
- between the 2nd and the 4th centuries in Rome,
- in the 16th and the 17th centuries in Western Europe, and
- at the end of the 19th and in the first half of the 20th centuries in Western Europe and North America.

Table 3.1. Waves of development; the Western hemisphere

Taxon	Substitution phase (years)	Quasi-Eq. phase (years)
Image of the world/civilization	100–300	400–1000
Image of the society/political order	50–100	200–300
Image of the economic system/economy	30–60	100–150
Epistechne/epistemological and technological systems	10–30	40–120
Paradigm (scientific and technological)	5–10	30–60

The period around the 6th century BC is a singular period in the history of humankind. It is marked by the activities of: the great Greek philosophers, the prophet Isaiah (concluding the work of the Jewish prophets), Confucius and Lao-tsy in China, Gautama Buddha in India, Zarathustra in Persia and King Numa – Numa Pompilius – in Rome. It is reasonable to claim that at that time the main evolutionary lines of cultural development in the history of humankind were initiated.

EPIGENETIC PARAGONS

The results of research in psychology, physiology, ethology and other social sciences in the last 30–40 years suggest the existence of many categories of cognition and perception in man which depend strongly on our biological nature. The idea of the existence of some *a priori* categories of our brain and *a priori* forms of human cognition comes from Immanuel Kant. The examples of categories in this taxon are: some *a priori* categories of space and time (Immanuel Kant); inborn categories of language structures (Noam Chomsky), disjunctive thinking, that is, thinking in categories of opposition (Konrad Lorenz); some expressive forms like inviting, leave-taking, quarrelling, consternation, fearing, delighting, courting (Irenäus Eibl-Eibesfeldt), thinking in terms of analogy and the search for similarities; classification abilities and recognition of common traits in different objects; and anticipation of impending events and building mental models of our action.

Karl Popper (1979, p. 71) writes that 'if it were not absurd to make any estimate, I should say that 999 units out of 1,000 of the knowledge of an organism are inherited or inborn, and that one unit only consists of the modification of this inborn knowledge; and I suggest, in addition, that *the plasticity needed* for those modifications is also inborn.' Similar opinions are expressed by Lorenz (1977, p. 294) and François Jacob (1987, p. 95). Jacob claims that the genetical programme of human beings set up something that may be called 'assent structures'. These structures enable a child to react to stimuli in the environment, to search for and to determine their regularities, to remember, and finally to 'reshuffle' all elements into new combinations. Contemporary research on 'phylogenetically programmed behaviour' extends our knowledge of '*a priori* categories of cognition', see for example, the works of Lorenz and Chomsky.

We are equipped with the senses which enable us to recognize things stretched in space, but we have no parallel senses to recognize things stretched in time. It may be expected that thanks to the natural selection mechanism which affects different species, the living species are at the state of optimal, or near to optimal, adaptation to the real world. If so, then this important difference between the characteristics of events (stretched in time) and those of space as observed in human perception ought to correspond to something real in the universe (see, for example, Denbigh, 1979).

Described by Anne M. Sullivan, the case of Helen Keller, blind and deaf following an illness when she was 18 months old, who learned to speak English at the age of seven, may be treated as evidence of the existence of inborn language structures. Helen was born on 27 June 1880 and until 6 March 1887 her mother almost ceaselessly kept her on the knees so that Helen could explore her sense of touch. At that time she knew only how to express her need for food and drink, and did not understand any symbolic or language communication. Anne Sullivan started to write full words and statements on Helen's palm, using the finger alphabet. She gave Helen a doll as a gift and wrote on her palm the word 'doll', letter by letter, without using any pictograms. After that she used to do this with different objects. It is almost incredible that a blind and deaf person is able to learn to read using such an approach, without the prior ability to speak, but Helen was able to connect mentally the signals on her palm with given objects. Of course, she did not recognize single letters, but the whole pattern of a series of impulses, which she next tried to reciprocate. Helen tried to communicate with her dog by 'writing' on its paw the first known word 'doll' on 20 March. By 31 March she knew 18 nouns and three verbs and she started to ask questions by simply bringing things to her teacher and holding out her palm for Anne Sullivan to write the names of the things. At the beginning Helen did not recognize differences between nouns and verbs, for example, she used the same word *doll* for doll as a thing and to name the act of playing with a doll. Three months later Helen wrote her first letter to her friend using the Braille alphabet. By the end of July she had learned to write in pencil very quickly and used it to communicate. At that time also she discovered questions using *why* and *what for*, and in September she correctly used pronouns and the verb *to be*. The next year, in September 1888, she acquired a knowledge of the subjunctive mood, making perfect use also of two others, the indicative and the imperative moods. Helen Keller became a writer and in one of her books she described the history of her life. The case of Helen Keller, especially her ability to acquire all grammatical rules and logic of the language within 18 months (from March 1887 to September 1888), when she was 7 years old, seems to confirm the theory of Noam Chomsky on the existence of innate linguistic structures.

Results of research by Alan Gevins and his co-workers based on computer analysis of EEC brain waves of people who were examined by the Finger Pressure Test seem to confirm the hypothesis that the human mind first builds a model of future performance, then evaluates correctness and speed of action on the basis of the mental model, and in the end undertakes relevant action. It is almost certain that the abilities to build such models are genetically determined.

Comparative ethology is one of such disciplines in which the results of research confirm the existence of numerous inborn modes of behaviour. Irenäus Eibl-Eibesfeldt (1970) filmed the behaviour of people from different cultures using a special camera with a built-in prism to make pictures which were perpendicular to the apparent direction of the camera. Analysis of the slow-motion films revealed that expressive forms in situations involving greetings, leave-takings, quarrels, courtships, joy, fright and dread are identical in Bushmen from Kalahari, Otj-Himba from the grasslands of Kaoko, Papuans from New Guinea, Waika Indians from Orinoco, inhabitants of Samoa, aborigines from Australia and so-called civilized French, Americans and other representatives of Western culture.

IMAGE OF THE WORLD

The main categories of paragons associated with the image of the world are the following:

- *existential categories* – paragons of these categories enable us to find answers to secular questions concerning: the sense and aim of human existence; the meaning of human suffering, torment, pain and death; the role of evil and the attitude of human beings to evil; the meaning of community spirit; understanding of the mind-body problem; the attitude of man towards nature; the place and role of man in the Universe.
- *aesthetic categories* – paragons of these categories enable us to evaluate the beauty of ideas and the beauty of physical objects; they define general categories of beauty.
- *cosmogonic* and *cosmological categories* – paragons concerning origin, evolution, structure and the essence of the Universe, its end and the goal of its evolution.
- *perception categories* – paragons of these categories refer to: general apprehension and knowledge of the world; ways of noticing phenomena, events and processes in the world; categories allowing the acceptance of some explanations of real phenomena (theories, hypotheses, ideas, and so on) as sufficient, adequate and satisfactory; attitudes of man to the incomprehensible, mysterious, inscrutable and transcendental phenomena; perception of man's surrounding spaces such as life space, social space, geographical space, and so on; nature of spaces – physical and theoretical; nature of time, awareness and experience of time; relation between space and time.

The existential paragons are identified by Bell (1985, p. 6) with culture, but what is important to us is that he emphasizes the importance of this kind of paragon for the development of societies. Culture for him is the domain of everlasting problems. Technological possibilities, in his opinion, may grow, we may observe technological progress, scientific knowledge may overcome nature, but the existential questions always remain. Different answers to existential questions are found but the questions always come back. Coherent sources of the existential paragons, and partially also of the cosmogonic paragons, are religions (Bell, 1985, p. 17). Religion is not a controlling force of social life – as Karl Marx and Emile Durkheim claimed. Religion is also not the owner of human essence – as stated by Friedrich Schleiermacher, Rudolph Otto, and religion phenomenologists (for example, Max Scheler). The foundations of any religion have an existential character, people are conscious of their finiteness and inexorable confinements. Therefore, they consequently search for a cohesive answer which enables them to adapt to their human conditions.

Bell does not write about other existential categories, such as sense of pain and suffering, but it seems that these, and probably many others, should be considered as 'essential questions pervading all societies'. The core part of all concepts and philosophical systems directed by great thinkers of religion and philosophy were always recommendations about how to proceed with individual and social suffering, and how to overcome and eliminate it (e.g., Scheler, 1986).

Aesthetic categories play a very important role in the activity of any creative person, not just a fine artist (Heisenberg, 1979). As was stated long ago by the ancient Greek philosophers, there are two main categories of beauty: (1) beauty as a harmony of all parts (elements) among themselves and with the whole (Pythagoras),[2] and (2) beauty as an emanation of everlasting brightness of 'Absolute Unity' by material objects (Plotyn).[3]

Paul Dirac and Louis Pasteur can be quoted to illustrate such an understanding of these two categories of beauty in science. In Dirac's opinion it is much more important to see beauty in an equation than to ensure an exact concordance of that equation with results of experiments.[4] A researcher who focuses his (her) efforts on the harmony within equations is on the very right route to make progress in his (her) research. Deviations of theoretical findings from the experimental results are no reason to be upset, the discrepancy may be caused by insignificant features neglected at the first stages of research, and all problems may be overcome in the further development of the theory. Pasteur, in his inauguration speech to the French Academy of Sciences, confessed[5] that he recognized the presence of the immensity all around the world. This strengthens our in-heart faith in the supernatural. The idea of God is no more than one of the forms of this immensity. The ancient Greeks understood very well the secret power of hidden features of reality; they bequeathed us one of the most beautiful words of our language, the word enthusiasm, i.e. *en theos* – in divinity. Most human actions are measured by the inspirations leading to them. Happiness is a feature of a person who cultivates in his (her) heart the name of divinity – the ideal of beauty – and who is submissive to the ideal of art and science. All is illuminated by the reflection of the immensity.

Different attitudes to describe the reality may be categorized as follows:

1. cause–effect explanation – worked out by Galileo and Descartes (frequently called the deductive model of explanation, the Popper model, or the Hempel–Oppenheim model), and
2. explanation by understanding – conceived by Aristotle, who asserted that to make something understandable it is enough to point out an aim

---

[2] 'Beauty – the adjustment of all parts proportionately so that one cannot add or subtract or change anything without impairing the harmony of the whole', Leon Battista Alberti (1404–72).

[3] 'Heat cannot be separated from fire, or beauty from The Eternal', Dante Alighieri (1265–1321). 'Beauty is a manifestation of secret natural laws, which otherwise would have been hidden from us forever', Johann Wolfgang von Goethe (1749–1832).

[4] *Scientific American*, 208(5), 1963, quotation from Heller and Życiński (1986).

[5] See Koestler (1967), pp. 261–2.

and sense (teleonomy) of existence of this something (Krasnodębski, 1986).

Research on the development of the idea of space and time in different cultures and by different scientific disciplines has generated an enormous literature. An outline of this problem is beyond the scope of this work. In every person there exist many categories of space and time, and each of these categories refers to different spheres of reality. Obviously all these categories are mutually related, and, what is important, depend on the *a priori* categories of space and time, which, as was mentioned, belong to the higher taxa, namely the epigenetic paragons. Human spaces reflect conditions of the human mind. It is possible to distinguish three basic types of human space: mythological, pragmatic and theoretical (Tuan, 1987). Naturally all three spaces overlap each other. The mythological space, which is mainly a conceptual scheme, is also the pragmatic space, in the sense that it relates to some practical human actions, for example, sowing and harvesting. Differences between the mythological and pragmatic spaces may be found in the fact that the latter is more constrained by the economic activity of man; the discovery of strips of fertile and barren soil is the achievement of intellect, of mind. When imaginative man tried to describe the arrangement of fertile and barren pieces of soil in the form of a cartographic map he, or she, used symbols, and this may be considered as the next step to conceptualization of the space. In the Western hemisphere the abstract (theoretical space) was created on the basis of everyday experience, i.e. pragmatic space. Theorems of the Euclidian space are founded on human experiences based on such human senses as touch and visual perception.

Association between different categories of space and time may shed light on the topology (structure) of space, for example, perception of distance in the same physical (geographical) space is different for those who use a horse as the quickest means of travelling, and for those who use a plane for moving from one place to another.

Two general categories of time are: the objective time (physical, philosophical) and subjective, or human, time (Siciński, 1974, and Sachs, 1978). Three main classes of time experienced by human beings are cyclical, mechanical and psychological (Murphy, 1973). Perceptions of space and time are fundamental for human intellectual and pragmatic activity, and so is the perception of relationships between space and time. Two essential types of relationship between objective time and physical space are:

1.   Substantive relationship – time and space are the absolute and steady entities, having their self-essence just as matter has. This idea was invented by the ancient Greek philosophers, Leukippos and Democrytus, and in the most advanced form was developed by Isaac Newton.

2. Relativistic relationship – time and space are properties of matter; nature and properties of time and space depend on the coexistence and interactions of material objects. This concept was founded by the Medieval philosopher, Maimonides (1135–1204), who said, in opposition to Aristotle, that time is a measure of movement. Maimonides claimed that time is an 'aspect of matter', and time emerged when *ex nihilo* the whole matter was created. This idea was developed by Gottfried W. Leibniz, who may be considered to be the founding father of the contemporary concept of the idea of time-space in Albert Einstein's theory of relativity.

The last shift of the image of the world in the Western hemisphere (European Civilization) was observed in the 16th and the 17th centuries, and two previous changes took place in the periods from the 6th to the 4th centuries BC in Ancient Greece and between the 2nd and the 4th centuries AD in Western Europe. A new image of the world in Ancient Greece emerged from *Theogony* – genealogy of the gods and cosmological vision of genesis of the Universe by Hesiod (about the 7th century BC) – and from the *Iliad* and *Odyssey* by Homer (probably also from the 7th century BC), two works which linked different tribes, becoming their common property and creating an alliance to face the danger of the neighbouring barbarians. The essential role in shaping the ancient image of the world was played by Greek philosophers from the 6th to the 4th centuries BC, searching for coherent and lucid ideas relating to the origin and evolution of the Universe and trying to find answers concerning the place of man in the Universe. The most fundamental philosophical and existential questions pervading humankind for centuries were established at that time, questions with probably no final answers. In my opinion the work of Plato (427–347 BC) ended the process of shaping this ancient image of the world.

The next transformation of the image of the world was observed in two centuries between the 2nd and the 4th centuries AD. Two names encompass the period of shaping this image of the world – Ptolemy (AD 100–178) and St. Augustus (AD 354–430). The geocentric concept of the two-spherical Universe, the development of coherent mathematical theory describing the movement of the planets by deferents, epicicles, equants and eccentrics, and the cosmological concepts of Ptolemy, described – among others – in Almagest (*Mathematicae Syntaxis*), had dominated Western thinking until the 15th century. The 2nd and 3rd centuries witnessed the dissipation of Christianity in the Roman Empire. This process was almost finished by the 4th century – on 30 April, AD 311, caesar Galerius issued an edict granting toleration to Christians; caesar Constantine the Great was personally committed to Christianity by AD 313, when he issued the Edict of Milan extending toleration to Christians, and was baptized in AD 337, shortly before his death. From that time Christian symbols were placed on shields (coat of arms) and army banners; in AD 380 Theodosius I (Flavius Theodosius) proclaimed Christianity the official state religion. After heavy rioting in Alexandria in AD 391, as the direct consequence of a special edict of Theodosius, Christians destroyed the Serapeum, sanctum of the Ptolemaic cult, one of the most beautiful temples and the centre of pagan worship. This act may be treated as the symbolic end of the Christianization process in the Roman Empire. Christianity was a coherent source of the existential paragons, and also caused the replacement of cyclical time by axis time, with a clear partition of the time-scale into the past, the present and the future. This period of shaping the new image of the world is crowned by the work of St. Augustus, who incorporated the philosophy of Plato and neo-platonism into the Christian tradition. The philosophy of St. Augustus became an integral part of the Christian doctrine.

The transformation of perception (topology) of the geographical and life spaces was connected with the invasion of the barbarian tribes from the north of Europe and later on the partition (in AD 395) of the Roman Empire into the East Empire (with the capital in Constantinople) and the Western Roman Empire. If we look at the map of the Roman Empire before its partition we see that its territory around the Mediterranean sea was, from a topological point of view, consistent and this consistency was lost after the year AD 395.

The transformation of the image of the world in the 16th and the 17th centuries was initiated by a series of great geographical discoveries, which changed the perception of the Earth and visualized its sphericity, and also made evident the existence of different cultures and continents. The discoveries instigated various types of research, for example, relating to cartography, navigation, or measurement of time.

The 16th century witnessed also the wide diffusion in Western Europe of the Reformation idea. The day Martin Luther proclaimed his Ninety-Five Theses, on 31 October 1517, in which he attacked various ecclesiastical abuses, may be seen as the pivotal moment for the Reformation process.

Two outstanding and crucial works which initiated revolutionary changes in the idea of man's physical world and that of man as a biological organism were published in 1543: *De revolutionibus orbitum coelestium* by Nicolaus Copernicus (1473–1543) and *De humani corporis fabrica* by Andreas Vesalius (1514–64).

The philosophical reflections on the nature of man and the structure of the Universe, mainly of Erasmus from Rotterdam, Machiavelli, Montaigne, Descartes and Francis Bacon, is the next intellectual stream which shaped the emergence of the new image of the world. As with the two previous processes of worldview transformation, this Renaissance transformation was strictly connected with a new interpretation, a new reading, of Plato's ideas (see, for example, Kuhn, 1957, pp. 197, 204; Dodson, 1938, p. 196). Neo-Platonists transformed the dynamic, flowing and passing, real world into the everlasting ideal world of pure spirit, and mathematicians showed them how to make it. Mathematics, in its understanding of neo-Platonism, reflects what is real and eternal inside the imperfect and flowing world. Triangles and circles were archetypes of all Platonic forms.

The world before the 16th century was essentially static, with each thing or each being having its proper, natural place. Any movement in such a world was connected with the aspiration of things (or beings) towards their natural place. In the emerging image of the world we see the concept of the dynamic world, whose dynamics is governed by laws of movement (principles of mechanics). The world was perceived as an entity composed of circles, triangles and straight lines reducible to some basic entities, namely mechanical entities. Conclusions concerning the behaviour of the whole system were drawn through the investigation of well-defined sub-parts and laws which govern the behaviour of these parts. This idea of reducibility to mechanical entities was strictly connected with an atomic and corpuscular vision of the structure of matter. Revival of the ancient Greek atomic idea was connected with new editions of old classic works, for example, up to 1600, over 30 editions of Lucretius's *De rerum natura* (the first edition, in 1473, by Brescia) had been issued. The reductionist and mechanistic vision of nature was transferred to man. In the opinion of Descartes (*Discours de la méthode*) the person who is acquainted with

> the variety of movements performed by different automata, or moving machines fabricated by human industry, and that with the help of but few pieces compared with the great variety of bones, muscles, nerves, arteries, veins, and other parts that one finds in the body of each animal ... will look upon this body as a machine made by the hand of God, which is incomparably better arranged, and adequate to movements more admirable than is any machine of human invention.[6]

Space in the Renaissance image of the world was filled constantly with ether and there was no place for a vacuum. It was the Euclidean space and through this geometry the world was perceived. Similarly, time was also perceived as continuous and all changes in such a world evolved gradually. Later, in the 18th century, Linnaeus and Leibniz expressed this principle in the well-known maxim *natura non facit saltus* – nature does not make leaps. In the Renaissance image of the world, events, in any process, were connected in succession (cause–effect principle) and a deterministic perception of development predominated the thinking of that period. Cognition of the world was based on logic and deduction. Faith in the power of mind, infinite cognitive possibilities of man and non-restricted possibilities of shaping nature by man were all commonly accepted.

---

[6] Descartes frequently compared the human organism to a mechanical clock, see, for example, articles 6 and 16 in his *Les Passions de l'âme*.

Descartes postulated that science ought to enable man to be the master and the governor of Nature; either the external nature – through a knowledge of mechanics – or the internal nature of man – through the development of medicine. Francis Bacon in his *New Atlantis* expressed similar opinion, through the governor of Salamon's House (the College of Six Days' Work): 'The end of our foundation is the knowledge of causes, and secret motion of things; and the enlarging of the bounds of human empire, to the effecting of all things possible.'

The Renaissance image of the world, prevailing since the 16th century, was questioned at the end of the 19th century. Since that time we can observe the process of shaping a new, 20th-century image of the world. The transformation was initiated by the works of the great evolutionists Charles Darwin and Alfred Russel Wallace, and the sociologist Herbert Spencer. Very intensive development of the theory of biological evolution has been observed since the works of Darwin and Wallace (1859) appeared, later supplemented by the works on physiological and genetic mechanisms of evolution by August Weisman and Thomas Hunt Morgan, and the formal approach with mathematical models of J.B.S. Haldane, Ronald A. Fisher and Sewall Wright. In the 1940s this stream of development succeeded in formulating the so-called synthetic theory of evolution. For the first time in human history the exceptional place of man in the Universe, his uniqueness and difference, rooted in religion (Gen. 1, 27–28), were questioned.

The other research stream which shaped the emergence (fulguration) of a new image of the world was the work of James C. Maxwell (in the years 1864–73) on electromagnetic field theory, and the work of Ludwig Boltzmann – particularly his ideas concerning a statistical version of the second principle of thermodynamics (in 1884) and his reflections on the nature of reversible and irreversible processes. The work of Maxwell paved the way to the holistic view of the development of nature and the perception of the Universe evolution as a web of interconnected processes.

The 20th-century research in paleobiology, biology, anthropology, etiology and many other sciences proved how much we are 'the children of the Universe', and offspring of evolution. Increasing uncertainty in the unconstrained possibilities of controlling nature by man is the result of an ecological crisis which has been growing for decades in many regions of the Earth, and can now be observed on a global scale. As members of the human race, we are now conscious of the great complexity of nature and an enormous interrelatedness of apparently barely correlated phenomena in nature. Reductionism and mechanicism led to a perception of nature as a system of strictly hierarchical structures, with more and less important elements. Nature perceived in terms of categories of complexity and the mutual relationships of its, more or less distanced, parts forces a view of it as a web of events and processes with a weaker hierarchy.

As I have already mentioned, the perception of life space is one of the important categories of paragon defining the image of the world. The shift in the perception of space in the 16th century was connected mainly with the geographical discoveries of that time. The current shift in the perception of space is connected mainly with the dissemination of new media of communication at the end of the 19th century and the beginning of the 20th – through the development of telegraph, telephone and car, and now through the development of space telecommunication and supersonic planes. The traditional perception of distance has been shaken; small towns situated a few tens of kilometres away seem to be placed at the same distance as a metropolis situated a few hundred, or thousands of kilometres. Change of the topology of our life space is also connected with our growing consciousness of the Earth's limits – let us recall only the space travels (among them the landing on the Moon and seeing Earth from that perspective) and the famous reports of the Club of Rome, thanks to which the truth about the limited resources of the Earth was made known to the common man. The emergence of new topology and a new perception of our space is also caused by great ecological catastrophes witnessed by us in the last decades, which do not recognize the borders of countries and freely pass through them. Change of the perception categories, especially relating to our perception of time and space, is closely connected to the 20th-century development of physics, chemistry and biology. Ideas about quantum mechanics, a discrete genetic code (discovered by James Watson and Francis Crick in 1953), and an enormous development in computer technology with discrete representation of time and space, lead us to perceive time and space as discrete entities. Modern theories in physics explicitly assume the discreteness of space and time. So, as is frequently assumed, changes in nature also ought to be discrete, not continuous. The cause–effect determinism was replaced by indeterminism described by some stochastic and probabilistic categories.

The 16th-century image of the world imposing a specific attitude to solve socio-economic problems was observed. Using contemporary language, it was assumed that in socio-economic processes the formulation of an objective, a rational function (criterion) was possible; by means of this criterion, the quality of performance of different approaches, or techniques, solving particular problems could be evaluated. At the same time, the possibility of delimiting the set of constraints, inside which the optimal solution ought to be sought, was assumed. It seems that the contemporary image of the world undermines the views on such a strictly rational, or absolutely rational, approach to the solution of socio-economic problems. The possibility of constructing such an objective function as well as the possibility of delimiting the set of constraints are questioned. An alternative approach to the solution of such problems emerged, based on the perception of socio-economic development as an evolutionary and adaptive process. In such circumstances, knowledge of the optimal solution, which could be discovered at some point and remain valid for a shorter or longer period, lost its importance, and the search for better and better solutions in a changing environment on the basis of adaptive mechanism becomes essential.

Emergence of the 20th-century image of the world is also connected with a fresh reading of Plato's works and a revival of Kantism. In the opinion of Konrad Lorenz (1977, p. 54), the invention of the revolutionary, from a physical as well as from epistemological points of view, hypothesis about quanta of energy was probably not possible without a thorough knowledge of the philosophy of Immanuel Kant. Max Planck was well aware of the ideas of Kant; he treated causality as one of the human hypotheses and when he found it difficult to arrange the well-known physical facts on the basis of causality he simply put aside this hypothesis and replaced it with a stochastic and quantum approach.

In the new image of the world, logic and deductive approaches were not suspended as cognitive methods but other, alternative methods acquired equal significance, for example, a comparative-genetic method which seeks the sources of our knowledge in the historical process. The cognitive methods will be described in the section on *epistechne*.

IMAGE OF THE SOCIETY

The image of society consists of paragons concerning the arrangement of social activity and the institutional organization of society which make community life harmonious and amiable.

The main categories of paragons forming the image of society are as follows:

- *subjective categories* – paragons of these categories enable us to expound on the roles and duties of the basic units of societies such as the individual, family, lobby (group of interest), social class, and so on, and their relative influence on the course and tempo of development of the whole society;
- *notional categories* – paragons of these categories give meaning to such notions as equality, justice, law-abidance, responsibility and liability, sense of duty, freedom of the individual, sovereignty of social groups and nations, and so on;
- *governing categories* – paragons of these categories denominate ways of judging the conflicts between basic units of the society; ways and scope of using force, constraint and violence; ways of assuring the security of every individual within the society and the security of the society in relation to other organized societies.

A predominant model of organized society in the Western hemisphere is the model based on the idea of the state as a social contract. For the first time in the history of humankind, and yet in the most conclusive and fundamental way this model was accepted by the societies of the United States of America in their constitutional law signed on 17 September 1787. The idea of such an organized society was the direct result and crowning moment of protracted efforts made by philosophers of the English and French Enlightenment – Locke, Montesquieu and Rousseau, creators of political democracy based on such principles as individual freedom, democratic representation and the separation of powers. The restriction of government to the exercise of its proper function was provided by the system of checks and balances of such government agencies as the legislature, the executive and the judiciary. In the successive stages of development of this system an important role was played by political parties as the representatives of main social groups (classes).

An attempt to build an alternative concept of the state was undertaken by Karl Marx at the end of the 19th century. For him the state is an instrument of class rule and robs man of his freedom. In the future classless society there is no place for the state. In the extreme opinion of anarchists the state is an instrument of oppression to be eradicated in all social situations, and therefore, they conclude that it is necessary to abolish the state immediately. At the end of the 19th and the beginning of the 20th centuries, Peter Kropotkin, and some Russian anarchists, propagated an idea that the state would gradually disappear with the growth of voluntary cooperation, even in the capitalist society. Many other anarchists, among them Mikail Bakunin, agreed with the Marxist idea about the necessity of revolution but declared that the state should be abolished immediately.

Current efforts to rebuild the social order within contemporary capitalist society are clearly visible. Such essential features of a contemporary model of social order as the principle of democratic representation, the place and role of political parties, and the function of government are questioned (for example, Drucker, 1971; Bell, 1976; Miller 1983, 1984). Miller (1983, p. 259) wrote: 'As the United States counts down to the 200th anniversary of its only constitutional convention, it is becoming increasingly clear that major changes are necessary in the oldest *written* fundamental law. Social institutions, for example, political, economic, legal, are under severe challenge ... Both the *formal* and the *living* (or *operative*) constitutions require thorough study and revamping.'

Peter F. Drucker guesses that

ultimately we will need new political theory and probably very new constitutional law. We will need new concepts, and new social theory. Whether we will get these and what they will look like, we cannot know today. But we can know that we are disenchanted with government – primarily because it does not perform. We can say that we need, in a pluralist society, a government that can and does govern. This is not a government that 'does'; it is not a government that 'administers'; it is a government that governs. (Drucker, 1971, p. 297)

IMAGE OF THE ECONOMY

Paragons of this taxon relate to ways of the fulfilling material needs of members of the society. The main categories of paragons in this taxon are as follows:

- *categories of needs* – paragons of these categories refer to the material human needs which it is possible to satisfy at the current stage of socio-economic development;
- *management (organizational) categories* – paragons of these categories concern (1) economic criteria (objectives) to be applied during the manufacturing process, (2) manufacturing structure and manner of manufacture of material goods, and (3) ways of distribution of material goods and services;
- *relational categories* – these paragons determine (1) the role of political power in the economic process, that is, intensity of connections or separation of political power (e.g. of the state), and economic 'power' (for example, of economic agents), and (2) the role and weight of organized labour (for example, guilds, trade unions) in the economic process.

The 'classical' image of the economy, which lasted over 100 years from the middle of the 18th century until the end of the 19th century, was based on the liberal ideas of David Hume, Adam Smith and Jeremy Bentham.[7] There is no space and no necessity to describe in detail the liberal economy, but in a few words this concept may be characterized as follows: as little intervention by the state as possible;[8] free market economy; free entrepreneurship, employment and price settings; quick turnover of the

---

[7] See especially, the following works: Hume's *Essays Moral, Political and Literary* (1741 and 1742), and *Of the Balance of Trade* (1752); Smith's *Theory of Moral Sentiments* (1759) and *An Inquiry of the Nature and Causes of the Wealth of Nations* (1776); and Bentham's *Defence of Usury* (1787), *Deontology*, and *Science of Morality*, posthumously published in 1834.

[8] The state ought to play the role of the night watchman with only three, albeit very important, duties: 'first, the duty of protecting the society from the violence of other independent societies; secondly, the duty of protecting, as far as possible, every member of the society from the injustice or oppression of every other member of it; or the duty of establishing an exact administration of justice; and thirdly, the duty of erecting and maintaining certain public works and certain public institutions, which it can never be for the interest of any individual, or small number of individuals, to erect and maintain' (Smith, 1776, Vol. I. p. 325, Book II, Chap. III, edited by Edwin Cannon, 5th edn, London: Methuen & Co., Ltd., 1930).

financial capital. The essence of liberal economy lies also in the specific mode of production based on the principle of division of labour. Free competition (the *invisible hand* of Adam Smith) forms the basis of the economy and allows the optimal allocation of resources, rational balance of all production factors, wages, workforce, profit for capitalists and rent for landlords. In the opinion of Adam Smith, as a consequence of putting such principles into practice, we should observe continuous economic progress and 'the wealth of nations'.

The 20th-century image of the economy was shaped in the last 30 years of the 19th century. During that period the image of the economy which had prevailed in Western societies since the end of the 18th century was significantly modified.

Under the influence of socialist ideas (of the Fabians in Great Britain, the social democrats in Germany and of Marx and Engels) the role of the state government in economic life has changed. Since the end of the 19th century it has been claimed that the government should take care of the redistribution of national income to provide social justice. Active involvement of the state in the economy was initiated by Bismarck after the Vienna Congress in 1878 (Bismarck *Sozialpolitik*, and *Solidarzollschutz*). Albeit less promptly, a similar propensity towards greater government intervention was observed in the USA. One of the favourable indices of the role played by government in the economic process is reflected in the fraction of government spending in the gross national product. Until the 1870s US government expenditure was less than 2% of GNP; during the 1870s it increased to 4%, was around 3% in the next 40 years, grew to 7% in 1920 and since that time steadily increased to reach 10% in 1939, 19% in 1950, and since 1960 the proportion of government spending stabilized at the level of 25%. Similar trends have been observed in all modern capitalist states and public spending is much higher in all modern capitalist European countries – probably the extreme case is Sweden with its public spending in the 1980s running at over 60% of the national GNP.

Concurrently with the process of switching the government's place in the economic process, the expansion of trade unions and their much greater influence on the economic decisions of entrepreneurs and on the political decisions of the state governments were observed. The state, with the cooperation of big head offices of trade unions, started to play the role of 'economic governor and social functionary'. This idea was expressed in extreme form in the politics of the New Deal in the 1930s, and expounded as a coherent theory by J.M. Keynes in his *General Theory of Employment, Interest and Money* (1936).

The shift of the image of the economy at the end of the 19th century was also associated with a new management and organization approach in industry and a new posture in agriculture. Innovative practice in management was mainly connected with a new vision of organization of working processes in factories. Frederick W. Taylor, inventor of 'scientific methods of management' has shown how it is possible to improve the working conditions of a worker in a factory by using 'systematic enquiry of the workplace'. Contrary to the almost universal belief that the main aim of Taylor's approach was to increase capitalists' profits, Taylor's primary intention was the improvement of workers' conditions of labour. Henry Ford, by introducing his assembly line to manufacture his famous model T, opened the way to mass production and mass markets. He has shown that it is possible to accumulate large global profits by gaining only small unit profits. He demonstrated and established the advantages of what is now termed economies of scale. The essence of this philosophy of production and fulfilling material needs is expressed in Ford's famous statement that he was able to produce and to sell cars of 'any color you want so long as it is black'.

Changes within agriculture at the end of the 19th century were coupled with the structural changes of whole societies. Agriculture since then has not been the predominant form of employment for the majority of 19th- and 20th-century societies, but concurrently farmers had to provide a sufficient quantity of food for the growing society. This demand imposed a flow of capital and an increase of technological progress in agriculture (especially in the United States). The organization and mode of production in agriculture became more and more similar to those in industry. A farmer became an agronomist and technologist, who organizes the production of food not only to feed his family but principally to manufacture a surplus of food to be sold.

The predominant category of material needs in the 20th-century image of the economy were any mechanical and automatic mechanisms (goods, things) of households, especially those facilitating household labour (refrigerators, washing machines, kitchen robots, and so on). Fulfilment of these needs was possible thanks to the application of mass production (economies of scale).

Opinions on future ways of production and the future image of the economy are diversified and heterogenous. But there is a common understanding that the emerging image of the economy will be essentially different from that predominant in the last decades. All categories of paragons mentioned at the beginning of this section will be modified or have been modified since the beginning of the 1980s.

The emerging category of needs will also include mechanical and automatic household devices but the predominant position will be occupied by devices fulfilling higher-order needs – connected with entertainment, sport, hobbies, craft, art, and so on. The basic difference between needs in the last decades and the future category of needs rests in the possibility of buying any commodity according to individual preferences, taste, relish and fancy. A leading slogan of the previous image of the economy was 'economies of scale' and it seems that in the emerging image of the economy this slogan will be replaced by a new one, namely 'economies of scope'. In the emerging image of the economy production of different products on the same set of plants will be as cheap (or even cheaper) as the production of one product on different plants. Potentialities of mass production will be much less important than elasticity of production and flexibility of design for individual requirements (for example, Jelinek and Goldhar, 1984). The new manner of production will be based on current highly developing technologies in microelectronics, computer science and the computer industry, telecommunication, and so on, and will result in the integration of currently separated technologies. First attempts have already been made, for example, CAD, CAM, CAE – Computer Aided Design, Manufacturing, Engineering; CIM – Computer Integrated Manufacturing; FMS – Flexible Manufacturing Systems; and computer trade technologies based, for example, on EFT – Electronic Funds Transfer.

In the emerging image of the economy we will also witness modification of the objectives of economic activity; besides contemporary predominant objectives focused on effectiveness and profit maximization, future consequences of current economic activities will also be taken into account.[9] The modification of economic objectives is forced by the growing consciousness of the ecological problems facing contemporary societies.

Economic analysis of industrial processes in the last decades suggests that besides two 'classic' factors of production, namely labour and capital, there exists a third 'residual' one, sometimes called knowledge, related to technological progress. Results of some statistical analysis show that this third, 'residual' factor of production is responsible for 70 to 80% of observed economic growth, and only 20 to 30% of economic growth is related to the classical factors – labour and capital. In the following chapter this problem will be discussed in more detail; here I would like to say only that the discovery of the third factor of production will have a significant influence on the economic policy of the state. Even now we observe further and further divergence from Keynesian economics and macro-planning towards a more decentralized economy based on the philosophy of self-organizing processes. In the new conditions the role of the government in economic process will be much less significant (for example, Friedman and Friedman, 1979), but probably there will be no radical retreat from state interventionism, which has been growing steadily since the beginning of this century. Probably the future model of the state in economic life will be

---

[9] See, for example, the special issue of FUTURES 9/1977 on this subject, with: D. Preace, 'Accounting for the Future', R.H. Haveman, 'The economic evaluation of long-run uncertainties', A.M. Freeman, 'Equity, efficiency, and discounting: The reasons for discounting intergenerational effects', T. Page, 'Discounting and intergenerational equity' and R.J. Mishan, 'Economic criteria for intergenerational comparisons'.

something intermediate between the model of the state as the 'night watchman' and the 'welfare state' – contemporary state monopoly. This process of shifting towards the new model of the state is observed all around the world – starting from the United States, through the European states (Sweden, Germany, Great Britain and many others), and ending in the East European states, former communist states, Poland, Hungary, the Czech Republic and Slovakia, and former Soviet republics.

A new subsequent feature of the emerging image of the economy will be a shift from the international to the world economy. International economy has been a subject of research for economists since the days of Adam Smith. What we have witnessed in the last decades is a tendency towards the strong cooperation of domestic economies and the creation of a world economy. One of the challenges for modern economic thought is how to explain the domestic economy as part of the world economy. The 19th-century separation of domestic and international economy is an obsolete concept. Economists must go beyond the traditional limitation of economic analysis focused on the concept of the domestic economy (see, for example, Drucker, 1971, p. 200).

In contrast to the very influential role of trade unions in the former image of the economy, the importance of trade unions in the succeeding image of the economy will be much smaller. This process is clearly visible now in the high-tech industries (computers, microelectronics, biotechnology) where trade unions do not exist or are very rare and weak. Drucker (1971, p. 81) states that:

> The greatest obstacle to economic growth in the United States and Great Britain is the craft organization of work and especially the craft union, which puts a tremendous premium on doing things the way they used to be done. The craft union with its 'jurisdictions' and 'demarcations' (the former, the American – the latter, the British, term for union restrictions) prohibits, by definition, the learning of new skills by its members, and at the same time forbids access to skilled job by outsiders.

The new shape of the future society will also impose changes in the modes of work and the basic subject of labour – in the former image of the economy the worker-proletarian was the basic subject of labour. Different authors expose different features of the future society, and this is reflected in different names for that society, for example, Drucker (1971) and Toffler (1985) speak about the knowledge society, others speak about a post-industrial, information, informal or dual society (for example, Halal 1985; Huber 1985; Marien 1977). In Toffler's opinion a specific class of workers will arise, namely those whose work will be based on knowledge, and he proposes naming this class *cognitariat*. Drucker (1971, p. 350) writes that:

> What the knowledge worker needs to be positively motivated is achievement. He needs

a challenge. He needs to know that he contributes. This is in complete contradiction to what we have come to consider 'good management' of the manual worker. The essence of our experience here is summed up in the popular phrase, 'A fair day's work for a fair day's pay'. Knowledge workers, however, should be expected to do 'an exceptional day's work' – and, they should then also have a chance to earn 'exceptional pay'.

Bell (1976) proposed the concept of a public household. In his opinion it is not the third sector of the future economy – congruous to the private household and the economic market – but one embracing the two. Bell claims that in this sector the market mechanisms would act whenever possible, but within well-defined social goals. In this concept an individual would be the basic unit of society and individual achievement would be rewarded. In this sense it is a liberal concept, but the central problem of the public household is how to reconcile the claims of one group with the claims of the other group, in cases where it is clear that the problem is not to choose between two alternatives, right-wrong, but to choose one alternative from two equally rational ones. The other problem is how to reconcile the claims of a whole group with individual rights; how to find a balance between freedom and equality, between justice and effectiveness.

EPISTECHNE

The name of this taxon comes from the Greek *episteme* (i.e. knowledge, acquisition, understanding), and *techne* (i.e. art, craft, proficiency, wiliness). It is my intention to include in this term both cognition research, which extends man's knowledge about the world, and practical knowledge, which decides on a degree of suppression of nature by man. So, *epistechne* includes both types of research activity of man, or what is now called science and technology.

Paragons of the *episteme* describe:

- research domains recognized by a researcher as important, interesting and suitable to undertake;
- ways of carrying out research activity and its organization; forms of interchanges and protection of knowledge and research achievements;
- type, place and meaning of experiment/observation in a research activity; type of instruments, devices, plants, installations, and so on, applied in experiments/observations;
- types and forms of mathematics (for example, computation methods, formal methods) applied to describe and explain results of experiments/observations.

Until the 17th century the fields of research of *episteme* and *techne*

were almost fully separated. *Techne* was mainly connected with craft work, and, since the 15th century, also with manufactures, and was developed through the transmission of practical skills from generation to generation. Innovations within *techne* were made mainly through trial-and-error processes, by making prototypes and testing their performance on material objects, not by using any systematic methods of research.

In the Middle Ages, *episteme* consisted of the so-called classical system of colleges' *trivium* (grammar, rhetoric and dialectics) and universities' *quadrivium* (arithmetics, geometry, astronomy and music). In the medieval system of knowledge an intellect, and mental experiments, were considered as the only source of truth. Information about the surrounding physical world was gained mainly through passive observations.

The transformation of higher taxa of knowledge development (the images of the world, the society and the economy) can be seen as a cyclical process, and an outline of such a description was presented in previous sections of this chapter. In this section, a proposition of looking at the development of *episteme* as the cyclical process in which each cycle consists of two phases, namely the substitution phase and the quasi-equilibrium phase, is also presented. It is a far-reaching idealization of the real process as observed in the last 350 years in Western Europe and North America. In fact, what we observe in the development of science and technology is the concurrent existence of numerous *epistemes* and *technes* (*epistechnes*) at any moment in time (for example, it is possible to identify in contemporary science and technology the following dominant *epistechnes*: in science – Cartesian, Baconian, comparative and holistic; in technology – industrial and complex). In fact, each *episteme* ought to be described separately with its own periodization. But a more detailed description of this process is outside the scope of this work, so I confine the presentation to a short description of all *epistemes* as one cyclical process. This stylized approach seems to be justified by the observed high correlation and significant synchronization of the development of all *epistemes*. In the last 100 years similar correlation and synchronization has been observed in the development of *epistemes* and *technes*.

I will not present a description of the periodic development of the *techne*, as this process is widely documented and described by different authors as so-called long waves or Kondratieff cycles (for example, Freeman (ed.), 1983; Freeman et al., 1982; Freeman and Perez, 1988; Tylecote, 1992). It has been estimated that each cycle lasts 50 to 60 years. The first cycle (*industrial revolution* – name proposed by Freeman and Perez, 1988) lasting from the 1770s to the 1830s, was connected mainly with innovations and the rapid development of textile industries (also related textile chemicals and textile machinery) and iron industries (and related steam engines and machinery). The second Kondratieff cycle lasted from the 1830s to the 1880s (*Victorian prosperity*), and was associated with the development of steam engines, machine tools and railways. The third Kondratieff cycle (*Belle epoque*) lasted from the 1880s to the 1930s and was connected with the development of electrical engineering and machinery, and also with the wide availability of cheap steel. The fourth Kondratieff cycle (*Golden age of growth and Keynesian full employment*) from the 1930s to the 1980s, was distinctive for its mass production of automobiles and trucks, consumer durables, synthetic materials and petrochemicals. The fifth Kondratieff cycle probably started in the 1980s and most likely will be identified with the revolutionary development of computer, information and telecommunication technologies.

The First Cycle of *Episteme* – From 1620 to 1677

The substitution phase is marked by two dates: 1620 – publication of Francis Bacon's *Novum Organum*; and 1644 – publication of René Descartes' *Principles of philosophy*. In the period 1620–44 there appeared the fundamental works of Galileo Galilei (*Dialogue Concerning the Two Chief World Systems – Ptolemaic and Copernican* in 1632; and *Dialogues Concerning Two New Sciences* in 1638), Descartes' *Discourse on Method* (1637) and Bacon's *New Atlantis* (1627).

Predominant domains of research in this cycle were related to:

1. Explanation of common principles of movement of macroscopic bodies 'on the Earth and in the sky' (for example, ballistic trajectories of artillery bullets and the planets' trajectories in the solar system). By using more powerful telescopes the scope of observations was extended to the solar planetary system and the Sun itself.[10]
2. Development of experimental methods in anatomy, initiated by Andreas Vesalius (1514–64). The efforts of many researchers in this stream of research were focused on the direct observation of physiological processes, and on the extension of the field of observation in this domain. The most spectacular result of that time was the discovery of the blood circulation system, announced by William Harvey (1578–1657) in his treatise *On the Motion of the Heart* (1628).

The substitution period, 1620–44, is marked by the emergence of two *epistemes* – Cartesian and Baconian. The Cartesian *episteme* was in great part an extension of the idea of scientific enquiry formulated by Galileo. The essence of the Cartesian *episteme* lies in the assumption of the

---

[10] Galileo was the first to use the telescope to study the skies. At the end of 1609 and the beginning of 1610 he announced a series of astronomical discoveries, among them irregularities of the Moon's surface, observations of the Milky Way as a collection of stars, and the satellites of Jupiter.

possibility of formulating the laws of nature (or common laws – in the words of Descartes) by pure activity of the human intellect (mind) and of cognition of observed phenomena by using the deductive method – starting from the most simple and the most general laws. An alternative to the Cartesian *episteme* was the Baconian one.[11] As may be estimated from a contemporary perspective, the Baconian *episteme* was the first attempt to build a bridge between the classical *episteme* (science) and the classical *techne* (technology). Francis Bacon emphasized the importance of active experiment with the main objective of compelling Nature to manifest its properties in conditions never, or rarely, observed in natural processes. The main aim of such experiments is to uncover the unknown. In the opinion of Baconian researchers, such experiments 'take the bull by the horns'. In the Baconian *episteme* the relation between theory and experiment was radically different from those in any former *epistemes*. In contrast to the Medieval *episteme*, where experiment or observation ought to prove the theory, theory was considered by Bacon as the consequence of an experiment. In extreme cases some researchers claimed that only the results of experiments are worth consideration, and any theory is essentially futile. In *Novum Organum*[12] Bacon stated:

> there are two ways, and can only be two, of seeking and finding truth. The one, from sense and reason, takes a flight to be the most general axioms, and from these principles and their truth, settled once and for all, invents and judges of all intermediate axioms. The other method collects axioms from sense and particulars, ascending continuously and by degrees so that in the end it arrives at the most general axioms. This latter is the only true one, but never hitherto tried.

Research made within the framework of the Cartesian *episteme* resulted in the development of the theory of gravitation by Isaac Newton, and experiments made within the framework of the Baconian *episteme* allowed for a better understanding of electrical and chemical phenomena and put the foundations for the development of these disciplines in the 18th and 19th centuries.

Experiments accomplished within the Baconian *episteme*, and the collection of files of their records encouraged close cooperation and frequent meetings of researchers within this circle. Necessity for close cooperation led to the creation of many informal groups of researchers in Great Britain, France, Italy, the Netherlands and many other European countries. The best known of these informal groups in Great Britain were the 'Gresham philosophers', named after the place of their meetings at Gresham College

---

[11] The roots of the Baconian *episteme* may be found in the activity of Roger Bacon (1214–94) and the work of Paracelsus (*circa* 1493–1541).

[12] Book I, xix, see also Book I, x, xi.

in London, and the group of researchers named by Boyle the 'Invisible College' (1646). The meetings within informal groups resulted in the creation of many scientific societies at the beginning of the 17th century; later on some of these societies were nominated to become National Academies of Sciences, of which probably the best known is the Royal Society of London for the Promotion of Natural Knowledge, with its first written constitution approved in 1662. The difference between the former *epistemes* of the Middle Ages and the ones discussed, which may be considered as the first *epistemes* belonging fully to the Renaissance image of the world, lies also in the distinction of financial sources of research support; in contrast to former ages, a significant portion of research in the 16th century was sponsored by private persons, frequently by the researchers themselves.

The post and communication media were notably improved at the beginning of the 17th century, which allowed more frequent interchange of correspondence and created new ways for the exchange of results of scientific research, and of critical comments.

The most significant improvement during this period, related to the formal (mathematical) tools, was the invention of analytical geometry by Descartes and of the application of this tool to research on the theory of movement of material bodies.

The Second Cycle of *Episteme* – From 1677 to 1787

Roughly speaking, the scope of the substitution phase is marked by the improvement of the microscope by Antoni van Leeuwenhoek in 1677 (with a magnification of around 300 times) and the publication of Isaac Newton's *Philosophiae naturalis principa mathematica* in 1687.

The extension of observatory scope of astronomers (outside of the solar system) and the significant improvement in the accuracy of observations were possible thanks to the use of new reflecting telescopes – built by Newton (and improved by William Herschel) and N. Cassegrain (the so-called Cassegrain reflector, designed in 1672). In 1684, Ole Romer, after his return from England to Denmark, designed and set up an instrument with altitude and azimuth circles, which greatly improved the accuracy of measurement of the position of celestial bodies.

Leeuwenhoek's new microscope initiated the revolution in biology, enabled observations of objects unseen by the naked eye, and allowed the discovery of the worlds of infusoria and bacteria. The possibility of observing small details of the structure of living organisms led to the emergence of new disciplines, such as histology, cytology and embryology.

The end of the 17th century was marked also by revolutionary ideas of comparative and systematic biology. These achievements in comparative biology may be considered as the direct result of the huge number of descriptive records about flora and fauna, collected in the previous decades. The first step was made by John Ray (1627–1705) in his works *Methodus plantarum nova* (1683), *Synopsis methodica animalium quadrupedum et serpentini generis* (1693) and *Methodus insectorum* (1704). The research was continued by Carl von Linné (Carolus Linnaeus, 1707–78) and resulted in his famous systematics of three kingdoms of animals, plants (vegetables), and minerals (the first edition of his *Systema naturae* was published in 1735). The principles formulated by Linnaeus became the foundation of future international agreement on systematics; his binomial classification system was commonly accepted by biologists within a few years of its publication.

After publication of Newton's *Principia*, astronomical, cosmological and ballistic problems, which had been at the centre of research since the 16th century, were considered as solved. Efforts of researches in the 18th and 19th centuries were focused on mathematical precision and experimental confirmation of principles stated by Newton. The interest of researchers was attracted to the mysteries of heat, pneumatics, electricity and chemistry. These resulted in essential modifications of the Baconian and Cartesian *epistemes*. Newton's work on 'mechanical philosophy' was continued within the Cartesian *episteme*. This was the domain of mathematics, so the Cartesian *episteme* became more theoretical and some purely mathematical explorations were initiated within this *episteme* (for a similar opinion, see Kuhn, 1985, p. 89). The Baconian *episteme* started to apply some mathematical approaches used within the Cartesian *episteme* and many Baconian disciplines became the quantitative sciences. An important feature of the Baconian *episteme* in this cycle was the close cooperation of Baconian researchers with craftsmen (*techne*) who built the scientific machinery used in the experiments. It turned out that making scientific equipment could be a profitable business for craftsmen and since then there has been a vigorous development of the scientific instrument industry.

The role of scientific societies had changed at the end of the 17th century. To a lesser extent they were places for the exchange of ideas; rather they became places where methodological problems (the modes of undertaking research) were debated. In contrast to earlier discussion, which focused on the benefits of scientific research to humankind and civilization, more and more frequently the problems of the benefits of scientific research to the nation and the national economy were disputed in official sessions of the scientific societies. Probably for the first time, problems of national interest were discussed in France by the founders of the Académie des Sciences (Hall, 1966, p. 238; 1962, pp. 200–201), and very clearly this was stated by members of the Berlin Academy of Sciences (founded by Frederick I in 1700). Gottfried Wilhelm Leibniz, also the adviser to Frederick I, wrote explicitly in a letter to Prince Eugene, discussing the proposed scientific academy in Vienna (Hall, 1966, p. 240; 1962, p. 202) that observatories, laboratories, botanical and zoological gardens, collections of natural and artificial peculiarities, records of physico-medicine history, and so on are necessary for improvements in art, craft, agriculture, civil and military construction, description of countries, working conditions of miners, as well as employment of the impoverished, for incentives of inventors and entrepreneurs, and in the end for anything that influences economy, technology and military strength of the state.

The first scientific journals (for example, *Philosophical Transactions* founded in London in 1665) announced only general information about scientific developments (about activities of scientific societies, minutes of scientific meetings, letters, and so on); results of original research or reports from ongoing research were not published there. The situation had changed by the end of the 17th century, when journals became the place where original results of research started to be published. The publication of original research results and their wide dissemination stimulated discussion and resulted in much polemic. The number of scientific journals grew significantly by the end of 17th century, and since the 1680s a geometrical growth of the number of scientific journals can be observed.

The meaning and the role of experiments had also changed in that period. Experiments were not treated as 'art for art's sake'. More frequently experiments and observations were intended to verify existing theories (two examples of such endeavours are mentioned by Hall, 1966, pp. 397 and 398).

The development and application of differential and integral calculus to physics may be considered an essential improvement to mathematical (formal) tools in natural sciences. The fundamentals of this calculus were published by Newton in his *Method of Fluxions* (1671). The development of this calculus and the application of better and more practical notation were accomplished, probably independently, by Leibniz who published it for the first time in his work in 1684.

The Third Cycle of *Episteme* – From 1787 to 1859

The substitution phase in this cycle spans from the publication of new terminology in chemistry by Antoine Laurent Lavoisier and three of his French adherents in 1787 (see Hall, 1966, p. 337) to the manufacture of the first electrical battery on the basis of 'chemical effects' by William Nicholson in 1802. Fundamental discoveries shaping the development of chemistry, biology and electricity in the first 70 years of the 19th century were made in the period 1787–1802. Only a few of them will be mentioned here: the publication by Lavoisier of *Truite élémentaire de chemie* (1789); discovery of the law of interaction (attraction or repulsion) of two electrical charges by Charles de Coulomb in 1785 (he measured the forces between two charges using a very sensitive instrument, the so-called torsion-balance, especially designed by him to measure small forces); the introduction of the notion of magnetic moment by Coulomb in 1789; the construction of the electrometer by Abraham Bennet in 1792; the explanation of the Galvani effect by Alessandro Volta (1792) and the construction of the Volta battery (the first 'artificial electrical organ') in 1800; and the discovery of the stoichiometric law by Joseph Louis Proust, John Dalton and Jeremias Beniamin Richter (1799–1804). In this period Charles de Bonnet (1720–93) introduced the notion of 'evolution' in biology and Georges Cuvier, William Smith and Jean Baptiste de Lamarck established the foundations of a new science – paleobiology.

The discoveries of the sixth planet of our system (Uranus) by William Herschel in 1781 and the first planetoid (Ceres) by Giuseppe Piazzi in 1801 changed the conception of the structure of our planetary system and demonstrated the possibility of the existence of other planets; these discoveries encouraged astronomers to make a systematic search of the solar systems. Publication of the five volumes of Pierre Simone Laplace's *Mécanique céleste* (1799–1825) was started during the substitution phase of this cycle. The cosmological hypothesis about the creation of the solar system presented in the work of Laplace was accepted by astronomers by the end of the 19th century.

The Baconian *episteme* was sanctioned by the universities as a matured science; some of the Baconian disciplines, for example, experimental physics, chemistry, heat science and electricity, were subject of university lectures and were considered equally as important as the classical sciences (for example, as mechanics). The École Politechnique is a symbol of these changes – in the 1790s the Baconian sciences were for the first time approved as normal courses in that university. As a consequence of the maturation process of Baconian sciences, a deep mathematization of empirical sciences was observed, for example, Siméon D. Poisson – mathematical research on electrostatic forces; Augustin L. Cauchy and Benoit P. Clapeyron – the mathematical theory of flexibility; Thomas Young and Augustin J. Fresnel – the wave theory of light. Mathematization of empirical sciences resulted in the development of formal tools, for example, partial differential equations (especially of the Laplace and Van der Pol type, wave and diffusion equations[13]), the theory of complex function (Carl F. Gauss and Augustin L. Cauchy), and the mathematical theory of probability (Pierre S. Laplace).

The demonstration of the finiteness of our galaxy and an approximate evaluation of its shape by William Herschel in 1783–84 not only gave a good example of the extent to which the mysteries of nature had been penetrated, but also heralded the invention of a specific mathematical

---

[13] Mathematical theory of partial differential equations was founded by Jean Le Rond d'Alembert, Leonhard Euler and Daniel Bernoulli in the middle of the 18th century.

method based on a statistical sample approach.[14] His work prompted the development of a new discipline – the study of stars and nebulae astronomy.

The Fourth Cycle of *Episteme* – From 1859 to 1912

This cycle is shorter than the previous ones, and may be considered as a transition cycle between the two images of the world – the Renaissance image and the emerging 20th-century image. It is very difficult to distinguish the substitution phase in this cycle; in fact the whole cycle is a series of fundamental discoveries which shaped the emerging image of the world, and future domains of scientific research. The cycle is conventionally assumed to begin in 1859, with the publication of the hypothesis about natural selection as a driving force of biological evolution by Charles Darwin[15] and independently by Alfred R. Wallace. Dmitrij I. Mendeleyev in *Principles of Chemistry* (1866–70) announced his discovery of the periodic classification of elements (the so-called Mendeleyev classification). In 1869 Johann Friedrich Miescher discovered the nucleic acids, and in 1887, Heinrich Rudolf Hertz announced the discovery of the photoelectric effect.

The unification of physics and chemistry as disciplines with the same root, as initiated by Stanislao Cannizzaro, was worked out and accepted by many researchers in the period 1869–88. The beginning of the cycle is also marked by the rapid development of such disciplines as statistical physics and the kinematics theory of matter – the fundamental research was accomplished by Rudolf E. Clausius, James C. Maxwell, and Ludwig E. Boltzmann between 1856 and 1868. This period is also marked by the discovery of the electromagnetic field theory by James C. Maxwell (from 1864 to 1873),[16] and the development of microbiology, the etiology of

---

[14] Herschel counted all the stars of a chosen magnitude in the 3,400 patches of sky which he was able to see in his 46 cm telescope. He drew the results on the map of the sky and in this way he was able to obtain an approximate shape of our galaxy and the distribution of the stars. The diameter of Herschel's telescope allowed him to observe $1/4°$ (i.e. 1/20 square degree) of the sky during a single observation. It means that he estimated the distribution of stars of the whole sphere (with 41,000 square degrees) on the basis of an observation of only 170 square degrees.

[15] Charles Darwin published his *Origin of Species by Means of Natural Selection* in 1859, and applied his general ideas to the evolution of humankind in *The Descent of Man and Selection in Relation to Sex* (1871).

[16] Maxwell's work on the model of the electromagnetic field has become the symbol of this cycle – from one point of view the final result and the consequences of the model belong to the new image of the world, but the principal ideas of electromagnetic theory as presented by Maxwell in the papers of 1861–61, and 1864 are rooted in the mechanical reductionist image of the world originating in the 16th and 17th centuries. Hermann L. Helmholtz (1872) describes the principal model of Maxwell as 'a system of cells with elastic walls and cylindrical cavities ... in which elastic balls can rotate and be flattened out by the centrifugal force. In the walls of cells there must be other balls, of invariable volume, as friction rollers ... their centre of gravity ... would merely be displaced by elastic yield of the cell-wall ... displacement of [the friction rollers] gives dielectric

infectious diseases and immunology (detailed in the works of Louis Pasteur between 1860–65), and physiology (Claude Bernard). Pivotal experiments having an essential influence on the future development of physics, were also undertaken during that time – probably the most important were: the experiments of Albert A. Michelson and Edward W. Morley (1881–87; proving that the speed of light is independent of the chosen system of coordinates); the discovery of thermoemission by Thomas A. Edison (1883); the condensation of oxygen and nitrogen (Zygmunt F. Wróblewski and Karol Olszewski, 1883); and the discovery of electron (Joseph J. Thomson, 1896; the existence of an electron had been foreseen by G.J. Stanley in 1868).

In 1859–60 Gustav R. Kirchhoff defined a black body as an object that re-emits all of the radiant energy incident upon it, that is, it was a perfect emitter and absorber of radiation. In 1884, Ludwig Boltzmann, applying the principles of thermodynamics, proposed the law of the radiation of the black body (now known as the Stefan–Boltzmann law). Max Planck was particularly attracted by the formula of the black body's radiation as proposed by his colleague Wilhelm Wien in 1896. He subsequently made a series of attempts to derive Wien's law, on the basis of the second law of thermodynamics. By October 1900, other colleagues from his institute had found definite indications that the Wien's law, while being valid at high frequencies, broke down completely at low frequencies. To explain this discrepancy (at the end of 1900) Planck had to relinquish his favourite belief that the second law of thermodynamics was an absolute law of nature. Instead, he had to accept Boltzmann's interpretation that the second law is a statistical law. Planck had to assume also that the oscillators comprising the black body and re-emitting the radiant energy incident upon it could not absorb this energy continuously but only in discrete amounts, in quanta of energy. The work of Planck, together with the work of Albert Einstein published in 1905 on the light quanta (later called photons) paved the way for the quick development of quantum physics.

In the paper 'On Electrodynamics of Moving Bodies' (1905), Albert Einstein published his special theory of relativity which together with four other papers published in that year in *Annalen der Physik* initiated new attitudes to nature, a new perception of space and time and a new view of the universe. This period is also marked by a substantial enlargement in the scope of research: (1) in physics to the subatomic level (thermoelectric effect, radiation of the black body), and (2) in biology to sub-cell level (karyokinesis in animal cells – Wacław Mayzel, 1873 – and the discovery

---

polarization of the medium; streaming of the same, an electric current; rotation of the elastic balls corresponds to the magnetizing of the medium, the axis of rotation being the direction of the magnetic force'. Quotation from Alfred M. Bork, 'Physics Just Before Einstein', *Science*, 29 April 1966, pp. 597–603. There is also a relevant bibliography.

of the nucleic acid by Johann F. Miescher in 1869). For the first time in human history the economic development of the whole society was strongly subordinated to the progress of the sciences (especially of those of the Baconian *episteme*). The emergence and development of electrical and chemical industries relied directly upon the former and ongoing research in electricity and chemistry. Concurrent with the emergence of new science-based industries the convergence process of *techne* and the Baconian *episteme* was observed. Industry and business encouraged the university research. Close cooperation between industry and universities led to widespread changes in the structure of universities. Formerly, teaching was the main obligation of universities; the scientific research was, in a sense, a private matter undertaken in addition to the main university commitment. University teaching was focused on general education at a high level. But since the 1870s in the United States an important objective was also the education of future researchers, which gave rise to the so-called graduate schools (the first one was established at Harvard University in 1873) where the main aim of education was acquaintance with utilitarian research. Since that time engineer–inventors' and scientists' careers have become profitable professions. Strong cooperation between industry and science also spurred the rapid development of the scientific equipment industry, for example, in 1881 Horace Darwin founded the Scientific Instrument Company, which still exists today. In 1876 in Menlo Park (USA) Thomas Alva Edison started the first 'invention factory'.[17] Edison's laboratories and workshops were equipped with any scientific equipment necessary to undertake systematic research. Edison had 'bought' all the most talented people, and he even worked out special tests for each candidate for admission to his invention factory. His laboratories may be considered as the transition organizations between 'old' and 'new' *technes* – organization of work and financial conditions were very similar to the upcoming 20th-century research units, but methods of research were rooted in the former image of the world, based mainly on making prototypes and experimenting with them, in contrast to the systematic research of contemporary industry research so closely related to those within the Baconian or Cartesian *epistemes*.[18] Edison initiated the establishment of outside university research units. Funds earmarked for research in such units grew very quickly, for example, in the United States in the Rockefeller Institute research funds had grown to $120 million within the first 5 years of activity.

---

[17] His aim was to build an 'all-purpose laboratory' in which he proposed 'to make inventions to order'.

[18] The classical example is the innovation of bulb fibre; after spending over $40,000 on fruitless experiments, in the end, on 21 October 1879, he used a carbonized cotton thread which glowed in a vacuum for more than 40 hours. Edison searched for the proper fibre not by using any systematic method of research, i.e. as indicated by the properties of the required material, but instead of that he searched at random by trying approximately 6,000 different materials.

The period 1870–90 was also marked by the very rapid development of new media of knowledge communication, the so-called abstract journals. The first three abstract journals originated around 1835 (D. de Solla Price, 1965, p. 98), but in the next 40 years no new journal of this type was launched. This may suggest the premature emergence of such journals. Since 1875 the number of abstract journals grew exponentially, for example, in 1900 about 20 journals were issued, and in 1925 about 100.

Concerning new mathematical methods, the advanced method of probability theory (for example, thermodynamics, statistical physics), integral and partial differential equations (the theory of electromagnetic field), and operational calculus (the basics of which were worked out in the 1880s and published by Oliver Heaviside in *Electrical Papers* (1892)) deserve a mention.

The Fifth Cycle of *Episteme* – From 1912 to the 1980s

The substitution phase lasted, approximately, from 1912, with diffraction of Roentgen's rays on the crystal net and formulation of Bragg's law in 1913 until 1932, with the foundation of population genetics by Tchetverikov (1926), Fisher (1930), Wright (1931) and Haldane (1932). Research in subsequently new regions of reality was initiated in that period. In physics it was sub-nucleus research – the construction of the first accelerator of charged molecules in 1931 (the cyclotron by Ernest O. Lawrence and M. Stanley Livingstone), and the development of the foundations of quantum mechanics in 1924–34 (Louis V. de Broglie, Erwin Schrödinger, Werner Heisenberg, Niels H. Bohr, Pascual Jordan, Wolfgang Pauli, Paul A. Dirac and Max Born). In biology and chemistry research was at sub-cell and sub-molecule levels – research in these fields was possible thanks to the discovery of Roentgen's rays (1912), the demonstration of the diffraction of molecules (among them the diffraction of electrons by C.J. Davisson, L.H. Germer and G.P. Thompson) and the designing of the first electron microscope in 1931 by Ernst Ruska.

This period was also marked by a new penetration of macrocosms and the emergence of new cosmology – Einstein's general relativity theory (1916) and his cosmological treatise (1917), and the first observation of a star not belonging to our galaxy by Edwin P. Hubble.[19] The development of astronomy and astronomical instruments in that period allowed the observation of far regions of the Universe and initiated discussion on the origin of the Universe – observations of radio waves coming from space by Karl Guthe Jansky in 1931–32 and Grote Reber in 1935 (since that time there has been a very rapid development in radio-astronomy); the invention

---

[19] It was cepheid, belonging to M-31, plate no. H-335-H, 5–6 October, 1925; observations were made with a 2.5 m. telescope sited on Mount Wilson.

of the catadioptric system in 1931 (Schmidt's telescope and Maskutov's telescope); and improvements in spectroscopic technology.

The development of observatory instruments in biology allowed research in micro-scale (cell and nucleus research) to be undertaken. Applications of specific mathematical approaches in biology allowed research at the population level – population genetics (Ronald A. Fisher, Sewall Wright and J.B.S. Haldane) and ecology (A.J. Lotka and Vito Volterra).

Fundamental research on the theory of information (for example, R.W.L. Harley, 1928) and solid-state physics (the streaked theory of conductors and semi-conductors – A.H. Wilson, N.F. Mott, F. Bloch and L. N. Brillouin) opened the way to the contemporary development of electronics and information technology (computers).

The development of quantum mechanics and the discovery, in 1927, of the uncertainty principle (Heisenberg's indeterminacy principle) changed the place and the role of the observer in experiments.[20] New perspectives in the perception of reality as proposed by quantum mechanics suggested an alternative to the principles of the reductionist approach and the endless search for 'basic units of matter'. The founders of quantum mechanics initiated a radically new school of thinking in the physics of elementary particles – according to this idea, 'nature, at the atomic level, does not appear as a mechanical universe composed of fundamental building blocks but rather as a network of relations, and that, ultimately, there are no parts at all in this interconnected web' (Capra, 1985).

Such a view of the world represented by physicists, philosophers (for example, Alfred N. Whitehead) and biologists, expressed in the philosophy of holism, caused the emergence of a new *episteme*, which I propose to call the holistic *episteme*. The appearance of this *episteme* is closely associated with the new image of the world which had been emerging since the end of the 19th century. The main features of the holistic *episteme* are as follows:

- perceiving the universe (nature) as a dynamic web of interrelated events; no part of this web may be considered as fundamental, elementary or basic;
- thinking in the categories of ongoing processes rather than a static structure (the structure is a consequence of ongoing processes);
- properties of any component of the system arise essentially from the dynamics of the whole system.

The emergence of the new image of the world resulted also in a revival of the comparative method. This method was applied in the past mainly in

---

[20] By analogy, the active role of an observer in experiments and his (her) influence on the results of observations, were accepted in other disciplines, for example, sociology and anthropology.

biology.[21] The first application of the comparative *episteme* in non-biological disciplines was made by Max Müller in his *Essays in Comparative Mythology* published in 1856. This book is regarded as the first important publication in the comparative study of religions. Müller developed his approach in *Lectures on the Science of Language* (1864). In 1871, Edward Burnett in *Primitive Culture* presented the reconstruction of the emergence and evolution of religious experiences and religious faith. Numerous applications of the comparative *episteme* were observed in the first decades of the 20th century by historians of cultures (for example, Oswald Spengler), anthropologists (for example, William H. Rivers), historians of religions (for example, Christopher Dawson), and ethologists (for example, Konrad Lorenz and Nikolaas Tinbergen). In the 1920s, the comparative *episteme* was built into the emerging image of the world and since that time has been put on an equal footing with the two 'classical' *epistemes* – Baconian and Cartesian.

The primary features of the comparative *episteme* are the following:

- presence of, at least, an elementary classification of 'units' to be the subject of the comparative analysis; during the research process this classification could be modified; the efficiency of the comparative approach depends directly on the correctness of classification, and vice versa, a good classification is the result of proper application of the comparative method;
- in principle, not active experiment but passive observations are the basic sources of information (knowledge); frequently, a single historical observation is the only source of knowledge;
- perception of all phenomena in historical (dynamical) perspective;
- much more important than questions on causes are questions on mechanisms of development;
- search for the mechanisms of development is based principally on thinking by analogy, not on 'true forever' laws of development; usually great pieces of knowledge on natural mechanisms of development are acquired through observation of pathological behaviour of the 'units' under investigation.

In the 1920s and 1930s a new *techne* emerged, which I propose to call the complex *techne* (Waszkiewicz (1982) calls this type of research

---

[21] The sources of the comparative method may be found in Aristotle (384–322 BC). This method was applied occasionally in the 16th century by, among others, Belon, Fabrizio, Camper, Hunter and Vicq-d'Azyr. The first methodical application of the comparative method was performed by George Cuvier (1769–1832) in his classification of animals. He succeeded mainly due to the formulation, and proper application, of two principles: the principle of *the correlation of parts* and the principle of *the subordination of characters*; (Cuvier, 1800, *Leçons d'anatomie comparée*, I:51 quoted in Mayr, 1982b).

'supertechnic'). The emergence of a new *techne* is closely related to new large economic ventures (organized by the 'omnipotent governments') for example, in the 1920s, the GOELRO PLAN – the plan for developing large industrial centres in the USSR and their uniform distribution over the whole territory of the USSR – and, originating in 1933 in the USA, the government's Tennessee Valley Authority (TVA), which was intended to meliorate the Tennessee river and to control the complex economic development of the South Appalachian Mountains. Experience gained during such economic ventures made it possible to prepare so-called great research programmes – the best known are the Manhattan Programme (to build the first atomic bomb), Polaris (a system of strategic missile defence) and the space programmes of the NASA.

The essential features of the complex *techne* are:

- large scale of a venture (regional, global);
- treating the problem on a broad basis; the research programmes are realized by interdisciplinary research groups, all technological, social, ecological and residual effects of realization of the basic goal of the venture are taken into account;
- thinking in the categories of ends and means;
- uniqueness of each venture of each research programme.

So it may be said that in the first decades of the 20th century six basic research modes co-existed, modified, according to the spirit of the emerging 20th-century image of the world: four *epistemes* – Cartesian, Baconian, holistic and comparative – and two *technes* – industrial (instituted by Edison) and complex.[22]

The Sixth Cycle of *Episteme* – The Substitution Phase, *circa* 1980s

The shape of the sixth cycle is still very unclear and in contrast to the

---

[22] The most important difference between the Cartesian and Baconian *epistemes* in the 20th century lies in different functions of mathematics in both approaches – for the Cartesian-rooted researchers, the primer is hypothesis (theory) expressed in the mathematical form (the hypothesis is created with a rather weak relationship to current results of experiments), and after coherent and logical elaboration of the hypothesis, the theory is empirically verified. For the Baconian researchers, the primer is an experiment and the results of this experiment; in the succeeding phase of research, on the basis of obtained results, attempts are made to build hypotheses–theories using existing formal (mathematical) apparatus (obviously the experiments are designed on the basis of some hypotheses, but frequently existing in non-verbal fashion, and almost never formulated in a mathematical form).

Close cooperation of researchers working within the industrial *techne* and the Baconian *episteme* may lead to the amalgamation of both research streams into one research programme. Research within the industrial *techne* made in the 1920s and 1930s was carried out with the close cooperation of university researchers. The innovations resulting from this research initiated the emergence of the fourth Kondratieff.

description of the other five cycles, the description of this cycle is not systematic, and is not based on the categories of *epistechne* presented at the beginning of this section.

New insights into the Universe, extending the exploration of nature, will be the result of concurrent development of some specific mathematical techniques and advanced hardware and software computer technologies (for example, tunnel microscope, tomograph). A distinguishing feature of this cycle will be the penetration of reality created by human civilization (it seems to be the general feature of the 20th-century image of the world). The scientific status, similar to that enjoyed by physics, chemistry and biology, will be achieved by disciplines studying this part of reality (artifacts). Symptoms are visible now in areas related to: (1) high technologies (Artificial Intelligence, Computer Science, Knowledge Engineering, Expert Systems, telecommunication), (2) material sciences – synthesizing materials of required properties, materials which do not exist in natural processes, and to some extent (3) social systems, for example, large urban societies; global-scale social problems (among them modes of cooperation between the poor and rich societies). Essential modifications of the existing *epistemes*, or even the emergence of new ones, specific to the new problems, may be expected.

Modifications in the organization of research may be foreseen; one of the features of this new organization of research will be the growth of 'institutional science' (financed by governments and large industries) and the emergence of 'non-institutional science', that is, research undertaken by small groups of researchers, or even scattered individual researchers, communicating through large telecommunication networks and using extended data banks. Non-institutional science will be financed mainly from private funds, frequently from funds allocated to these researchers for doing 'service' work for industrial organizations and governments. New ways of storing, distribution and exchange of knowledge (among others, through telecommunication and electronic media) will facilitate the development of non-institutional science. Modes of education, especially at the university level, will be deeply transformed. This transformation process will be closely related to the ongoing emergence of a new knowledge society (see the section on the image of the economy above).

Until the 1980s patents were issued only for technological innovation, that is, research made within the *techne*. Scientific knowledge was considered to be freely disseminated, and in fact the rule of free render of results of scientific research was dictated by scientific ethics. Precedents of patenting of scientific knowledge (for example, genetic engineering) have changed our understanding on this matter, and probably will have a noticeable effect on the modes of scientific research process in the future.

PARADIGM

Paragons of this taxon relate to forms, patterns and designs of conducting scientific and technological research in some well-defined research domains. The term 'paradigm' is adopted from Kuhn (1962). After publication of his *The Structure of Scientific Revolutions* in 1962, the concept of paradigm was very popular and readily accepted, even by the opponents of his concept, but, as Kuhn (1985, p. 407) himself emphasized, also differently understood. Our intention is to use the concept of paradigm as it was interpreted by Kuhn in his 'Second Thoughts on Paradigms' (Kuhn, 1985), that is, a pradigm as a pattern of research or as a disciplinary matrix. The only difference is that we use this concept as personal knowledge of a researcher, not in a broader Kuhnian sense, that is, the knowledge which is common to a specific scientific community, and only to them. Perception of the paradigm as relating to an individual enables better understanding of the emergence process of common beliefs and judgements, and, at least partly, allows the elimination of troublesome consequences of a vicious circle (and a kind of tautology) – that what is common for some community of researchers is called a paradigm, and vice versa, the paradigm forms the community (partnership) from a dispersed group of researchers. Kuhn is conscious of these troublesome consequences and comments on this problem (Kuhn, 1985, p. 408). The long debate about paradigms after publication of *The Structure ...* induced Kuhn to broaden the concept of a paradigm. In contrast to the earlier understanding of a paradigm as 'a standard example' (as in Kuhn, 1962), now Kuhn comprehends the paradigm as 'the disciplinary matrix' which consists of symbolic generalizations, models and exemplifications (standard examples) (Kuhn, 1985, p. 411). Standard examples are still the most important components of the disciplinary matrix (Kuhn, 1985, pp. 424–5) and frequently serve as a practical and customary discriminant of a particular scientific community.

In technology, an analogous concept was proposed by D. Sahal (1981, p. 33), who used the term 'technological guidepost', but its meaning is very similar to the meaning of paradigm in the Kuhnian sense. G. Dosi explicitly uses the term technological paradigm:

> A scientific paradigm could be approximately defined as an 'outlook' that defines the relevant problems, a 'model' and a 'pattern' of enquiry. ... In broad analogy with the Kuhnian definition of a scientific paradigm, we shall define a technological paradigm as a model and a pattern of solution of selected technological problems, based on selected principles derived from natural sciences and on selected material technologies. (Dosi, 1983, p. 83)

Examples of paradigms are numerous, so only a few will be given here:

- in physics, successive paradigms are: Galileo's mechanics (1609), Descartes' physics (1644), Newton's mechanics (1687), the modification of Newton's mechanics made by Hamilton (1853), the special theory of relativity of Einstein (1905), quantum mechanics (1920s);
- in biology, theories of the development of living organisms: Lamarckism (1809), Cuvier's catastrophism (1825), the theory of evolution based on the principle of natural selection (Darwin and Wallace, 1859), Weisman's neo-darwinism (1892), the synthetic theory of evolution (1946);
- in technology: in aeronautical engineering – the design of the famous DC-3 aeroplane in 1935 (followed by the Lockheed Electra in 1936), which was a pattern for numerous aeroplane designs in the next 30–40 years; the design of digital computers as proposed by J. von Neumann (1947) – probably neuro-computers or so-called fifth generation of computers (for example, field computers, transputers) may be considered as an attempt to design digital computers on the basis of a new paradigm.

New hypotheses and theories, and new technologies, are worked out by individuals within paradigms accepted by them. It is a kind of direct influence, but higher knowledge taxa also delimit individual thinking and form chreodic modes of individual, and social, thinking (see modes of development in Chapter 2, page 25).

PART II

Economics and Evolution

4. Neoclassical and Evolutionary Perspectives in Economics

Once again the revival of interest of economists in long-term development was observed in the 1950s. In developing a theory, efforts were concentrated on the search for appropriate tools of analysis of the dynamic view of economic development. The best-known models of economic development of that period are the Keynesian models of Harrod and Domar and the neoclassical models of Meade, Solow and Swan. The models aimed to find explanations of observed dynamics of production, engaged capital and labour, and fluctuation of prices.[1]

Concurrently with those theoretical works an extensive empirical research on the evolution of long-term characteristics of development (overall production, capital, employment, worker's productivity, price index, and so on) was undertaken. Abundant statistical material collected in that period suggested that in the former decades the rate of growth of national product was almost equal to the rate of growth of capital engaged and was much higher than the rate of growth of labour (measured in man-hours); it means that the ratio of capital to production was constant during that period but production per worker and the ratio of capital to labour had grown in the same proportion. These results were in apparent disagreement with the classical interpretation of the growth process as a movement along the neoclassical production function. The growth ratio per worker ought to be lower than the growth ratio of capital to labour. This 'residual' production was comparable to the part of production growth associated with the classical factors of production – capital and labour. In the empirical research the residual production was branded as 'technical advance'. A few decades earlier Schumpeter (1912 (1960)) and Hicks (1932) suggested that innovation (technical change) should be discerned as an independent factor of production – change of the production function, as it was called by Schumpeter (1939, p. 87) – in contrast to factor substitution as a shift along the production function. In theoretical analysis this component was treated as one of the forms of capital represented, for example, by the R&D research funds. The empirical research of Robert M. Solow in the 1950s was a principal contribution to the process of understanding the residual factor of production – technical change. Solow (1957) proposed to relate production Q with capital K, labour L and technical advance A at time t in

---

[1] For an excellent and very original review of the literature on economic growth and technological change see Chapters 2 and 3 of Verspagen (1993); see also Fiedor (1986).

the formula:

$$Q = A(t)F(K,L).$$

For the discrete time and making some additional assumptions, Solow found the following relationship between technical advance, production and capital:

$$\frac{\Delta A}{A} = \frac{\Delta(Q/L)}{(Q/L)} - b\frac{\Delta(K/L)}{(K/L)},$$

where b is the ratio of capital to production; $\Delta A/A$ is the measure of the part of growth of the national product per capita which is associated with all factors of production except the capital per worker. Using the above formula it is possible to calculate values $\Delta A/A$ for each year of available data. The last step is to calculate the cumulative changes of technical advance. Solow assumed arbitrarily that A was equal to 1 in 1909 and used the following formula to calculate cumulative changes in the year t:

$$A(t+1) = A(t)\left(1+\frac{\Delta A(t)}{A(t)}\right).$$

Solow calculated that for non-agriculture, the private sector of the American economy in the period 1909–49, A(1949) = 1.809, which means that 80.9% of production growth in the USA within the forty years could be attributed to the technological advance. Estimations for different sectors of various economies were more or less similar; technological advance was responsible for the observed production growth of 70 to 90%. But we should say that the remaining 10 to 30% of the production growth is related to a specific type of investment, namely investment in plants and equipment, which does not change the quality and structure of manufactured products. Therefore, the share of 'technological advance' in these estimations is always overestimated. Denison (1962) in his study of the GNP growth in the United States in 1929–57 applied a specific method, the so-called Total Factor Productivity, to estimate the share of an advance of knowledge in the production growth per worker and the result was that it was about 20%, that is, much less than in the former estimations. Many critical opinions on this type of approach to the estimation of the shares of different factors of production in the production growth were expressed. The two main objections are: (1) the relationship between capital, labour and technical advance is far more complicated than it was assumed, and the changes of one of these factors influence interactively all the others, and (2) in such an approach it is not possible to take into consideration disruptive, non-continuous economic and social changes observed in real processes.

Putting aside all this discussion it should be said that in the 1950s and 1960s the problem of the search for explanations of the role of technological and knowledge advance was stated clearly and explicitly.

Some authors speaking of neoclassical economy use the notion of neoclassical paradigm, but – according to our classification (see Chapter 2) – what we understand by neoclassical approach ought to be placed slightly above the paradigm. Paradigm is related rather to some technical apparatus and tools used by researchers and not to their general views on methodological and epistemological problems of research. The notion of neoclassical and evolutionary approaches contains 'higher-order' views on the ways of undertaking the research, so it is proposed that we speak of neoclassical and evolutionary *epistemes* instead of neoclassical and evolutionary paradigms.

The main aim of the remarks presented in this chapter is to point out essential differences between the neoclassical and evolutionary *epistemes* (perspectives). To make the differences more apparent and explicit the picture will be strongly stylized. We see the essential differences between these two *epistemes* in attitudes to: (1) optimization, (2) knowledge, (3) concept of competing firms, (4) perception of time, and (5) the role of random factors. A short description of the above discrepancies is presented below, but first some general remarks concerning these two *epistemes* will be made.

The essential difference lies in the 'ideology'; the neoclassical *episteme* is rooted in the Renaissance image of the world, and the evolutionary *episteme* is rooted in the 20th-century image of the world, which emerged (fulgurated) at the end of the 19th century. From a certain point of view it seems to be a paradox – in the course of laying the foundations of neoclassical economics it was clearly visible (even among economists, for example, Alfred Marshall and Thorstein B. Veblen) that new revolutionary attitudes in sciences (especially physics) and a new perception of the world emerge. In spite of that, the neoclassical approach was based on the foundations of classical physics, namely on atomistic ontology and mechanistic metaphor. In the following decades neoclassical economists clung strictly to these principles, despite evident changes in the philosophical foundations of modern physics. Neoclassical economics, described as 'the pure theory of economics or the theory of exchange and value in exchange' ought to be considered as 'physico-mathematical science like mechanics or hydrodynamics' (Walras, 1954 (1874), p. 71). Probably the process of creation of the neoclassical *episteme* at the end of the 19th century is the result, and an example, of inertia of thinking and a kind of conservative posture, so frequently observed in a scientific community.

The neoclassical equilibrium theory, established by Léon Walras

(*Élements d'économie politique pure*, 1874) and William Stanley Jevons (*The Theory of Political Economy*, 1871), from the beginning was not able to deal with problems relating to the proper explanation of the role of technical progress as the most prominent driving force of economic growth. The problem of technical progress was one of the main topics given consideration by classical economists but it was not an object of concern for neoclassical schools.

The recent revival of interest in evolutionary approaches to economic analysis and technological change is at least partly due to dissatisfaction with the way the neoclassical economics dealt with processes of technological change, but also, more generally, with any type of change which transforms the economic system in a fundamental way. As a result of some tension observed between these two *epistemes*, common co-evolution of the orthodox and evolutionary economics is observed. Some of the evolutionary ideas are accepted by neoclassical economists and built into their theories.

Orthodox economists see the beauty of the models of economic behaviour based on assumptions of rational expectations, neoclassical natural rates of unemployment, marginal productivity, or disequilibrium models with varying fixed-price assumptions. They consider the mathematical models as an 'intellectual achievement of the highest order' but do not notice that the behaviour of these models reflects less and less the reality. Evolutionary economists, who were in a minority for decades but whose number seems to have grown in the last two decades, are dissatisfied with the orthodox approach and see many shortcoming in it, for example, the models do not deal with dynamic competition, do not get to grips with the sources and effects of technical change, and the decision-making process embraced in the models is evidently misleading.

Critical views on neoclassical foundations of economic theory are numerous, especially in the last two decades. The critical analysis encompasses discussions on the limitations of the mechanistic metaphor of neoclassical theory (Nicholas Georgescu-Roegen, 1971), as well as the identification of the roots of neoclassical theory in the outdated physics of the 19th century (Bruno Ingrao and Giorgio Israel, 1985, and especially Philip Mirowski, 1986, 1989). These numerous critical views resulted first of all in formal attempts to come to grips with the dynamic character of economic problems, and even in the building of neoclassical theories of technical progress and innovation (for example, Binswanger and Ruttan, 1978), the neoclassical interpretation of differential economic growth and development (Lucas, 1988; Romer, 1989), the neoclassical view of long-term institutional change (North, 1981), and in the end in efforts to develop elements of neoclassical interpretation of economic evolution (for example, Lehmann-Waffenschmidt, 1990).

An evolutionary view allows us almost in a natural way to search for explanations of the role of technological change and innovation in economic process. Attempts to perceive economic development in an evolutionary manner are not new, but in contrast to the neoclassical approach, the evolutionary view lacked the formal elegance and clear mathematical formulation. This seems to be one of the main reasons for far less popularity for this approach in the first half of the 20th century. In fact, it is very difficult to conceive evolutionary ideas in an adequate way in a rather simple mathematical model, as is done in the neoclassical *episteme*. The analytical treatment of the evolutionary models is rather difficult because of non-linear relations built into the models; hence, up to the early 1960s, they were formulated mainly in a verbal way, and therefore the most recent evolutionary models are formulated as computer simulation models. The evolutionary views of economic process may be found in the works of Thorstein Veblen (1899, 1919) and other American Institutionalists, Alfred Marshall (1890), and above all Joseph A. Schumpeter (1912, 1942). Evolutionary phenomena and evolutionary concepts seem to stir up interest, and contribute also to the creation of an image of the world ('worldview'), of different schools of thought in economics. The recent wave of publications on this theme is rooted in four different intellectual traditions: the Austrian school, the Schumpeterian tradition, institutionalism and the Western Marxist school. The present state of evolutionary economics is thus best characterized as being a new heterodoxy in economic thinking (Witt, 1991).

In the Schumpeterian tradition important objections to neoclassical economic thought have been formulated by Nelson and Winter (1982), Day and Eliasson (eds) (1986), Silverberg (1987), Dosi et al.(eds) (1988), Hanusch (ed.) (1988). The research within this school is focused mainly on the firm, on industrial development and growth, in long waves of development, technical progress, innovation and market structure. Little has yet been done to develop a more general framework which would cover the level of individual behaviour, the industrial level and phenomena at more aggregate levels.

Institutionalist writers have provided a thorough criticism of neoclassical economics (see, for example, Hodgson, 1988; Gordon and Adams, 1989, for recent surveys). Understandably, by its very nature, this school (especially the 'old institutionalists') tends to disregard some aspects related to individual behaviour in economics while focusing on patterns of change in institutions and aggregate phenomena (Langlois, 1986).

It is natural that, when constructing any theory, some assumptions are made unconsciously, and may be called hidden or latent. These latent assumptions are revealed either during further development of the theory (when 'something' is wrong and the theory does not fit the reality) or by its critics searching for alternative approaches. This awareness process also occurred during the development of neoclassical theory, for example, perception of irreversibility of development, or bounded rationality of economic actors. And naturally hidden assumptions are also present in current evolutionary theories of economic development and probably will be revealed, and modified, during further development of this approach.

OPTIMIZATION AND EQUILIBRIUM

When building a model, orthodox economists make specific assumptions, similar to those made in classical physics and engineering, on the possibility of: (1) isolating a specific sphere of socio-economic reality, (2) specifying all relations of phenomena within the sphere with the external environment, and (3) building the model which describes all important phenomena observed within the chosen sphere, and which also includes all essential influences of the external environment. On the basis of such a model some optimal control, or optimal path of development, is calculated.

Such a mechanistic approach to socio-economic processes turned out to be wrong and misleading. A lot of decisions made by policy-makers on the basis of such models caused strong social and economic tensions, especially visible in the 1930s and the 1970s, that is, during the period of radical structural changes of the economies of industrialized countries.

In socio-economic processes, the clear isolation of well-defined spheres of reality, the specification of important relations with the external environment, the building of relevant mathematical models and optimizing the choice of suitable policies are almost impossible. In this situation the basic questionnaire related to the finding of an appropriate and satisfactory description of social reality has changed. Questions concerning optimal decisions in the long-term perspective and in periods of structural changes have lost their significance. Far more important become the questions on the mechanisms of long-term development and on the possibilities of controlling the economic process to reach a prerequisite (not optimal) course of development. Those kinds of questions form the root of the evolutionary approach, not only in economics. Acceptance of an evolutionary perspective in dealing with a socio-economic system almost naturally enforces a specific way of subtly controlling the development of social systems, not through imposing optimal values of relevant parameters but through creating favourable conditions for suitable development.

Neoclassical economics focuses on the analysis of the properties of economic systems in equilibrium, and in contrast to the evolutionary approach, neglects a consideration of transition processes. The Walrasian auctioneer has to assemble, process, transform and communicate huge amounts of information (knowledge). All the information requisite in the process of price setting has to be in the auctioneer's hands. So knowledge has to be centralized. Clearly, this is against the spirit of a market system and against all rhetoric of neoclassical economics. 'It is not far from the truth to say that the current neo-classical approach to micro-foundations of macroeconomics is based on the representation of the economy as a *centralized* system' (Coricelli and Dosi, 1988, p. 130). The Walrasian 'market' model thus demands 'a totalitarian police state' rather than a decentralized, liberal market system.

KNOWLEDGE

The assumption of neoclassical economics about the possibility of making optimal choices requires a particular theoretical representation of the individual's cognitive situation. The individual is characterized as already having a complete overview of all possible choices and at least a rough understanding of their consequences. Neoclassical economics supposes that there is some theoretically imaginable, complete and perfect knowledge of the external world to which actors could conceivably aspire.

This attitude is completely opposite to the Austrian school idea of the partial ignorance and fallible knowledge prerequisite for discovery and learning. Decision problems are not inherent, but first have to be created in the mind of an individual. This question is completely left out of the neoclassical synthesis of constrained maximization and the notion of equilibrium. As shown by Hayek (1945, pp. 519–30), economic knowledge is always of a dispersed nature; a 'grass-roots' knowledge is available only to direct participants and not to any central bodies. So, a number of opportunities are missed in any centralized system, mainly due to the lack of relevant knowledge in decision-makers at the top of centralized hierarchy.

As I have mentioned in Chapter 2 it was Michael Polanyi (1967) who pointed out that a great part of individual knowledge exists in the unconscious, and it is very hard to verbalize it. He named this type of knowledge a tacit one. The concept of tacit knowledge was employed in economic analysis, typically embodied in habits and routines, by Nelson and Winter (1982). Tacit knowledge forms a large part of a number of skills, for example, swimming or landing an aeroplane. A lot of the skills used in management have a considerable tacit component. But, of course, besides the tacit knowledge there is knowledge which can be expressed in symbolic form and can be easily communicated. David Teece (1981) proposes to call it codified knowledge.

Apart from not being directly communicable, individual tacit knowledge has a few other properties which are of relevance to economic analysis – it is neither directly measurable, nor interpersonally comparable. We may draw some hypotheses about the form of this knowledge only by obtaining certain results of its application in particular circumstances – such as the solutions to particular problems, or the performance in particular tests or tournaments.

By making the assumption of perfect (unbounded) rationality of all economic agents, mainstream economics implicitly assumes that such knowledge is always perfect. The neoclassical economic agent is able to order all his (her) preferences, take into account all relevant constraints and make an informed choice to get the required results. The orthodox economists call this type of behaviour rational. It is simply impossible for this dispersed and decentralized knowledge to be gathered, either by a central planning authority or by a Walrasian auctioneer.

Quite the contrary, according to present observations of social and economic processes, such knowledge is rather scarce and unequally distributed. To describe our cognitive situation, Herbert A. Simon proposed the hypothesis of bounded rationality (Simon, 1955). The limitation of knowledge and computational ability of the human mind does not allow us to account for all factors necessary to make optimal decisions (choices) in any life situation. The only solution, worked out during the long process of human evolution, is that under severe time constraints, imposed by almost all life situations, and with huge amounts of information (knowledge) gathered, the human mind makes simplified models of every life situation and on the basis of such models makes relevant decisions (choices). In this sense all human beings are rational entities, and their choices ought to be called rational. But it should be added that the rationality of man, recognized as bounded, is highly diversified in all human societies and depends not only on the life histories (experiences) of every human being but also strongly depends on his (her) biological complexion (epigenetic paragons).

CONCEPT OF COMPETING FIRMS

Observed in real processes, the diversity of behaviour may reside in differences between the expectations, preferences, capabilities and cognitive proficiency of individuals (economic agents). The diversity cannot be captured by any model which starts from the representative agent, as is the case of the neoclassical models. The same applies to the individual behaviour of every human being as well as to the behaviour of economic organizations, for example, firms. In fact, the problem lies not in the assumption that human actors are rational, in any reasonable sense of this word, but that all rational actors are alike. Orthodox economics, to simplify consideration and to make calculation and analytical treatment of the mathematical models much easier, assumes that it is possible to replace all diversified firms which operate in the industry by a set of similar firms, and applies the concept of one standardized firm as the representative of all firms under consideration. This simplification may be understood as the first approximation only, but there is no reason to follow this method in the search for more adequate descriptions of the economic processes. The evolutionary *episteme* proposes to take into account all diversities, which in fact are essential for the long-term development of socio-economic processes. Close observation of evolutionary processes (in biology as well as in the socio-economic sphere), and some computer simulations (Kwaśnicka et al., 1983) show that in the short-term perspective, systems with relatively high diversity behave much worse than homogeneous systems (i.e. systems with similar 'actors'), but in the long-term perspective, highly diversified systems compensate for this deficiency thanks to much greater creativity, and much more frequent emergence of innovations, resulting in much higher, long-range rates of development. In the short-term perspective, diversity makes the average performance of a system much worse than the homogeneous system but, as Schumpeter (1942) writes 'A system ... that at *every* point in time fully utilizes its possibilities to its best advantage may yet in the long run be inferior to a system that does so at *no* given point in time, because the latter's failure to do so may be a condition for a level or speed of long-run performance.'

Neoclassical economics focused its attention on a specific type of competition, that is, price competition. Competition was viewed as analogous with Newtonian motion. Competition forced prices to the lowest possible values with resources approaching their optimal modes of utilization. So, it may be said that order and stability in the market were coerced by competition, which played a role similar to gravitation in the Newtonian system. Pure (or perfect) competition is most frequently mentioned in textbooks but relates to a state of equilibrium, and not to the process of rivalry and change. Perfect competition is related to the state where all firms are equal and therefore they cannot generate any qualitative change in their output or methods of production.

Close observation of modern industrial processes suggests different pictures of competition. Price competition ought to be viewed as just one of the possible ways of competition; competition related to the introduction of new products, new technologies, or new modes of organization of production seems to be much more important (see for example, Schumpeter, 1912).

In neoclassical analysis and also in most of its modern followers, attention is limited to the question of how resources are allocated. These theories regard organization of the economy as already given and everlasting. The essential question of how an economy adjusts its organization and structure to an incessantly changing world is simply ignored. Schumpeter was probably the first to note this limitation of neoclassical theories when he said that 'the problem that is usually being visualized is how capitalism administers existing structures, whereas the relevant problem is how it creates and destroys them' (Schumpeter, 1942). In his doctoral dissertation, published in German as *The Theory of Economic Development* (1912), Schumpeter pointed out that the main driving force underlying economic growth are radical innovations introduced by entrepreneurs seeking supernormal profits. Such profits arise from a temporary position of monopoly, attained by each successful entrepreneur until his imitators are able to enter the market. This concept provides a qualitative explanation of, and justification for, supernormal profits. To some extent it also explains capital accumulation (from profits). Naturally, it explains the observed fact of technological obsolescence, and its corollary of technological progress. It even explains, to some degree, the unevenness of technological change, and it also explains the great diversity of firms within almost all contemporary industries.

In orthodox thinking, a commonly used phrase is 'profit maximization', and in contrast, for the evolutionary approach, a formula of 'search for profit' or 'action motivated by profit' is closer (see, for example, Nelson and Winter, 1982). In a stable environment the differences between 'profit maximization' and 'search for profit' seem to be negligible, but a stable environment is rather a rare state in contemporary, vigorous industrial life. In a constantly changing environment it is very difficult to expound the set of options from which firms choose the best solution; during the decision-making process an important role is played by random factors, so it becomes essential to make a distinction between these two attitudes – profit maximization and search for profit.

PERCEPTION OF TIME

In the orthodox economy, all firms are always in the equilibrium state and each firm immediately reacts to environmental challenges, making decisions which lead them immediately to a new equilibrium.

Evolutionary economists assume that decisions are made continuously and independently by each firm, taking into account the expected decisions of its competitors as well as its own perception of the future development of the external environment. All decisions interfere, in a direct or indirect way, with routines applied by each firm and, importantly, the set of routines is the subject of a continuous adaptive process. The decision process is seen in historical perspective. The evolutionary approach does not assume anything about the equilibrium state; the industry may or may not be in equilibrium. What we observe in real processes is the incessant process of driving towards equilibrium, and it can happen that because of frequent variations in the external environment firms are not able to adjust to new situations, and for a relatively long time the industry remains far from any equilibrium. The main aim of the 'evolutionary' firm is to improve its situation using the experience of its competitors, so time plays an essential role in the evolutionary approach. Unlike the general equilibrium world, where everything happens instantaneously, real socio-economic processes are embedded in flowing time. Current actions affect future actions and future states of the world. Expectations about future states of the world are part of the conditions for present actions.

It is not far from the truth to say that neoclassical economics was economics without time; through making enormous efforts to study an economy in the state of equilibrium all problems relating to the states of disequilibrium were neglected – in particular no transition processes were investigated.

All problems relating to the passing of time, that is, relating to the problem of the existence of the 'arrow of time', were also neglected. Even when the subject of time was brought up for discussion by neoclassical economists, it was perceived as symmetrical (reversible) – similar to that in classical mechanics. Social processes, and economic processes in particular, are irreversible by nature, that is, with a recognizable direction of unfolding time, with no symmetry between the past and the future. Georgescu-Roegen (1971) points out that it is greatly misleading to model social or economic processes on mathematical models, all of which entail reversible time. He suggested that the social sciences could find closer correspondence with the irreversibility of thermodynamics and biological evolution.

RANDOM FACTORS

Differences between the two *epistemes* discussed are manifested also in the perception of random factors. In the orthodox models, random factors are placed in mathematical equations as stochastic variables with given distributions. The changes in any variable are seen as a trend with overwritten random noise. In further stages of the analysis of orthodox models, the random factors are filtered and attention is focused on the average values of important characteristics. Uncertainty, if present in the neoclassical models, is reducible to incomplete information described by some stochastic characteristics (for example, by probabilistic distributions). This still enables the (hyper-)rational behaviour of economic agents resulting in optimization, so admired by neoclassical economists.

In evolutionary economics random factors play an essential role, especially in the decision-making process and in the process of the search for innovation. It is frequently said that the evolutionary process is similar to the 'trial and error' process, that the search for improvements resembles the process of 'groping in the dark'. In many cases it is impossible to describe uncertainty in terms of stochastic characteristics (for example, probabilistic distributions). In contrast to orthodox economics, evolutionary economics treats the creative process as costly, involving the strong influence of random events. The possibilities of gaining relevant information are diversified. Some kind of information (especially that related to scientific knowledge) is freely available in the public domain, but important information, related, for example, to new technologies, is protected and access is restricted. Obtaining private information is costly and, as we know from experience, strongly associated with a bit of luck. This is a situation totally opposite to that assumed by neoclassical economists. In fact, in the economic situations as perceived by evolutionary economists there is no place for global optimization. Basically, because of lack of essential information, long-run optimization is impossible; at best economic agents may try to optimize their expectations in the very short perspective. The uncertainty in the evolutionary process also makes prediction of long-term developments impossible. In principle, it is possible to predict future developments of the evolutionary process if all actual alternatives are known and under the assumption that within a particular period of time no other alternatives will appear. It may be said that the prediction of future developments may be quite an easy task in the transition period (substitution phase in our terminology), but long-term prediction during the equilibrium phase is essentially impossible, because of the fundamental impossibility of predicting the fulguration (emergence) of novelty.

One of the fundamental questions of any theory of economy is the problem of the emergence of coherent behaviour of economic agents from the uncoordinated pursuit of self-interest. This question was formulated by Adam Smith over 200 years ago; his tentative, and still open, answer based on the concept of 'the invisible hand of the market', as well as neoclassical generalization ought to be conceived as first approximations. The current development of evolutionary economics suggests that this approach can throw new light on the 'central economic question'. The evolutionary approach is only at the initial stage of its development; its formal, mathematical tools are not so mature as those of neoclassical economics. Evolutionary economics is also far from being a coherent and complete theoretical system. The evolutionary perspective offers a number of improvements over the orthodox, mechanistic approach. Besides some particular new insight, for example, the concept of irreversibility or the 'arrow of time', it proposes a more general view of the development of the economic system on the basis of a concept of process rather than comparative statistics, and it includes disequilibrium as well as equilibrium situations. As can be observed in the last decades, evolutionary concepts are more and more frequently accepted by some neoclassical economists and also the new generation of economists is much more eager to accept an evolutionary perspective. All this arouses hope that the increasing efforts of many economic schools will bear fruit and a new theoretical system will emerge, with a maturity comparable to that of neoclassical economics.

5. The Evolutionary Model of Industry Development

The model presented in this chapter is focused on the economic features of industrial development with no technological change embedded; an extended version of this model, with the search for innovation process included, is given in Chapter 7. From an evolutionary viewpoint the basic model presented in this chapter contains only a self-organization mechanism of development and no hereditary information (represented, for example, in the form of firms' routines). Because the general intention is to include the evolutionary factors in that model I prefer to call it evolutionary, rather than the seemingly correct term 'self-organization model of industrial dynamics'. The first version of the model was presented at several conferences and published by Kwaśnicki and Kwaśnicka (1992). The main difference between the model of this section and the former presentations lies in the form of investment representation and the credit policy.

The model describes the behaviour of a number of competing firms producing functionally equivalent products.[1] It is important to note that the basic model presented in this chapter is deterministic. There are no random factors; fluctuations observed for some initial simulation conditions are caused only by the deterministic mechanisms of development embedded in the model.

The decisions of a firm relating to investment, price, profit, and so on, are based on the firm's evaluation of the behaviour of other competing firms and expected response of the market. The firm's knowledge of the market

---

[1] Broadly speaking, since the end of the 19th century economic analysis has split into two branches: micro- and macro-economics. The main subjects of micro-economic research are firms and consumers, and the main subjects of macro-economics are national economies or even the global economy. Micro-analysis of economic mechanisms leads to a great number of details plagued with idiosyncrasies and specificities of contexts of investigated institutions. It is very difficult to apply the same process of abstraction to build a model of economic development on the basis of such micro-observations. On the other hand, the macro-economic models use such aggregate entities (like GNP per capita, global investment, global unemployment, and so on) that some essential mechanisms of economic development are lost in the proposed models of growth.

What has been observed in the last 20 years of development of economic analysis is the tendency to operate on the same medium level, and to use industry as a basic unit of investigation. The main aim of such analysis is an investigation of processes and mechanisms occurring among firms. A process of abstraction is applied to characterize a firm, in which each firm is characterized by a relatively small number of entities (characteristics) related in some way to micro-observations and not as aggregated as in macro-analysis. *Meso-economics* seems to be the correct term to name this type of economic analysis. The model presented in this chapter may be placed at that intermediate level.

and knowledge of the future behaviour of competitors is limited and uncertain. There is no possibility of characterizing the limitation and uncertainty of knowledge in statistical terms, for example, in terms of probability distributions. Firms' decisions can only be suboptimal. The decisions are taken simultaneously and independently by all firms at the beginning of each period (for example, once a year or a quarter). After the decisions are made the firms undertake production and put the products on the market. The products are evaluated by the market, and the quantities of products of different firms sold in the market depend on the relative prices, the relative value of product characteristics and the level of saturation of the market. Frequently the products evaluated as the best are not sold in the full quantity offered, and conversely, the inferior products are frequently sold in spite of the possibility of buying better ones. But for long periods the preference for better products, that is, those with a lower price and better characteristics, prevails.

Figure 5.1. General structure of the evolutionary industrial model

The general structure of the evolutionary model of industrial dynamics is presented in Figure 5.1. The product's price depends on current innovation being in the hands of a firm, on the actual structure of the market and on the level of assumed production to be sold on the market. The two arrows between Price and Production indicate that the price is established in an interactive way to provide fulfilment of the firm's objectives (that is, to maintain a relatively high profit in the near future and to further the firm's development in the long-term perspective). Modernization of products through innovation and/or initiating a new production through applying a radical innovation depend on the investment capacity of the firm. So each firm managing innovation takes into account all the economic constraints, as they emerge during the firm's development. Therefore it frequently occurs that because of economic (financial) constraints some promising invention is not incorporated into the firm's practice. One of the distinctive features of the model is coupling technological development and economic processes. Current investment capacity is also taken into account by each firm in the investment process and the price setting. The success of each firm in the search for innovation depends not only on the amount of R&D funds spent by each firm in the search for innovation but also on the extent to which the competitor's private knowledge is made public. Making the private knowledge of a firm known to competitors can in some cases speed up a whole industrial development but also diminishes a firm's incentives to spend more funds on R&D projects. The advantages of making public the private knowledge of the firm should be weighted against the disadvantages.

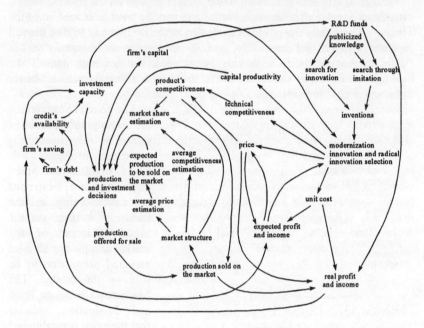

Figure 5.2. Causal relationships in the evolutionary industrial model

The causal relationships between the main variables of the industrial model presented in the following sections are shown in Figure 5.2. In some way it is a more detailed description of the structure presented in Figure 5.1. A firm's investment capacity depends on the firm's savings and the availability credit, and also, through an indirect way, on the firm's debts. Production and investment decisions rely on the firm's expectations related to the future behaviour of its competitors, market structure, expected profit and the actual trend of the firm's market share. The current technical and economic characteristics of products offered for sale (in terms of their technical competitiveness, being the measure of the products' technical performance), and the characteristics of the technology used to manufacture the products (in terms of unit production cost and productivity of capital) are taken into account in the setting process of price, investment and production. Because of inevitable discrepancies between a firm's expectations and the real behaviour of the market, the quantity of the product offered for sale on the market is different from that demanded by the market (it can be either smaller or greater than the demand). The firm's savings and its ability to pay current debts depend on the real profit and income of that firm.

We distinguish between innovation and invention (that is, a novelty being considered for introduction into practice and thus becoming an innovation). There are two general ways of searching for inventions, namely autonomous, in-house research by each firm and by the imitation of competitors. Publicized knowledge does not only permit imitation by competitors. The public knowledge can also relate to the methods of research, indicated by the arrow from the publicized knowledge to autonomous research. From a number of inventions only a small fraction are selected to become innovations. Innovation allows the modernization of current production, but also can initiate new, radical ways of production, that is, by implanting essentially new technology. In general each innovation can effect a reduction in the unit cost of production, increasing the productivity of capital and improvements in technical product performance, but frequently it happens that an improvement in one factor is accompanied by a deterioration in the two other. Therefore firms usually face the problem of balancing the positive and negative factors of each invention and allow it to become an innovation if positive factors indicate that the firm's objectives will be attained.

FIRMS' DECISIONS

It seems that one of the crucial problems of contemporary economics is to understand the process of decision-making. Herbert Simon states that 'the dynamics of the economic system depends critically on just how economic agents go about making their decisions, and no way has been found for discovering how they do this that avoids direct inquiry and observations of the process' (Simon, 1986, p. 38). The other problem is how to model this process using some formal apparatus. A lot of attempts have been made to imitate real decision-making processes, some of which are very sophisticated and very close to reality. The purpose here, being the first approximation, is to catch the general and the most essential features of firms' decision-making processes, and at this stage of the model's development there is no necessity to feature this process in detail. What is proposed is only an initial, very rough approximation of the decision making-process on the firm's level. This proposition does preclude further development of the procedure modelling decision-making processes in subsequent versions of the model.

Here the procedure is presented for evaluating the production, investment, expected income and profit in succeeding periods of time of firm i selling its product at product price $p_i(t)$. The problem of choosing the appropriate price $p_i(t)$ will be discussed later on.

(a) Calculation of the product competitiveness $c_i(t)$

Two kinds of product competitiveness are distinguished: technical competitiveness and overall competitiveness (or simply competitiveness). The technical competitiveness reflects the quality of technical performance of the product on the market, and depends directly on the values of the product's technical characteristics, such as reliability, convenience, lifespan, safety of use, cost of use, quality and aestheticism. The overall competitiveness describes product attractiveness on the market and depends on technical competitiveness and the product price. There is no search for innovation in the model presented in this chapter, therefore all characteristics of products are constant and the same for all products. This assumption imposes the corollary of the uniformity of technical competitiveness of all firms. In Chapter 7 this assumption will be weakened and the technical competitiveness will alter because of emergence of technical innovations. Competitiveness, as a measure of attractiveness of a product, grows with a reduction in its price and an improved technical performance. It is assumed that a product competitiveness at a price $p_i(t)$ is equal to

$$c(p_i(t)) = \frac{q}{(p_i(t))^\alpha} \qquad (5.1)$$

where q is the technical competitiveness (constant during the simulation of the basic model), α the elasticity of price in the competitiveness; α is a characteristic of the market and describes the sensitivity of the market to price fluctuations. Let us denote by $c_i(t)$ the competitiveness of products of firm i at time t, that is, $c_i(t) = c(p_i(t))$.

(b) Estimation of the average price and average competitiveness

It may be said, without much exaggeration, that all man's decisions are made on the basis of his expectations, but as Herbert Simon asserts: 'economists do not disagree about many things, but they disagree about a few crucial things, in particular, how people form expectations' (Simon, 1986, p. 504). It is rational to assume that, in general, a firm knows nothing about current and future decisions of competitors. It is assumed that decisions of any firm are made independently on the basis of its

expectations of what other firms (competitors) will decide. The simplest
assumption is that next time the competitors will behave in a similar way as
in the past. Therefore the firm i estimates that in the succeeding period
$(t, t+1)$ the average price will be equal to

$$p^e(t) = p^P(t)(1-f_i(t-1))+p_i(t)\,f_i(t-1) \tag{5.2}$$

Similarly, the average competitiveness is expected to be equal to

$$c^e(t) = c^P(t)\,(1-f_i(t-1))+c_i(t)\,f_i(t-1) \tag{5.3}$$

where $f_i(t-1)$ is the market share of firm i at the previous instant, and $p^P(t)$
and $c^P(t)$ are trend values of average price and average competitiveness,
respectively.[2] It is assumed that prediction of the trend values $p^P(t)$ and $c^P(t)$
is made outside the industry and that these values are known to all firms.
Different formulae to calculate these values are built into the model (for
example, moving averages, linear and exponential trends) but in all
simulations presented below the exponential trend $[A\exp(Bt)]$ is assumed;
values of the average price and the average competitiveness in the last five
years of industry development are suitable for calculation of the optimal
values of the parameters A and B.

Equations (5.2) and (5.3) enable us to model diversified situations faced
by different firms, for example, the weight of a small firm to form the
average price is much smaller than that of a large firm. So, small firms are,
in general, 'price takers' in the sense that they assume that the future
average price will be very close to the trend value, and vice versa, large
firms play, in general, the role of 'price leaders' or 'price makers' so their
weight in the formation of the future average price is much more significant.

(c) Estimation of the global production

After estimating the average price of all products on the market, the global
production sold on the market, that is, the global demand $Q^d(t)$, can be
estimated. It is assumed that all firms know the demand function,

$$Q^d(t) = \frac{M(t)}{p^e(t)}, \tag{5.4}$$

---

[2] The expressions (5.2) and (5.3) have the same mathematical form for each firm. It is a
simplification, made intentionally to catch the most essential features of the industrial processes.
From an evolutionary perspective the formulae ought to be firm specific, and the knowledge (firm's
routines) and firm's experience ought to be embedded in them. We hope to make the next
'stepwise concretization' in this direction after gathering the results of the first elementary
experiments with the model.

where $M(t)$ is an amount of money which the market is inclined to spend to buy products at an average price $p^e(t)$. It is assumed that

$$M(t) = N\exp(\gamma t)(p^e(t))^\beta \qquad (5.5)$$

where N is a parameter characterizing the initial market size, γ the growth rate of the market size, and β the elasticity of the average price. The consumption theory and results of empirical research (for example, McConnell, 1984, p. 415) show that almost all price elasticities in demand functions are negative: for primary needs (for example, food, clothing) the elasticities are between 0 and -1, those of secondary (or 'luxury') needs are below -1. So, it may be expected that for commodities fulfilling primary needs β is greater than zero and smaller than one and for commodities fulfilling higher-order needs (for example, entertainment) β is smaller than zero.

(d) Estimation of the market share of firm i

After estimation of the average competitiveness of all products offered for sale on the market and perceiving the competitiveness of its own products, firm i may try to estimate its future market share. I propose deterministic selective equations similar to those used in former models of evolutionary processes (Kwaśnicki, 1979; Kwaśnicka, et al., 1983). The share of firm i in period $(t, t+1)$ is equal to

$$f_i(t) = f_i(t-1)\,\frac{c_i(t)}{c^e(t)} \qquad (5.6)$$

It means that the share of firm i increases if the competitiveness of its products is greater than the average competitiveness of all products offered for sale on the market and declines if the competitiveness is smaller than the average competitiveness.[3]

---

[3] There is the possibility of applying stochastic selective equations. Probably the stochastic equations would be closer to reality because of the essentially random process of 'meeting' a specific product with a specific buyer, but at the actual level of development of the model the deterministic selective equations deal with the problem and give satisfactory results. The proposed selective equations may be treated as the first approximation and the possibility of making them stochastic after a thorough investigation of the deterministic model is still open. My intention is that at the initial stage of investigating the model the random factors ought to be related to the innovation process only, to enable full evaluation of the influence of innovation on the behaviour of the model. The search for innovation is by nature a stochastic process and assumption of the deterministic process of emergence of the innovations leads to a significant departure of the model's behaviour from patterns of development observed in real processes.

(e) Estimation of the production of firm i

Having the expected share and the expected size of the market, firm i is able to estimate the quantity of production to be accepted by the market (i.e. the supply of production of firm i) on the basis of the simple equation,

$$Q_i^s(t) = f_i(t)Q^d(t). \tag{5.7}$$

The capital needed to get output $Q_i^s(t)$ is equal to

$$K_i(t) = Q_i^s(t)/A. \tag{5.8}$$

A in the above equation is the productivity of capital. Because there is no R&D process, then firms do not improve the productivity of capital and in the basic model the productivity A is constant and uniform for all firms during simulation runs.

If the required growth of the capital of firm i is greater than the investment capability of firm i, then it is assumed that the capital of firm i at time t is equal to the sum of the investment capability and the capital at $t - 1$, minus the capital physical depreciation (the amortization). For the capital calculated in such a way, the production $Q_i^s(t)$ is recalculated as

$$Q_i^s(t) = K_i(t)A. \tag{5.9}$$

(f) Estimation of the expected income and profit

The last step in the decision-making procedure is calculation of the expected income and profit of firm i, which are equal to

$$\Gamma_i = Q_i^s(t)(p_i(t) - Vv(Q_i^s(t)) - \eta), \tag{5.10}$$

$$\Pi_i = \Gamma_i - K_i(t)(\rho + \delta), \tag{5.11}$$

where Γ_i is the expected income of firm i at time $t + 1$, Π_i is the expected profit of firm i at time $t + 1$, $Q_i^s(t)$ the output (supply) of firm i, V the unit production cost (because there is no innovation, V is constant and uniform for all firms during the simulation), $v(Q_i^s)$ is the factor of unit production cost as a function of a scale of production (economies of scale), η is the constant production cost, $K_i(t)$ the capital needed to obtain the output $Q_i^s(t)$, ρ the normal rate of return and δ the physical capital depreciation rate (the amortization).

For a given price $p_i(t)$ the expansionary investment, the production in the next year, and expected profit and income are calculated by applying the procedure presented above. The problem to be discussed is the way of setting the product price $p_i(t)$. It is assumed that a firm takes into account its investment capabilities and estimates the values of an objective function for different prices of its products. The price for which the objective function reaches the maximum value is chosen by a firm as the price of its products. It is not a maximization in the strict sense. The estimation of values of the objective function is not perfect and is made for the next year only; so this is not a global optimization once and for all as the firms apply this rule from year to year.

Different price-setting procedures (based on different objective functions and the markup rules) have been scrutinized, the results of which are presented in the work of Kwaśnicki and Kwaśnicka (1992) and will also be discussed in the succeeding chapter. The results suggest that firms apply the following objective function:

$$O_1(t+1) = (1 - F_i) \frac{\Gamma_i(t+1)}{\Gamma(t)} + F_i \frac{Q_i^s(t+1)}{QS(t)},$$

$$F_i = a_4 \exp\left(-a_5 \frac{Q_i^s(t+1)}{QS(t)}\right),$$

(5.12)

where F_i is the magnitude coefficient (with values between 0 and 1), Q_i^s the supply production of firm i in year $t+1$, Γ_i the expected income of firm i at $t+1$ (defined by equation (5.10)), QS is the global production of the industry in year t and Γ the global net income of all firms in year t. $\Gamma(t)$ and $QS(t)$ play the role of constants in equation (5.12) and ensure that the values of both terms in this equation are of the same order. The function O_1 expresses short- and long-term thinking of firms during the decision-making process (the first and second terms in equation (5.12), respectively). The plausible values of the parameters are $a_4 = 1$ and $a_5 = 5$; it means that the long-term thinking is much more important for the firms' survival and that the firms apply flexible strategy, that is, the relative importance of short- and long-term components changes in the course of firms' development (the long-term one is much more important for small firms than for the big ones).

The decision-making procedure presented above with the search for the 'optimal' price-setting procedure based on the objective concept constructs a formal scheme for finding the proper value of the price. I treat this scheme as an approximation (abstraction) of what is done by real decision-makers. They, of course, do not make such calculations from year to year, they rather think in the routine mode: 'My decisions ought to provide for the future prospects of the firm and also should allow income (or profit) to be maintained at some relatively high level'. Decisions on the future level of production and the future product price depend on the actual investment capabilities of the firm. It is possible to embody in the model different ways of calculating the firms' investment capabilities. I propose to investigate two formulae. One as proposed by Nelson and Winter (1982), and Winter (1984) in which the investment capability of the firm i in period $(t, t + 1)$ is a function of profits (Π) of the firm i in period $(t - 1, t)$ and the second in which the investment capability depends on the firm's current savings (SV). Let us call these two the Π-investment and the SV-investment strategies, respectively. Investment capability of firm i in the Π-investment strategy is equal to:

$$IC_i(t) = \max\{0, \delta K_i(t-1) + \mu \ \Pi_i(t-1)\}, \qquad (5.13)$$

where δ is the physical capital depreciation, μ the coefficient equal to one for $\Pi_i < 0$, and equal to μ_0 for $\Pi_i > 0$. The credit parameter μ_0 is greater than, or equal to, one. If μ_0 is greater than one, firm i takes credit if its overall investment $I_i(t)$ at time t exceeds the sum of the amortization and the profit of the firm at $(t - 1)$. Nelson and Winter (1982) say nothing about the method of taking credit and its future repayment. It would seem that a firm takes credit from banks if required investment exceeds its current profit, without an eye to future repayment..

I propose to incorporate more explicitly the process of credit taking and its future repayment. In the SV-investment strategy it is assumed that every year a firm spares a fraction of its current profit to be invested in its future development. If at any time required investment exceeds current savings, then the firm takes credit and its debt increases. The debt is repaid within an assumed period. The savings and debts increase every year at the assumed interest rate ρ_1. If it is assumed that credit ought to be repaid within μ_1 years on average, then the compensation (the debt repayment) in the next year is equal to

$$DR_i(t) = D_i(t-1)/\mu_1. \qquad (5.14)$$

The investment capability of firm i at time t depends on current savings SV and current compensations DR_i, and is equal to (the meaning of parameters δ and μ as in equation (5.13)):

$$IC_i(t) = \max\{0, \delta K_i(t-1) + \mu(SV_i(t-1) - DR_i(t))\}. \qquad (5.15)$$

It may happen that the required investment of firm i exceeds the firm's own funds (equal to the sum of amortization $\delta K_i(t - 1)$ and current savings $(SV_i - DR_i)$). If this is the case and μ is greater than one, the firm accepts credit to finance the exceeding investment. Let us denote by ICr_i the investment financed by credit and by IS_i the investment financed by the firm's own savings (that is, the capital depreciation funds $\delta K_i(t - 1)$ excluded). To simplify the calculations, the structure of the debt is not considered (that is, the moment at which credit is accepted is not recognized), so it is assumed, as the first approximation, that the debt at time t is characterized by its total value, that is, equal to

$$D_i(t) = (D_i(t-1) - DR_i(t))(1 + \rho_1) + ICr_i(t). \tag{5.16}$$

The debt is diminished by the current repayment and increases according to the interest rate (the first term) and is enlarged by current investment financed by credit, ICr_i. Each year the firm i spares a fraction of its current profit for savings. It is assumed that the fraction of profit allocated to savings depends on the relation between current savings and the firm's capital; the greater the savings, the lower the proportion of actual profit (if positive) which is set aside for savings. A parameter *ToSave* controls the fraction of profit for savings. To delimit the amount of money passed for saving SP_i we use the following formula (the expression $\exp(\cdot)$ is a fraction of positive profit spent for saving):

$$SP_i(t) = \max\{0, \Pi_i(t)\} \exp\left(-\frac{SV_i(t-1)}{ToSave\ K_i(t-1)}\right).$$

The savings at time t are reduced by current obligations related to repayment of debt DR_i, multiplied in accordance with the interest rate ρ_1, reduced by the investment financed from the firm's own resources IS_i, and raised by current savings from profit, so the saving is equal to

$$SV_i(t) = (SV_i(t-1) - DR_i(t))(1 + \rho_1) - IS_i(t) + SP_i(t). \tag{5.17}$$

FIRMS' ENTRY

In each period $(t, t + 1)$ a number of firms try to enter the market. Each firm enters the market with assumed capital equal to *InitCapital* and with the initial price of its products equal to the predicted average price. The larger the concentration of the industry, the greater the number of potential entrants (that is, firms trying to enter the market).

In general, any firm may enter the market and if a firm's characteristics are unsatisfactory, then it is quickly eliminated (superseded) from the market. But because of the limited capacity of computer memory a threshold for potential entrants is assumed; namely, to control the number of entering firms it is assumed that a firm enters the market if the estimated value of objective O_1 of that firm is greater than an estimated average value of the objective O_1 in the industry.[4] By making this assumption a more competitive environment is provided for all firms – for operating firms and for entrants.

---

[4] It may be expected that a similar threshold exists in real industrial processes.

As a result of competition the market shares of firms with competitiveness smaller than average decrease, and the shares of firms with competitiveness greater than average increase. A firm is driven from the market if it does not keep pace with competitors (that is, in the long run, competitiveness of its products is smaller than the average). To limit the number of very small firms it is also assumed that a firm is eliminated from the register of firms if its market share is smaller than some assumed minimum share, for example, 0.1%.[5]

COMPETITION OF PRODUCTS IN THE MARKET

All products manufactured by the entrants and the firms existing in the previous period are put on the market and evaluated. After that all decisions are left to buyers; these decisions primarily depend on the relative values of competitiveness of all products offered, but quantities of products of each firm offered for sale are also taken into account.

It is assumed that the global demand $Q^d(t)$, for products potentially sold on a market is equal to an amount of money – $M(t)$ – which the market is inclined to spend on buying products offered for sale by the firms divided by the average price, $p(t)$, of the products offered by these firms, as was presented in the decision-making procedure; see equations (5.4) and (5.5) defining the demand function, where instead of $p^e(t)$ it is necessary to put $p(t)$. The only difference is that in the decision-making process firms use their estimated values of the average price, as a result of their expectations of the future market and behaviour of competitors, and here the average price in the demand function is counted using the whole pool of products offered for sale on the market (that is, the supply). Therefore the average price of products is

$$p(t) = \sum_i p_i(t) \, \frac{Q_i^s(t)}{Q^s(t)}. \tag{5.18}$$

The global output offered for sale (the supply) is equal to

$$Q^s(t) = \sum_i Q_i^s(t). \tag{5.19}$$

Global production sold on the market is equal to the smaller value of the

---

[5] It is possible to add other criteria for withdrawing a firm, for example, bankruptcy, if the firm's current debt exceeds an assumed fraction of the firm's current capital.

demand $Q^d(t)$ and the supply $Q^s(t)$,

$$QS(t) = \min\{Q^d(t),\, Q^s(t)\}. \tag{5.20}$$

The general selection equations of a firm's competition in a market have the following form (for comment see also footnote 3 on page 89),

$$f_i(t) = f_i(t-1)\frac{c_i(t)}{c(t)}, \tag{5.21}$$

where $c(t)$ is the average competitiveness of products offered for sale,

$$c(t) = \sum_i f_i(t-1)c_i(t). \tag{5.22}$$

This means that the share (f_i) of firm i in global output increases if the competitiveness of its products is greater than the average of all products present on the market, and decreases if the competitiveness is less than the average. The rate of change is proportional to the difference between the competitiveness of products of firm i and average competitiveness.

The quantity of products potentially sold by the firm i on the market (that is, the demand for products of firm i) is equal to

$$Q_i^d(t) = QS(t)f_i(t). \tag{5.23}$$

The above equations are valid if the production offered by the firms exactly fits the demand of the market. This is a very rare situation and therefore these equations have to be adjusted to states of discrepancy between global demand and global production, and discrepancy between the demand for products of a specific firm and the production offered by this firm. Equation (5.23) describes the market demand for products of firm i offered at a price $p_i(t)$ and with competitiveness $c_i(t)$. In general, a real production (supply) of firm i is different from the specific demand for its products. The realization of the demand for products of firm i does not depend only on these two values of the demand, $Q_i^d(t)$, and the supply, $Q_i^s(t)$, but on the whole pool of products offered for sale on the market. The alignment of the supply and demand of production of all firms present on the market is an adaptive process performed in a highly iterative and interactive mode between sellers and buyers. In our model, we simulate the iterative alignment of the supply and the demand in a two-stage process in which a part of the demand is fulfilled in the first stage, and the rest of the demand is, if possible, fulfilled in the second succeeding stage of the alignment. If there is no global oversupply of production, then in the first stage of the supply–demand alignment process all demands for production of specific firms, wherever possible, are fulfilled, but there is still the shortfall in production of firms which underestimated the demands for their products. This part of the demand is fulfilled in the second stage of the supply–demand alignment process. At this stage, the products of the firms which produce more than the specific demand are sold to replace the shortfall in production by the firms which underestimated the demand for their products.

The supply–demand alignment process is slightly different if the global oversupply of production occurs. It seems reasonable to assume that in such a case the production of each firm sold on the market is divided into (1) the production bought as the outcome of the competitive process (as described by equations (5.21) and (5.23)), and (2) the production bought as the outcome of the non-competitive process (let us call it the cooperative process) – in principle, this part of production does not depend on the product competitiveness but primarily depends on the volume of production offered for sale, that is, random factors play a much more important role in the choice of relevant products to be bought within this part of the production. In general, the division of the production of each firm into these two parts depends on the value of the global oversupply. The higher the oversupply, the larger is the part of the production of each firm which is sold on the basis of the non-competitive preferences.

To evaluate the shares of these two parts of production we construct the coefficient w which depends on the global demand and the global supply, namely

$$w = \min\left\{1, \frac{Q^d(t)}{Q^s(t)}\right\}. \tag{5.24}$$

The coefficient w divides the behaviour of the model into two regimes: w is equal to one if the demand exceeds the supply, and is smaller than one for the oversupplied market. If there is no global oversupply (that is, $w = 1$), then, as has been said, the products of the firms which produce more than the demand are sold instead of the potential production of the firms which produce less than the demand (this is done in the second stage of the supply–demand alignment process, see below). If there is a global oversupply, then maximum $w\,100\%$ of the demand is supplied by the production of each firm in the first, competitive stage of the alignment process, and the rest $(1 - w)100\%$ of the demand is supplied in the second, cooperative stage (if such production is available).

Usually the global oversupply, if such occurs, is small so the major part of production is distributed under the influence of the competitive mechanisms and only a small part is distributed as a result of cooperative distribution. But to understand the necessity of distinguishing the two proposed stages of the selling–buying process let us consider the following, albeit artificial, situation: except for one firm, the production of all other firms exactly meets the demand for their products. The atypical firm produces much more than the demand for its products. The question is: what is the result of the market selling–buying process? It may be assumed that the production sold by all firms is exactly equal to the specific demands for their products, which is equivalent to the assumption that the volume of overproduction of the atypical firm does not influence the behaviour of the market. In an extreme case, we may imagine that the volume of production of the atypical firm is infinite and the rest of the firms continue to produce exactly what is demanded. Does it mean that the excessive production would go unnoticed by the buyers and that they would remain loyal to firms producing exactly what is demanded? It seems that a more adequate description requires the incorporation of the assumption that the future distribution of products sold on the market depends on the level of overproduction of all firms, and particularly the level of overproduction of the atypical firm. And it seems that in the case of the overproduction of one firm its share in the global production sold will increase at the expense of all firms producing exactly what is demanded. In the extreme case, when overproduction of the atypical firm tends to infinity (i.e. the coefficient w is approaching zero), the only products sold on the market belong to that firm, and the shares of all other firms are going to be zero. But it does not mean that producing more than is demanded is an advantageous strategy for the firm and that it is an effective weapon to eliminate the competitors; in fact, the bulk of the overproduction is not sold on the market and is lost by the firm. In effect the atypical firm's profit is much smaller than expected, or even may be negative; after some time the firm's development will be stopped and in the end it will be eliminated from the market.

Incorporation of coefficient w also permits the entry of new competitors into the market. Without the assumption of the two-stage distribution in the supply–demand alignment process the entry of a new firm might be very difficult, and it would be necessary to add a special procedure to allow the entry in the case of the global oversupply. In such a case, when all firms' production meets the demands for their products, there would be no place for new entrants. The competition process, as described by the selection equation (5.21), cannot be initiated because of the zero value of the share of the entrant at the previous instant, $f_i(t-1)$. The assumption that the $(1-w)$ fraction of the global demand is fulfilled in the cooperative stage of the alignment process enables the entry of new firms. Similarly, the entry is possible if there is no global oversupply (that is, $w = 1$). In such a case, there is a place on the market for the new entrant and, in general, all its production is sold on the market.

It is assumed that at the competitive stage of the supply–demand alignment process the demand is partially fulfilled by production OS_i^{comp},

$$QS_i^{comp}(t) = \min\{Q_i^s(t), wQ_i^d(t)\} = \min\{Q_i^s(t), wQS(t)f_i(t)\},$$

$$QS_i^{comp}(t) = \min\left\{Q_i^s(t), wQS(t) \, f_i(t-1)\frac{c_i(t)}{c(t)}\right\}. \tag{5.25}$$

The remaining $(1 - w)$ fraction of the demand may be fulfilled in the cooperative stage if there is such production available, that is, if $Q_i^s(t) > wQ_i^d(t)$. It is assumed that this fraction of the demand is fulfilled in the cooperative stage according to the distribution of unsold products in the competitive stage. After completion of the competitive stage of the supply–demand alignment process the global production sold is equal to

$$QS^{comp}(t) = \sum_i QS_i^{comp}(t) = \sum_i \min\{Q_i^s(t), wQ_i^d(t)\}. \tag{5.26}$$

So, the unfulfilled global production after the first stage, to be supplied in the second cooperative stage of the alignment, is

$$QS^{coop}(t) = QS(t) - QS^{comp}(t). \tag{5.27}$$

The unsold production $QN_i(t)$ of firm i is equal to

$$QN_i(t) = \min\{0, \, Q_i^s(t) - wQ_i^d(t)\}.$$

The fraction of unsold products of firm i in the global production unsold in the first stage of the alignment process is equal to

$$f_i^{coop} = \frac{QN_i(t)}{\sum_j QN_j(t)} = \frac{\min\{0, \, Q_i^s(t) - wQ_i^d(t)\}}{\sum_j \min\{0, \, Q_j^s(t) - wQ_j^d(t)\}}.$$

It is assumed that the fulfilment of the demand for products of firm i in the cooperative stage of the alignment process is proportional to the fraction f_i^{coop}, so

$$QS_i^{coop}(t) = QS^{coop}(t)f_i^{coop} = (QS(t) - QS^{comp}(t))f_i^{coop}.$$

Finally, the production sold is the sum of production accepted in the competitive and the cooperative stages of the supply–demand alignment process,

$$QS_i(t) = QS_i^{comp}(t) + QS_i^{coop}(t),$$

$$QS_i(t) = \min\{Q_i^s(t), wQ_i^d(t)\} + (QS(t) - QS^{comp}(t))f_i^{coop}. \qquad (5.28)$$

The general meaning of the supply–demand alignment process as described above parallels that of equations (5.21), (5.22), (5.23). If supply exactly meets market demand (that is, if $Q^s(t) = Q^d(t)$ and $Q_i^s(t) = Q_i^d(t)$ for all i), equations from (5.24) to (5.28) are equivalent to equations (5.21) to (5.23).

The market share of the production sold of firm i is

$$f_i(t) = \frac{QS_i(t)}{QS(t)}. \qquad (5.29)$$

The real income and profit of firm i are as follows:

$$\Gamma_i = QS_i(t)(p_i(t) - Vv(Q_i^s(t)) - \eta), \qquad (5.30)$$

$$\Pi_i = \Gamma_i - K_i(t)(\rho + \delta) - D_i(t)/\mu_1. \qquad (5.31)$$

$K_i(t)$ in equations (5.30) and (5.31) is the value of capital allocated by firm i to produce $Q_i^s(t)$, so profits are smaller than expected if the firm inappropriately evaluates the required level of production and manufactures more than it can sell in the market.[6]

Effective capital of the firm is expressed as

$$K_i(t) = QS_i(t)/A,$$

---

[6] There arises the question of what is to be done with the excess production. It is assumed that this part of the production is lost. It is possible to incorporate the backlogs into the model, but this leads to much greater complexity of the model in the presence of innovations (see Chapter 7). The production may be modernized due to innovations applied, so it would be necessary to remember the quantities of orders and unsold production at different moments together with the technical characteristics. It seems that our assumption on excess production does not lead to large errors, bearing in mind that (1) the model is focused on long-term industry development, (2) yearly overproduction is normally not very high, and (3) to consider backlogs and delivery delays it would be necessary to take into account also all related costs, for example, of storing of the unsold production.

and global sales are equal to

$$GS(t) = \sum_i QS_i(t)p_i(t).$$

The market share of firm i in global sales is

$$fs_i(t) = QS_i(t)\, p_i(t)/GS(t).$$

6. Economic Analysis and the Model

This section concentrates on the equilibrium analysis of the model's behaviour. However, at the end of this chapter, results of experiments with the variable cost of production and variable size of the market, and preliminary results of simulation with the possibility of innovations emergence are presented, mainly to show how infringement of basic assumptions of neoclassical economics causes the emergence of the positive profit. But the main aim of this chapter is to show to what extent the model's behaviour resembles industrial processes. It is also hoped that some results presented in this chapter will allow us to understand better the industrial mechanisms of development.

Using the concept of supply and demand functions traditional economic theories (classical or neoclassical) demonstrate the emergence of positive profit and show how this profit disappears over time. A stylized illustration of this process is presented in Figure 6.1 (see, for example, McConnell's *Economics*, 1984, pp. 43–59, and 408–23); the upward-sloping supply curve in the left-hand chart of Figure 6.1

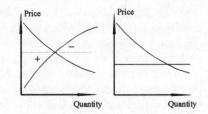

Figure 6.1. Neoclassical supply and demand functions

aggregates all diversified costs of production of existing firms in the industry. Its intersection with the demand function (the downward-sloping curve) determines an equilibrium price. The areas marked by (+) and (–) determine the profit (sometimes called the pure profit) acquired by the whole industry. This describes the state of affairs only in the short-run perspective. Due to the competitive process and free entry of new firms, the supply curve more and more conforms to the horizontal line determined by the equilibrium price; this process continues until the supply curve becomes totally horizontal (as in the right-hand chart of Figure 6.1) and the possibility of making positive profit disappears. So, in the long run, at equilibrium, the only profit made by firms is the 'normal' profit embedded into the supply function in the form of the opportunity costs. The normal profit is identified by neoclassical economics with the long-run interest rate. But all the time we should bear in mind the assumptions under which the results have been obtained. The most essential assumptions seem to be: perfect competition (that is, competition of an infinite number of firms on

101

the market – or at least a large number of equal-sized firms), constant size of the market, constant value of the unit cost of production (that is, no external influence, for example, through the price of raw materials, changes of wages), infinite 'computing power' of decision-makers allowing them to find optimal decisions (perfect knowledge and objective rationality). Any violation of the above assumptions leads to the emergence of long-run positive profit. Innovation is one of the best-known causes of positive profit. But, as we will see, there are other causes of positive profit, such as the finite 'computing power' of decision-makers (bounded rationality). The simulation results of our model show that, at least theoretically, even with the fulfilment of the neoclassical assumptions there are two domains of the so-called cost ratio (defined as multiplication of the unit cost of production by the productivity of capital) in which industries behave in a qualitatively different way (see page 122). For the cost ratio below some threshold value industries behave as classical (or neoclassical) theories suggest, namely the profit at the equilibrium state is equal to zero. But for the cost ratio greater than the threshold value the equilibrium profit is greater than zero and increases very quickly with increasing values of the cost ratio. The other question is whether any real industry is characterized by the values of the cost ratio greater than the threshold value. Our result is purely theoretical and needs to be empirically verified. Numerous simulation experiments with the presented model suggest that the model reflects phenomena observed in real industrial processes and allow us to get confidence in that model. I believe that the result related to the cost ratio is not only a theoretical one but will be confirmed by empirical study of industrial development.

Our model makes it possible to create extreme conditions and to investigate the behaviour of the industry in highly artificial situations, never, or very rarely, observed in our complex socio-economic life but very important for a better understanding of the mechanisms of economic development. The model also enables us to investigate the influences of a single factor on industry behaviour, as well as to investigate the mutual impact of a set of such factors and observe how non-cumulative the simultaneous influences of these factors are.

HOW ARE PRICES SET?

The problem which seems interesting to us and which should also be solved before further systematic study of the model is 'how are prices set?'. It has been assumed that the price in the decision-making procedure of a firm (equations (5.1) to (5.11) in the preceding chapter) is set by a firm by using some 'external' procedure. Production and investment in the next period (year or quarter) are estimated on the basis of this 'external' price. In this section a plausible mechanism of the price determination will be suggested.

The importance of price determination as a part of the market process was recognized by economics long ago. The interest of neoclassical economics in price determination is based on the assumption that comprehension of the market-price determination explains virtually all that is important in the economic process. In Kaldor's opinion (1985, pp. 13–14),

> the price mechanism is the key to everything, the key instrument in guiding the operation of an undirected, unplanned, free market economy. The Walrasian model and its most up-to-date successor may both be highly artificial abstractions from the real world but the truth that the theory conveys – that prices provide the guide to all economic action – must be fundamentally true, and its main implication that free markets secure the best results must also be true. (Quoted from Tool, 1991)

The institutionalist's generalization about price-setting practices states that 'virtually all significant prices are set as discretionary acts of identifiable persons – that existential markets are, in large part, shaped and staffed by *price makers* rather than by *price takers*' (Tool, 1991). Shackle (1972, p. 227) suggests a reason for habitual patterns of behaviour as conventions in price-setting: 'Prices which have stood at a particular level for some time acquire thereby some sanction and authority. They are the "right" and even "just" prices. But also they are the prices to which the society has adapted its ways and habits, they are prices which mutually cohere in an established frame of social life.'

Using phrases with 'price makers', 'price takers', or 'habitual patterns of behaviour' may be useful to explain short-term practices of price determination, but they seem to say nothing about the long-term practices. Institutional theorists understood that and proposed some operational criteria for price discrimination, for example, Means and Blair perceived price determination to be accomplished by the calculation of a 'target rate of return on capital' (Means et al., 1975, pp. 33–67). An objective is the highest rate of return on capital 'consistent with a healthy growth of business'. As will seen, proposed objective, being the result of independent investigation, comes very close to that proposition.

The problem of how prices are set is discussed by Silverberg (1987). He rejects the marginalist theory as well as monopoly price/output criterion (marginal revenue equal to marginal cost) as inapplicable to his model. Silverberg proposes difference equations for price dynamics on the basis of the markup theory – 'firms determine average unit cost at some standard operating capacity, and add a fixed percentage to arrive at a price which is otherwise independent of demand and competitive pressures'. His dynamic adjustment equations 'capture the main aspect of the problem, and at the same time allow for shift in the price structure due to long-term changes in relative cost competitiveness' (Silverberg, 1987). Silverberg uses continuous time in his model. To adjust his formula to our model, it has to be reformulated as a system of difference equations (using discrete time). Using our notations the parallel price dynamic equation applied in our model has the form,

$$p_i(t+1) = p_i(t)(1 + a_1 \ln(a_3 V/p_i(t)) + a_2 \ln(c_i/c^e)), \qquad (6.1)$$

where $p_i(t)$ is the price of products of firm i at time t, a_1, a_2, a_3 are parameters, V is the unit cost of production (variable and constant), c_i the competitiveness of products of firm i, and c^e the average competitiveness of products on the market.

It is agreed that Silverberg's equations 'capture the main aspect of the problem' and reflect what some firms are doing. Our model enables us to compare the effectiveness of different price-setting procedures (PSPs) and observe how the distribution of firms using different PSPs changes in the course of development of the industry. What is proposed is to invent different price-setting procedures and allow each firm to choose (for example, randomly) the price-setting procedure applied by this firm during its lifetime. By making a number of such experiments we are able to evaluate which PSP wins in such a game and which class of behaviour is more likely to allow them to coexist or to dominate the market. The proposition of Silverberg is regarded as one of these PSPs (rules). The others which are investigated are based on the assumption that a firm estimates values of some objective function for different values of the price of its products. The price for which the objective function is maximized is chosen by a firm as the price of its products. It is not maximization in the strict sense. The estimation of the values of the objective function is not exact and made only for the next year (it is not a global optimization, once and for all, since firms apply this rule annually – or quarterly, depending on the strategy used by the firm, and the unit of time in the model).

Two objective functions are proposed:

$$O_1(t+1) = (1-F_i)\frac{\Gamma_i(t+1)}{\Gamma(t)} + F_i \frac{Q_i^s(t+1)}{QS(t)},$$

$$O_2(t+1) = (1-F_i)\frac{\Pi_i(t+1)}{\Pi(t)} + F_i \frac{Q_i^s(t+1)}{QS(t)}, \qquad (6.2)$$

$$F_i = a_4 \exp\left(-a_5 \frac{Q_i^s(t+1)}{QS(t)}\right),$$

where F_i is the magnitude coefficient, Q_i^s the expected production of firm i in year $t + 1$, Γ_i the expected income of firm i at $t + 1$, defined by equation (5.10), Π_i the expected profit of firm i at $t +1$, defined by equation (5.11),

QS the global production of the industry in year t, Γ the global net income of all firms in year t, and Π the global net profit of all firms in year t. If we assume that a_4 is equal to zero, then the objective of a firm is equivalent to net income in the first case, and profit in the second case. For a_4 greater than zero the objective of a firm is in some sense a combination of short-term thinking (search for profit or income in the next year) and long-term thinking (obtaining a larger market share in the future). The parameter a_5 controls the variation of magnitude of short- and long-term thinking for small and large firms. For a_5 greater than zero the long-term thinking is more important for the small firms than for the large firms. This parameter is added to check if it is essential for firms with larger market shares to change their strategies or to stick to a rigid strategy (as defined by parameter a_4).

A formal procedure is used to find the price and this procedure is treated as an approximation of what is done by decision-makers in reality. They, of course, do not make such calculations from year to year; rather they think in a routine mode: 'My decisions ought to provide for the future prospects of the firm and also should allow profit (or income) to be maintained at some relatively high level'.

The values of the parameters a_1, a_2, a_3, a_4, and a_5 for each firm are randomly drawn from defined sets of values for each firm in the year of its entry into the market. This gives an opportunity to observe the competition of firms applying the same rule for different values of relevant parameters as well as competition between firms applying different rules. The following series of experiments have been made. (1) All firms entering the market apply the same price-setting procedure (the markup rule, the O_1 rule, or the O_2 rule). Values of relevant parameters are randomly drawn for each firm. (2) At the time of entry a firm chooses randomly one of two (or three) price-setting procedures (there are four combinations: (a) markup and O_1; (b) markup and O_2; (c) O_1 and O_2; and (d) all three price-setting procedures). The initial conditions in all experiments are the same.[1] These experiments have been repeated for two values of the unit cost of production V (assumed to be constant during simulation) that is, equal to 1.3 and 2.6.

In the markup rule values of parameters a_1, a_2, and a_3 are drawn from sets $(0, 1)$, $(0, 0.5)$, and $(1, 3)$, respectively. The results of 20 simulation runs for each cost of production for the markup rule are summarized in Figure 6.2 (a) and (c). Coordinates a_1 and a_3 for the largest firms (that is, firms with market shares in the last year of simulation ($t = 100$) greater than 4%) are marked by rectangles.[2]

---

[1] The rate of market growth γ is equal to 1%, the other parameters as in the Appendix.

[2] We ought to present the results in a three dimensional space (a_1, a_2, a_3), but to make the picture readable we confine the presentation to the plane (a_1, a_3). The distribution of the parameter a_2 is almost uniform, that is, similar to that of a_1.

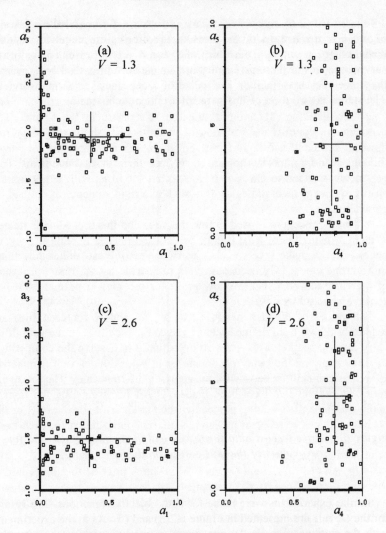

Figure 6.2. Coordinates of the parameters for the largest firms; the markup PSP ((a) and (c)), the O_1 PSP ((b) and (d))

If all firms which enter the market in these simulations had been marked in these pictures, then the distributions of these firms would have been uniform in the rectangle defined by the minimum and the maximum values of parameters a_1 and a_3. The distribution of the largest firms is far from being uniform. Average values of parameters a_1, a_2, and a_3 for the largest firms are equal to: 0.364, 0.132 and 1.939 (for $V = 1.3$), 0.357, 0.138 and

1.489 (for $V = 2.6$), respectively. These points are marked by the crosses in Figure 6.2, the lengths of the arms of the crosses are equal to standard deviations of a_1 and a_3. The values of a_1 and a_2 are not essential for firms' survival; values of these parameters are almost uniformly distributed within the scope of their variability. But values of a_3 are crucial for firms' survival. The standard deviation of this parameter is relatively small.

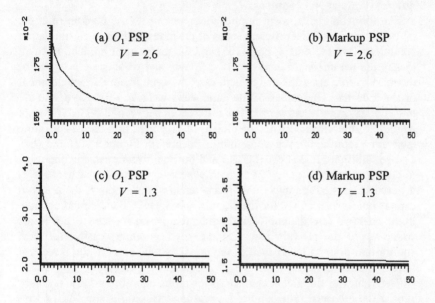

Figure 6.3. Price to cost ratio for the O_1 and the markup PSPs, and for two values of the unit cost of production

Similar experiments were made for both objective functions. The results for the O_1 rule are presented in Figure 6.2(b) and (d). As in the experiments with the markup rule, the largest firms are marked within the rectangles defined by the minimum and the maximum values of parameters a_4 and a_5 (it is assumed that a_4 varies between 0 and 1, and a_5 between 0 and 10). Average values of parameters a_4 and a_5 are equal to 0.783 and 4.26 (for $V = 1.3$); 0.803 and 4.52 (for $V = 2.6$), respectively. Parameter a_5 is almost uniformly distributed within assumed borders, which means that a_5 is not so essential for firms' survival as a_4. The average value of a_4 suggests that long-term thinking is decisive for firms' survival. Reaching high income (or profit) is important but considerably more important is concern with the future of a firm. Average values of the parameters a_4 and a_5 are almost the same for different costs of production. The pictures in Figure 6.2(b) and (d) are very similar. This implies that firms may apply the same O_1 rule for different costs of production (experiments were made for the O_1 rule under different initial conditions and the results suggest that the 'optimal' O_1 rule is invariable for different simulation conditions). The situation is different for the markup rule, where the average values of parameter a_3 for two levels of the cost of production are significantly different (1.94 and 1.49, respectively). This suggests that the 'optimal' markup rule is different for different simulation conditions.

The following experiment implies that, contrary to the markup rule, the O_1 rule is invariable for different states of the industry. For given simulation conditions (see footnote 1, page 105) and the unit cost of production equal to 2.6, the parameters a_4 and a_5 of the O_1 rule and parameters a_1, a_2, a_3 of the markup rule are estimated in both cases to result in similar development of the industry. The values of the parameters were: $a_1 = 0.115$, $a_2 = 0.05$, $a_3 = 1.5928$, $a_4 = 1$, and $a_5 = 5$. The differences between these two runs are negligible; the characteristics of global development are almost the same (see, for example, the price/cost ratio presented in Figure 6.3(a) and (b)). The equilibrium price is equal to 4.3 and the equilibrium value of the price to cost ratio is equal to 1.5928 in both experiments. Small (but negligible) differences existed for some other characteristics, for example, the profit to capital ratio was 1.015% for the O_1 rule and 1.016% for the markup rule. In the next two runs the unit cost of production V was reduced to 1.3. Firms which apply the O_1 rule adjust to the new conditions easily; the new equilibrium price is lower than in the previous run (3.0) but the price/cost ratio is higher (2.14).

The values of the global characteristics at the equilibrium state are very similar in both runs, for example, the profit/capital ratio is equal to 1.015% for $V = 2.6$, and 1.017% for $V = 1.3$ (Figure 6.4(a) and (c)). The average price in the second run with the O_1 PSP is lower than in the previous experiment, so the global production is larger in this run (Figure 6.4(b) and (d)). The adjustment to the new conditions is not observed in a similar run with firms applying the markup rule. Because of the stable value of the a_3 parameter, the price in this case is lower than in all previous runs (equal to 2.23), the equilibrium price/cost ratio is the same as in the previous experiment with the markup rule (equal to 1.593). Because of the low price the profit of the firms falls below zero (Figure 6.4(e)), firms have no funds to invest (the investment/capital ratio is equal to 3.5%, that is much less than the capital physical depreciation, which is 10%) and global production also falls (Figure 6.4(f)). To get similar results for the markup rule (as for the O_1 rule) in the case of the reduced cost it is necessary to adjust the markup parameters (for example, a_3 ought to be equal to 2.14). So to get plausible results it would be necessary to incorporate into the model some meta-rule for adjusting the markup parameters according to the changing state of the industry.

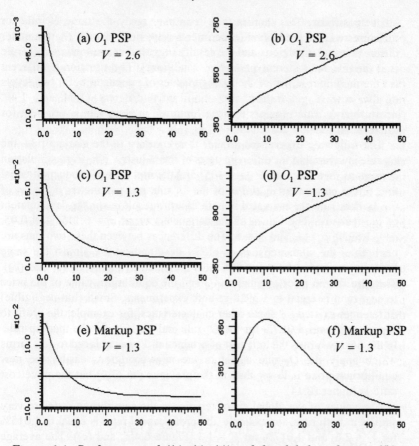

Figure 6.4. Profit to capital ((a), (c), (e)) and the global production ((b), (d), (f)); the O_1 and the markup PSPs

Hundreds of simulation runs with the O_1 rule with different simulation conditions (different number of competitors, different values of the model parameters, such as α, β, μ, γ, and so on) show that the industry adjusts to these conditions without changing the parameters a_4 and a_5. If we vary the values of a_4 between 0.6 and 1.0, the development of the industry does not change significantly (see the results presented in the next section). This means that the development of the industry is not sensitive to values of a_4 (for a_4 greater than 0.6) and it confirms our conjecture that firms need not apply the O_1 rule in such an analytical form as implemented in the model, that is, in reality the O_1 rule takes on the form of a general routine: 'Make decisions that provide for future prospects of the firm and at the same time allow income to remain at some relatively high level.'

The possibility of choosing all combinations of the price-setting procedures was available in a number of experiments (for each combination at least 15 simulation runs were made). There is no place to present in full detail the results of these experiments. The general findings are as follows: the O_1 rule wins against either the markup rule or the O_2 rule; the markup rule always wins against the O_2 rule. Similarly, the O_1 rule beats the markup rule and the O_2 rule in experiments with all three price-setting procedures available. To check to what extent the O_1 rule is better than the markup rule, the following experiments were made. During the first 20 years all firms choose only the markup rule, and after $t = 20$ entering firms choose, with the same probability, either the markup rule or the O_1 rule. In spite of the initial advantages of the markup rule over the O_1 rule firms which apply the O_1 rule dominate the market at $t = 100$ in all these experiments. Using the biological terminology, it may be said that the O_1 rule is an Evolutionary Stable Strategy (Maynard Smith, 1982).

It is necessary to say that the results presented in this section related to long-term advantages of the O_1 rule over the markup rule do not exclude the possibility that some firms may apply the markup rule in the short-term perspective. In fact, it is much easer to use the markup rule, but it seems that from time to time firms modify their markup rules, especially at crucial moments of industrial (or the firm's) development (for example, when business is not going on as expected); so in the long-term behaviour, the modified markup strategy overshoots (underestimates and overestimates) the 'optimal' route but goes very close to the 'ideal' O_1 strategy.

LONG- AND SHORT-TERM OBJECTIVES IN THE DECISION-MAKING PROCESS

In the majority of neoclassical models an assumed objective of firms' behaviour is simply profit maximization. Many students of economic behaviour questioned this simplified specification. Some of them proposed other objectives (for example, market value, market share, or 'stockholder unanimity'), while others doubt if any objective is applied by firms. The scope and thoroughness of discussion on this subject is so wide that there is no place, as well as no necessity, to review the whole spectrum of opinions. Simulation results of our model suggest that in the long-run perspective firms apply an objective as a base of their actions. Although the objective does not exist in any explicit form, rather it endures in the applied routines of each firm. In this sense we are very close to the major point of Cyert and March (1963) that possession of a comprehensive, clearly defined, objective function is not a necessary condition for firms' operation in the real domain.

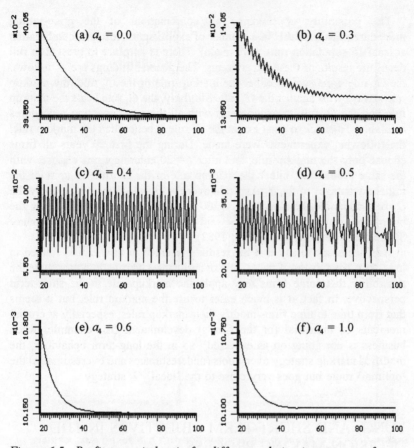

*Figure 6.5. Profit to capital ratio for different relative importance of
long- and short-term firms' objectives*

It is difficult to model such a 'verbal' and informal objective in any
simple mathematical expressions and for a proper description it is necessary
to apply more sophisticated procedures (for example, based on the Artificial
Intelligence and Expert Systems approach), nevertheless it seems that, as the
first approximation, it is possible to use the proposed idealization and try to
describe it using simple mathematical equations.[3] As the results of the
simulation presented in the preceding section reveal, the objective being a
combination of short-term and long-term components has distinguished
advantages over simple profit maximization or the markup approach.

---

[3] The representation of the firm's objective in the form of a simple equation(s) does not hinder
further development as the next stage of the 'stepwise concretization'.

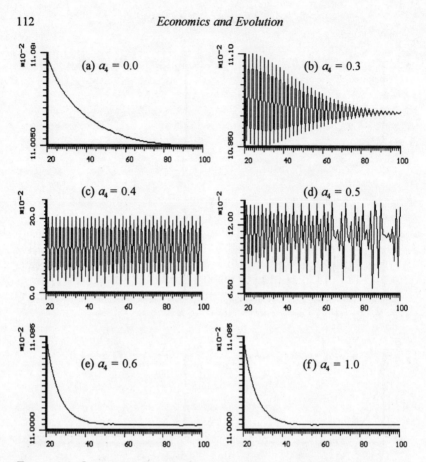

Figure 6.6. Investment to capital ratio for different relative importance of long- and short-term firms' objectives

Further investigation may reveal that there exist some better objectives but it seems that the O_1 objective proposed here adequately describes what the majority of firms are doing. The main aim of this section is to show the modes of behaviour of the industry for different relative weights of short- and long-term thinking, as well as under flexible and rigid strategies of the decision-making process. For the O_1 rule two series of experiments were made; in the first series, firms apply an inflexible strategy, that is, the parameter a_5 is equal to 0 and only parameter a_4 is changed. In the second series, firms apply a flexible strategy, that is, the parameter a_5 is a positive and variable factor, and the parameter a_4 is fixed.

The results of the first series of experiments are presented in Table 6.1,[4]

---

[4] The symbols used in the tables are as follows: n_H – average value of the Herfindahl firms'

and in Figure 6.5 (the profit to capital ratio) and Figure 6.6 (the investment to capital ratio). Values of the profit/capital and profit/sales ratios are very high (about 40%) for a_4 close to zero, that is, the short-term objective (the income) dominates; they diminish to a rather small value (slightly over 1%[5]) for a_4 close to one, that is, when the long-term objective dominates. The discounted profit rate for a_4 greater than 0.6 is almost zero. There is some kind of unstable firm's behaviour for values of a_4 between 0.35 and 0.55, that is, when both objectives are nearly equally important. For these settings the behaviour of the firm is apparently chaotic, with fluctuations of the profit/capital ratio of the same order as the mean of this ratio.

Table 6.1. Long- and short-term objectives (inflexible strategy); characteristics in the years 20–100

a_4	n_H [%]	Π/K [%]	Π^*/K [%]	Π/S [%]	I/K	p/V
0.0	11.65	39.647	38.627	37.290	11.020	2.063
0.1	11.68	29.418	28.403	30.616	11.015	1.865
0.2	11.70	20.988	19.976	23.950	11.012	1.701
0.3	11.72	13.919	12.907	17.272	11.012	1.564
0.4	10.61	8.035	6.031	10.793	12.004	1.460
0.5	10.56	2.932	1.698	4.213	11.234	1.353
0.6	8.89	1.021	0.010	1.508	11.011	1.314
0.8	8.89	1.020	0.009	1.507	11.011	1.314
1.0	8.89	1.020	0.010	1.507	11.010	1.314

The same kind of behaviour is observed for other characteristics of industry development, for example, the investment to capital ratio (Figure 6.6(c) and (d)). The fluctuations of the investment/capital ratio are so big that frequently the values of this ratio drop below 10% (that is, below the value of capital physical depreciation) and the global production is

---

number equivalent; K – average capital; Q – average production; V – average unit cost of production; I – average investment; Π – average profit; Π^* – average discounted profit;
$\Pi^* = \Pi - (I - \delta K)$, where δ is the capital depreciation rate.
The Herfindahl–Hirschman index of concentration of the industry is equal to:
$H = \Sigma_i (f_i)^2$,
The Herfindahl firms' number equivalent is defined as
$n_H = 1/H$,
and is the number of equal-sized firms that would have the same H index as the actual size distribution of firms.
  [5] The profit very close to 1% and the investment of about 11% are due to the 1% market growth rate ($\gamma = 0.01$), if there is no growth of the market ($\gamma = 0$) the profit disappears and the investment is 10%, that is, equal to the capital physical depreciation ($\delta = 0.1$) – for discussion of influence of the growth rate on the industry development see p. 136.

significantly reduced. No fluctuations of the industry development are observed if firms apply a flexible strategy, that is, the value of a_5 is greater than zero (see Table 6.2). It may be said that the a_5 parameter acts as a filter. The changes of the global characteristics are smooth, as in Figure 6.5(a), (e) and (f) and in Figure 6.6(a), (e) and (f). If we compare the values of the relevant characteristics of development in Table 6.1 and Table 6.2, we see that parameter a_5 shifts the characteristics towards the lower values of a_4, and the greater the value of a_5 the more significant is this shift; for example, the characteristics for $a_4 = 0.4$ and $a_5 = 3.0$ are similar to those for $a_4 = 0.3$ and $a_5 = 0.0$.

Table 6.2.   Flexible strategies in the decision-making process; characteristics in the years 20–100

a_5	n_H	Π/K [%]	Π^*/K [%]	Π/S [%]	I/K [%]	p/V
$a_4 = 0.4$						
0.0	10.61	8.035	6.031	10.793	12.004	1.460
1.0	11.87	9.754	8.763	12.763	11.013	1.483
2.0	11.93	11.524	10.509	14.737	11.015	1.519
3.0	11.96	13.219	12.203	16.547	11.016	1.551
5.0	11.99	16.397	15.383	19.740	11.015	1.613
10.0	12.00	23.118	22.113	25.749	11.006	1.743
$a_4 = 1.0$						
0.0	8.89	1.020	0.010	1.057	11.010	1.314
1.0	8.90	1.020	0.009	1.507	11.011	1.314
3.0	8.89	1.020	0.009	1.707	11.011	1.314
5.0	9.61	1.115	0.076	1.644	11.039	1.314
7.0	10.99	2.280	1.169	3.298	11.111	1.325
10.0	11.84	6.602	5.498	9.002	11.104	1.415

It seems that in real processes of industrial development firms change the relative importance of the long- and short-term objectives in the course of their development. The long-term objective is much more important in the initial phase of a firm's development. If firms achieve a significant share in global production, the short-term objective becomes more important. As the simulations suggest, the chaotic kind of development is not observed if firms use a flexible strategy, and it may be expected that real processes are far from the chaotic mode of development. However, short periods of chaos in industrial development cannot be excluded. The problem needs detailed study but it seems that when we look at the development of the capitalist system in the last two centuries we see some evidence of specific evolution of firms' objectives – in the early stages of capitalist development until the middle of the 19th century, gaining a maximal profit (or income) was the firms' main objective, by the end of the 19th century a distinguishable shift of thinking towards a long-run perspective was observed, so now, in the last few decades, the long-term thinking has dominated the firms' objectives. Using our notation we may say that parameters a_4 and a_5 in the firms' objective function are also the subject of evolution as a result of evolution of routines applied by the capitalist firms. At the early stages of capitalist evolution values of a_4 were small, or even close to 0, but from the mid-19th century they have gradually evolved to reach values close to 1 in modern capitalist firms.

CONCENTRATION OF INDUSTRY

Textbooks of traditional economics distinguish four typical industry structures and study them under the name of pure competition, pure monopoly, oligopoly and monopolistic competition.[6] To explain how prices and profits are formed in the typical industries, traditional economics uses such notions as: demand and supply functions, marginal cost, average total cost, average variable cost, average fixed cost, marginal revenue, total revenue, and so on. Usually, each typical situation is considered separately in different chapters. Reading these chapters and looking at diagrams supporting the reasoning one may get the impression that different mechanisms are responsible for the development of industries with different concentrations. It seems that the study of industry behaviour at different concentrations ought to be based on an understanding of the development mechanisms which are essentially invariable and do not depend on current industry conditions, particularly on the actual number of competitors. Variations in behaviour modes of differently concentrated industries ought to be an outcome of the cooperation of well-understood mechanisms of development, and not the result of juggling differently placed curves representing supply, demand, marginal revenue, marginal cost, average total

---

[6] What follows is only a short description of the essential features of these basic structures as understood by traditional economics (for example, McConnnell, 1984):

Pure competition is a feature of industry which consists of a large number of independent firms producing a standardized product; no single firm can influence market price; the firm's demand curve is perfectly elastic, therefore price equals marginal revenue.

Pure monopoly is where there is a sole producer of a commodity, and there are no straight substitutes for that commodity.

Oligopoly is characterized by the presence within the industry of a few firms, each of which has a significant fraction of the market. Firms are interdependent; the behaviour of any one firm directly affects, and is affected by, the actions of competitors.

Monopolistic competition – there is a large enough number of firms; each firm has little control over price, interdependence is very weak or practically absent, so collusion is basically impossible; products are characterized by real and imaginary differences; a firm's entry is relatively easy.

cost, average variable cost, average fixed cost and many other variables. I do not claim that the findings of traditional economics flowing from the analysis of 'curves placement' are wrong, quite the contrary, they are in accord with real phenomena, but does such analysis explain anything? To quote some findings from one popular textbook (McConnell, 1984): o n p u r e   c o m p e t i t i o n (pp. 485–6):

> Short-run profit maximization by a competitive firm can be analyzed by a comparison of total revenue and total cost or through marginal analysis. A firm will maximize profit by producing that output at which total revenue exceeds total cost by the greatest amount. Losses will be minimized by producing where the excess of total cost over total revenue is at a minimum and less than total fixed costs. ... Provided price exceeds minimum average variable cost, a competitive firm will maximize profits or minimize losses by producing that output at which price or marginal revenue is equal to marginal cost ... Applying the MR $(P) = MC$ rule at various possible market prices leads to the conclusion that the segment of the firm's short-run marginal cost curve which lies above average variable cost is its short-supply curve.

O n   p u r e   m o n o p o l y   (p. 506):

> The pure monopolist market situation differs from that of a competitive firm in that the monopolist's demand curve is downsloping, causing the marginal-revenue curve to lie below the demand curve. Like the competitive seller, the pure monopolist will maximize profits by equating marginal revenue and marginal cost. Barriers to entry may permit a monopolist to acquire economic profits even in the long run. ... Given the same costs, the pure monopolist will find it profitable to restrict output and charge a higher price than that of competitive seller. This restriction of output causes resources to be misallocated, as is evidenced by the fact that price exceeds marginal cost in monopolized markets.

O n   o l i g o p o l y (p. 537):

> Noncollusive oligopolists in effect face a kinked demand curve. This curve and the accompanying marginal-revenue curve help explain the price rigidity which characterizes such markets; they do not, however, explain the level of price. ... The uncertainties inherent in noncollusive pricing are conducive to collusion. There is a tendency for collusive oligopolist to maximize joint profits – that is, to behave somewhat like pure monopolists. Demand and cost differences, the presence of a 'large' number of firms, 'cheating' through secret price concessions, recessions, and antitrust laws, are all obstacles to collusive oligopoly. ... With cost-plus or markup pricing oligopolists estimate their unit costs at some target level of output and add a percentage 'markup' to determine price.

To prove that the long-run profit is equal to zero the traditional economic theories assume an infinite number of competitors on the market. In reality, as in our simulation, the number of competitors may be only finite, but we may expect that for a reasonably large number of competitors the results will be very close to the theoretical predictions. How many firms may be treated, from a practical point of view, as 'the infinite number of competitors'? Some characteristics of the industry at the equilibrium state obtained in a series of experiments with a different number of competitors, under additional assumptions that the initial size of all firms is the same (that is, equi-partition of the market is assumed) and that the size of the market is constant (that is, $\gamma = 0$), are presented in Table 6.3. All other parameters have values as presented in the Appendix. The controlling variable in the series of experiments is the number of competitors. The results presented in Table 6.3 are the outcome of the co-working of the same mechanisms of development embedded in the model described in the previous chapter. The results are grouped into two parts: for the normal rate of return, ρ equal to zero, and for the rate ρ equal to 5%. Our normal rate of return corresponds, in some way, to the normal profit embedded in the neoclassical supply function. The value of the normal rate of return may be considered as an effect of the development of the whole economy, and for any single industry may be treated as exogenous. In any real processes the normal rate of return is greater than zero, but the results of a simulation for ρ equal to zero are presented as an example

Table 6.3. Industry concentration; global characteristics at the equilibrium state

n $n_H(0)$	Π/K [%]	Π/S [%]	p/V
normal rate of return $\rho = 0$			
1	151.907	71.685	4.2382
2	52.692	46.757	2.2539
4	22.096	26.915	1.6419
6	11.450	16.026	1.4290
8	6.050	9.160	1.3210
10	2.804	4.464	1.2561
12	0.643	1.060	1.2128
13	0.000	0.000	1.2000
16	0.000	0.000	1.2000
32	0.000	0.000	1.2000
normal rate of return $\rho = 0.05$			
1	146.908	69.326	4.2382
2	47.692	42.321	2.2539
4	17.096	20.824	1.6419
6	6.450	9.028	1.4290
8	1.050	1.590	1.3210
10	0.000	0.000	1.3000
12	0.000	0.000	1.3000
16	0.000	0.000	1.3000
32	0.000	0.000	1.3000

of some extreme, theoretical case. The values of profit under $\rho = 0$ may be considered as a 'natural' normal rate of return. In both series of experiments close similarity of the model's behaviour to real industrial processes is observed and in this sense the results correspond to the findings of traditional economics. As in real processes of industry development, the greater the concentration of the industry, the larger the profit of the existing firms, but with the difference that, in contrast to the assumption of profit maximization of traditional economics, the objective of the firms in our model (the O_1 rule) is a combination of the short term (firm's income) and long term (firm's production, or expected firm's share). The one extreme is pure monopoly (with profit in excess of 150% in our simulations), the other is pure competition between an infinite number of firms with profit equal to zero. The profit drops very quickly with an increasing number of competitors. In our simulations, industries with the Herfindahl firms' number equivalent greater then 12 competitors may be considered as very close to the ideal situation of pure competition (profit to capital ratio for these industries is smaller than 10^{-7}). Dynamics of change strongly depends on industry concentration. Starting from the same initial conditions, the more concentrated industries reach an equilibrium state much more quickly. For fewer than eight competitors the equilibrium state is reached within 20–40 years but for a greater number of competitors the dynamics is much smaller and for industry very close to pure competition (over 15 competitors), equilibrium is reached within 80–120 years. Many other simulation experiments suggest that for plausible values of parameters the competition process may be considered as perfect for the industries with the Herfindahl firms' number equivalent greater than 12. We observe a trade-off between the profit rate and the normal rate of return, for example, for highly concentrated industry if the normal rate of return increases from 0 to 5%, as in Table 6.3, the profit rate decreases also by 5%, and the price is kept on the same level. But the trade-off acts up to the moment when a positive profit for the same price of products is maintained. If the profit for the same price becomes a loss, then firms decide to increase the price to keep a zero profit and are satisfied with the normal rate of return. In our simulation, for $\rho = 5\%$, the trade-off is observed for industry with fewer than nine competitors; for a greater number of firms the 'natural' normal rate of return is lower than 5%, and the firms increase the price to keep profit equal to zero (compare relevant values in Table 6.3). The positive normal rate of return also causes the profit to sales ratio to diminish but there is no full trade-off as between the normal rate of return and the profit/capital ratio. Reduction of the profit/sales ratio is always smaller than the increase in the normal rate of return (compare relevant values in Table 6.3).

Changes of the values of the capital physical depreciation δ have a similar effect on the characteristics of industry development as changes in the normal rate of return ρ, for example, we observe a similar trade-off between the capital physical depreciation and the profit as we observe in experiments with a positive normal rate of return; reduction of the capital physical depreciation (amortization) in highly concentrated industry by 5% leads to an increase of the profit/capital ratio, also by 5%. So it may be expected that for highly concentrated industries the rising of amortization δ or rising of the normal rate of return will not significantly affect the products' price, but for less concentrated industries we may expect higher prices to cover the higher opportunity costs.

The assumed capital depreciation δ was equal to 10% in all former experiments. But if we reduce amortization δ so that it approaches zero, providing also that there is a normal rate of return equal to zero (which, anyhow, seems quite an artificial and extreme situation), we observe the emergence of fluctuations in industry development for a relatively large number of competitors (in our simulations, for more than 16 competitors). The smaller the value of the sum of amortization and the normal rate of return, the larger are the fluctuations. Fluctuations of the profit/capital ratio for $\rho = 0$, and $\delta = 5\%$ are shown in Figure 6.7 (the upper chart), and for $\rho = 0$, $\delta = 2\%$ (the bottom chart). Similar fluctuations of all other characteristics of development (for example, the investment rate, the growth rate, the debt and savings) are also observed. The mode of fluctuations depends also on the number of competitors. Fluctuations presented in Figure 6.7 are for 25 firms, and, for example, for 32 competitors these are more regular (with a period of three years, and almost equal amplitude in the whole period of simulation). The average value of profit/capital ratio and the amplitude of fluctuations are much higher if we reduce ρ and δ so they are closer to zero. As we see in Figure 6.7, the average values of profit to capital ratio are about 0.07% for $\delta = 5\%$ and about 3.2% for $\delta = 2\%$, amplitudes of fluctuations are 0.02% and 0.15%, respectively. In the extreme case, of course never observed in reality, in which both

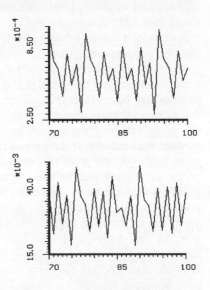

Figure 6.7. Fluctuations of the profit to capital ratio – perfect competition, small ρ and δ

δ and ρ are equal to zero the average value of the profit ratio is 5.4% (for 25 firms) and the amplitude of fluctuations is about 2.1%.[7] Therefore, it may be expected that even for pure competition, when all neoclassical

---

[7] During simulation experiments we also observe the instability of industry behaviour for highly concentrated industries, with less than four competitors, for a large normal rate of return (over 80%) and when the initial price is lower than the equilibrium price (that is, very close to the unit cost of production). Firms sell their products at higher and higher prices and concurrently reduce the production. The instability disappears if the initial price is comparable to the equilibrium price. In such a situation we observe over-pricing at the initial phase of industry development followed by a steady reduction of the price to reach the equilibrium price after a relatively short period.

assumptions are valid, there are still industrial regimes (although some of them quite unnatural) in which industry never reaches stable equilibrium and fluctuates around the steady state.

Table 6.4.   Concentration of the market. Non-uniform firms' size distribution

n	n_H (0)	n_H (100)	n_H (200)	T_e [year]	Π/K [%] (100)	Π/K [%] (200)	p/V (200)
2	1.02	2.00	2.00	14	47.692	47.692	2.2539
4	2.61	4.00	4.00	22	17.096	17.096	1.6419
6	4.18	6.00	6.00	47	6.450	6.450	1.4290
8	5.75	7.30	7.68	–	2.932	2.282	1.3456
12	8.93	9.76	9.81	–	0.216	0.033	1.3007
16	12.12	12.15	12.16	–	0.026	0.001	1.3000
32	25.52	25.59	25.59	–	0. 022	0.001	1.3000

Note: T_e is a year in which the H index is equal to the number of firms, i.e. $n_H = n$. The years of measurement of relevant characteristics are given in parentheses.

The dynamics of change also depends on the initial structure of industry. To investigate to what extent the initial firms' size distribution influences the dynamics of the process, the following series of experiments were made. Starting from highly diversified firms' size we measure the values of basic characteristics of industry over the course of time and observe the tendency towards uniform distribution for different concentrations of the industry. The initial Herfindahl firms' number equivalent and some general characteristics of development of the model for a different number of competitors for $t = 100$ and 200 are presented in Table 6.4. For relatively high concentration of the market (that is, for the number of firms smaller than eight) there are no significant differences in the dynamics of change between industries with uniform and non-uniform firms' size distribution. This is due to a very strong tendency towards uniform distribution for the highly concentrated industries. The more concentrated the industry is, the quicker the uniform firms' size distribution is reached – compare values of T_e in Table 6.4, for highly concentrated industries. For a small concentration of the industry the dynamics of reaching the equilibrium state is significantly lower and also there is no such strong tendency towards the uniform firm's size distribution; quite the contrary, some conservative tendency to stabilize the size distribution is observed. For industries very near to pure competition the distribution of the firms' size is almost the same as at the beginning of simulation (see in Table 6.4 relevant values of n_H for years 0, 50 and 100, when the number of firms is greater than 12).

In the following series of experiments an investigation has been made of the ability of free entrants to penetrate the industries of different concentrations, with no economies of scale present (values of the other parameters as in the Appendix). It was assumed that for a given number of equal-sized firms, at some moment, a small firm with an assumed capital (equal to *InitCapital* as stated in the Appendix) enters the market. From the moment of entrance we observe the evolution of the structure of industry, and particularly the market share of the entrant, namely if its market share grows to reach the same size as that of the initial firms (that is, if the firms' size distribution is uniform). As a measure of convergence we use time T_e which spans from the moment of entrance to the moment of the uniform firms' size distribution (let us call this

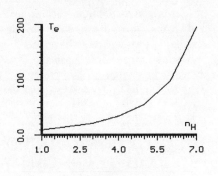

Figure 6.8. Free entry and the penetration time

time the penetration time). The results are summarized in Figure 6.8. As it turns out, the invasion is quite easy for a highly concentrated industry, for example, for the monopoly industry the newcomer is able to increase its initial market share of 0.5% to the equilibrium 50% market fraction in nine years: for two, three, and four firms the relevant values of T_e are 16, 22 and 35 years, respectively. But as we see in Figure 6.8 the penetration time grows exponentially (or even hyperbolically) with diminishing concentration of industry, for example, if the industry is dominated by six competitors, the newcomer needs 98 years to get the same fraction of the market as the initial firms, and for seven firms the relevant time becomes very long, namely 195 years. There is no possibility of penetrating the market if the number of firms is greater than seven. Because of much higher competitive conditions the average profit within the industry is very small, and the newcomer is not able to collect enough capital to invest and to raise its market share.[8] The invasion time for n_H greater than seven is infinite; at the equilibrium state the newcomer's market share stabilizes at a very low level, which is lower the smaller the industry concentration is, for example, for eight, nine, ten and fifteen competitors the newcomer's share at equilibrium is equal to 0.35%, 0.11%, 0.1%, and 0.09%, respectively.

In the basic model only the price competition is considered, and as we

---

[8] The raising of the price above that imposed by the 'old' firms, to get higher profit, is not possible because of diminishing competitiveness of the newcomer's products.

see it is very difficult to enter the market under pure competition. The prerequisite for successful invasion of the highly competitive market is concurrent introduction of the product's innovation, but this problem will be discussed in the next chapters, where the model which incorporates a search for innovation process will be presented. Traditional economics states that in oligopolist industries market shares are usually determined on the basis of non-price competition, such as advertising and product variations, so the real firms' size distribution deviates from the uniform one, and that oligopolists frequently have adequate financial resources to finance non-price competition. Basically it is true, and we observe such type of industry behaviour in the presence of incremental innovations (to some extent responsible for the 'product variations').

THE COST OF PRODUCTION AND THE PRODUCTIVITY OF CAPITAL

It is normal that the behaviour of the model does not depend on the applied units of measure (for example, of capital, production, productivity, price and costs of production). But as simulation experiments reveal, the development of the model is invariably for the same value of a factor equal to the multiplication of the productivity of capital and the unit cost of production, that is, the AV factor. If we look more closely at what this factor means, it transpires that it is equal to the cost ratio: the global cost of production to the global value of capital. Values of the cost ratio are simple real numbers and do not depend on the units of measure of capital and production. It seems that the cost ratio may be used as the practical characteristic for the classification of industries. Small values of the cost ratio indicate that in this type of industry a large capital is required to manufacture products at relatively low cost, and vice versa, a large cost ratio means that in this type of industry a relatively small capital is enough to manufacture products at high cost. Industries with large productivity of capital and low unit cost of production may have the same cost ratio as industries with small productivity of capital and high unit cost of production; and the result is that in all such cases the characteristics of the industry development, in the absence of innovations, are exactly the same. It may be expected that labour cost is a major part of the unit cost of production, so the invariability of development of different types of industries for the same value of the cost ratio resembles the classical finding of substituting labour with capital.

The equilibrium values of some global characteristics of development for different values of the cost ratio and for the diversified industry concentration (that is, for monopoly $n = 1$, duopoly $n = 2$, oligopoly $n = 4$

and 8, and for 'pure' competition $n = 16$) are presented in Figure 6.9.[9] More detailed values of some characteristics for pure competition are presented in Table 6.5. The dynamics of reaching the equilibrium values depends strongly on the value of the cost ratio; changes are very slow for small values of the cost ratio and relatively quick for larger values.[10]

From a qualitative point of view the relationship between the profit/capital ratio and the cost ratio is similar for different concentrations of the industry. Up to some threshold value of the cost ratio, which value depends on the industry concentration, the profit is equal to zero; from the threshold value the relationship is linear with the slope being the greater, the higher the concentration. The threshold values of the cost ratio are equal to 0.02, 0.1, 0.18, 0.25, 0.94, respectively for one, two, four, eight and sixteen competitors (see the upper chart of Figure 6.9). A different mode of relationship

Table 6.5.   The cost ratio; constant market size, uniform firms' size distribution

Cost ratio	Π/K [%]	Π/S [%]	p/V
0.01	0.000	0.000	16.00000
0.02	0.000	0.000	8.50000
0.05	0.000	0.000	4.00000
0.10	0.000	0.000	2.50000
0.25	0.000	0.000	1.60000
0.50	0.000	0.000	1.30000
0.60	0.000	0.000	1.25000
0.75	0.000	0.000	1.20000
0.80	0.000	0.000	1.18750
0.90	0.000	0.000	1.16673
0.94	0.000	0.000	1.15964
0.945	0.026	0.024	1.15901
0.95	0.106	0.096	1.15901
1.00	0.901	0.777	1.15901
2.50	24.752	8.542	1.15901
5.00	64.504	11.131	1.15901
10.00	144.008	12.425	1.15901

between the profit/sales ratio and the cost ratio is observed: after quick growth of the profit/sales ratio upon surpassing the threshold value we observe a slow down in growth as a saturation point is reached. The saturation level depends on the concentration of the industry, for example, for a monopoly it is about 76% and for pure competition it is about 14%.

---

[9] For a better presentation of the results logarithmic scales are used in all three charts in Figure 6.9. Using such coordinates the linear relationship between the profit/capital ratio and the cost ratio, after reaching the threshold values, becomes an exponential relationship. It ought to be underlined that all results of the simulation, and particularly the threshold values, are obtained for specific, although plausible, values of all other parameters of the model as presented in the Appendix. The results may be slightly different for different values of the 'basic' parameters, although the general findings relating to modes of development, shapes of curves, broad relationships, and so on, are valid for a wide spectrum of the model parameters' variability.

[10] For example, for the cost ratio equal to 0.02, for eight firms the equilibrium is reached within 100 years, and for the cost ratio equal to one the equilibrium is reached in 25 years.

124   *Economics and Evolution*

In a sense, a reverse mode of development of the margin of price is observed. Up to the threshold value the price/cost ratio (the price margin)

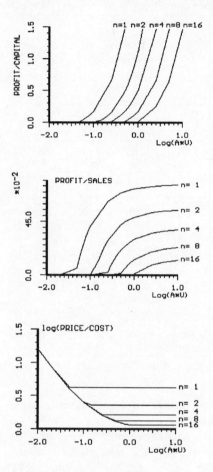

Figure 6.9. The cost ratio

is quickly reduced to be kept at the constant value for greater values of the cost ratio. What is interesting is that the development of the margin of price up to the threshold value is along the same curve for all concentrations of industry (see the bottom chart in Figure 6.9). As may be expected, the 'horizontal' price (for the cost ratio greater than the threshold value) depends on the concentration of industry; for example, for a monopoly, it is over four times greater than the unit cost of production, and for pure competition it is 16% higher (see also Table 6.5). Let us note that the log–log relationship between the price/cost ratio and the cost ratio becomes linear for very small values of the cost ratio; this means that if we keep the productivity of capital constant (for example, $A = 0.1$) and reduce the cost of production nearer and nearer to zero, the equilibrium price is not reduced to zero but approaches the asymptotic value[11] (for $A = 0.1$ the asymptotic value is 1.5, and, for example, for values $V = 0.01, 0.001$ and 0.0001, the

equilibrium price is equal to 1.51, 1.501 and 1.5001, respectively[12]).

The presented results are purely theoretical and ought to be the subject of further study and verification. In particular a comparative study of real

---

[11] The asymptotic value depends on other model parameters, for example, on the normal rate of return ρ, the capital physical depreciation δ, or the shape of demand function (β and γ).

[12] Obviously, to the same extent other characteristics of the model's behaviour reach asymptotic values, for example, profit tends to zero, production stabilizes at a value of 1770.92 units, and sales at 2656.40.

industrial processes focused on the modes of development related to different values of the cost ratio ought to be made. But even at the current stage of research, after the preliminary simulation studies and a rough comparison of the models' behaviour with real industrial development, it transpires that for plausible values of cost ratio the behaviour of our model strongly resembles the behaviour of real industries.

Table 6.6. The cost ratio ($\gamma = 1\%$)

Cost ratio	Π/K [%]	Π^*/K [%]	Π/S [%]	p/V
0.01	1.118	0.113	6.471	17.107
0.02	1.118	0.113	6.114	9.054
0.05	1.118	0.113	5.245	4.221
0.10	1.118	0.113	4.241	2.611
0.25	1.118	0.113	2.693	1.644
0.50	1.118	0.113	1.675	1.322
0.60	1.118	0.113	1.455	1.269
0.75	1.118	0.113	1.215	1.215
0.90	1.118	0.113	1.043	1.179
1.00	1.069	0.064	0.954	1.161
1.10	2.691	1.686	2.087	1.161
1.50	9.179	8.174	5.222	1.161
2.50	25.399	24.394	8.667	1.161
5.00	65.949	64.944	11.252	1.161
2.50	147.048	146.043	12.544	1.161

On the basis of the presented results one may draw the conclusion that it is possible to imagine situations (industry regimes) in which highly concentrated industries behave as if they are in a state of pure competition[13] (that is, for very small values of the cost ratio) and industry regimes in which numerous competitors behave as oligopolists (or even as a monopolist), that is, for high values of the cost ratio. The state of pure competition for highly concentrated industries is created for sufficiently small values of the cost ratio, and for example, in our simulations, monopoly may be considered as being in pure competition when the cost ratio is below 0.02, and duopoly for values below 0.1. The oligopolist mode of behaviour is observed in industries which have a large number of competitors for a relatively high value of the cost

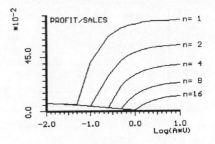

Figure 6.10. Profit to sales ratio for expanding market

ratio (for example, in our simulation, for 16 firms the oligopolist type of behaviour is observed when the cost ratio is greater than one). The

---

[13] So, it may be said that even a monopolist exploiting the advantages of economies of scale to keep his monopoly position, and in this way reducing steadily the costs of production, is himself creating more competitive conditions, leading to reduced profit, and keeping the production and sales at almost constant levels.

conclusions are purely theoretical; in real industrial processes we would probably not observe such small and large values of the cost ratio.

As a hypothesis, it may be stated that in the course of time since the industrial revolution a tendency has been observed for the cost ratio to be reduced,[14] and therefore it may be expected that in the course of economic development we shall observe higher competitive conditions of industrial development. In all experiments presented in this section the model parameters (specified in the Appendix) have values which generate plausible behaviour of the model. The second reason for choosing such values of parameters was the need to fulfil the most essential assumptions of neoclassical economics. Constant market size is one such assumption of the neoclassical approach under which the theorem of zero profit for pure competition is valid. To check how an expanding market influences the behaviour of industry, an experiment was made with the growth ratio of the market size γ equal to 1%. The equilibrium values of some characteristics for an industry with 16 competitors are shown in Table 6.6 and the profit/sales ratios for different industry concentrations are presented in Figure 6.10. The course of changes of the profit/capital ratio and the price margin are very similar to those obtained in the previous experiment (compare, for example, the results in Table 6.5 and Table 6.6). Two modes of development are also observed in these simulation runs – the first one, which may be called pure competition, for a cost ratio below the threshold values, and the second one, imperfect competition, for values of the cost ratio greater than the threshold values. If we compare the thresholds in both series of experiments we see that for the expanding market the values are slightly greater than those for the constant market, for example, for 16 firms the threshold value for the constant market is 0.94 and for a 1% expanding market it is 1.00. Because of a growth ratio of the market size equal to 1%, the profit/capital ratio is positive (1.118%) even for a cost ratio below the threshold value. Because of a capital physical depreciation equal to 10% and a rate of market growth equal to 1%, the equilibrium investment/capital ratio in all runs is about 11% (the exact value is 11.005%), so the equilibrium value of the discounted profit/capital ratio for the cost ratio below the threshold values is equal to 0.113%. In all simulations with a constant market size, the equilibrium for pure competition is reached smoothly, at which point the savings and debt are equal to zero. For some reason, in the case of an expanding market firms do not fully repay their debts, and also equilibrium savings are slightly above zero (in pure competition the equilibrium debt is 6.11% and the savings are 0.5%). Probably because of

---

[14] The analysis of industrial records suggests that at least since the beginning of the 20th century, because of the technological and organizational progress, the tempo of reduction of the unit cost of production is relatively higher than the tempo of increasing the productivity of capital, so the cost ratio AV also ought to be reduced.

this 6% debt at equilibrium the discounted profit is slightly above zero, equal to 0.11%. For the expanding market the profit/sales ratio is slightly different from the case of the constant size market. Because of non-zero profit at the equilibrium for the cost ratio below the threshold the profit/sales ratio is not a horizontal line (see Table 6.6 and Figure 6.10); it is relatively high for small values of the cost ratio, and is reduced in the course of the growing values of the cost ratio up to the threshold value, from which point the profit/sales ratio grows rapidly to reach a kind of saturation level as is observed in experiments with constant market size.

ECONOMIES OF SCALE

It is a well-known fact that economies of scale lead to greater industry concentration. To check to what extent these classical phenomena are observed in our model, a series of experiments for different modes of development of the economies of scale were made. It is assumed that the factor reducing the cost of production caused by the increasing level of production (learning by doing, labour and managerial specializations, efficient allocation of capital, and so on) has the form:

$$v(Q_i) = 1 - \exp(-bQ_i)(1 - \exp(aQ_i)), \tag{6.3}$$

where Q_i is production of a firm i. If b is equal to zero, $v(Q)$ is simply the exponential factor (i.e. $v(Q) = \exp(a\,Q)$). The curves of the economies of scale for two values of the parameter a (b equal to zero) are shown in Figure 6.11. It seems unreasonable to assume that the reduction of cost on account of economies of scale tends endlessly to zero. A more realistic assumption is that a reduction of cost is possible up to some 'optimal' level of production – for greater production the possibilities of cost reduction are exhausted and diseconomies of scale prevail, so the costs of production rise for larger production. Four such curves (for $b > 0$) are also presented in Figure 6.11. In two cases[15] (for $a = 15$, $b = 10$; and $a = b = 5$) the proficiency of the economies of scale is relatively quickly exhausted and the minimum unit cost is achieved at relatively low output (60 and 140 units, respectively); for $a = 5$ and $b = 0.5$ the diseconomies of scale are remote, so the minimum cost is for relatively large production (450 units); the last curve (for $a = 5$ and $b = 2$) represents the intermediate case, in which the economies and diseconomies of scale ensure that the minimum costs are

---

[15] To shorten the description we write, for example, $a = 5$, but the exact value of a is 0.005, which means that in order to get exact values of a and b the values presented below ought to be multiplied by 10^{-3}.

placed between the two previous cases (that is, for 250 units). It may be said that the three curves in which $a = 5$ and only b is changed represent a family of curves in which the economies of scale at the beginning develop along the same exponential curve and only the diseconomies of scale are placed at different distances. The curve for $a = 15$ and $b = 10$ is slightly different from the other three and is appropriate for comparing the effects of very quick exhaustion of the advantages of economies of scale. Later on in this section we will discuss the modes of industry behaviour for these four cases. First we will discuss the simple cases of exponential economies of scale (for $a > 0$ and $b = 0$).

Let us first assume that a number of equal-sized firms operate on the market where no diseconomies of scale are observed, that is, $a = 5$ and $b = 0$. The results for different numbers of firms are presented in Table 6.7. The initial unit costs of production are equal to five, and as can be seen, the monopolist fully utilizes the possibilities of economies of scale and at equilibrium its unit costs are very small (0.0007); this value is the result of the assumed shape of the demand function ($N = 3,000$, and $\beta = -0.3$) and the mechanisms of development related to the cost ratio described in the previous section. Further reduction of the unit cost does not result in the reduction of price and the profit of the monopolist is very close to zero (profit/capital is smaller than 10^{-6}%). For a larger number of firms the possibilities offered by the economies of scale are not fully utilized, and as can be seen in Table 6.7 the larger the number of competitors, the poorer the utility of economies of scale. The equilibrium profit is always very close to zero (it is largest for three competitors – 0.01%). As can be seen, with the growing number of firms the unit costs are reduced in a lesser and lesser degree, for example, for ten firms the cost at equilibrium is reduced only by 14% (from 5.0 to 4.3). This causes the equilibrium price to be higher, and the global production Q sold on the market to be much smaller – the global production for ten firms is

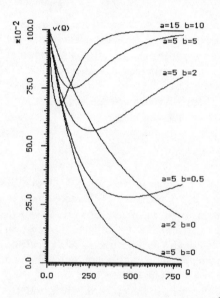

*Figure 6.11. Economies of scale –
six modes of
development*

almost six times smaller than that offered by the monopolists, and the price is almost four times the monopolist's price.

Table 6.7. Economies of scale – equilibrium values (a = 5, b = 0)

n	p	p/V	min V	Q	Q_i
1	1.501	2091.157	0.0007	1769.79	1769.79
2	1.580	19.805	0.0798	1655.17	827.59
3	3.040	1.975	1.539	706.92	235.64
4	4.390	1.519	2.891	438.36	109.59
5	4.929	1.437	3.429	377.16	75.43
6	5.240	1.401	3.740	348.00	58.05
7	5.447	1.380	3.947	331.26	47.32
8	5.594	1.366	4.094	319.97	40.00
10	5.791	1.350	4.291	305.88	30.59

Naturally, with the growing number of firms the production of each firm is reduced to a much larger degree, for example, for ten firms the firm's production Q_i^s is almost 60 times smaller than the production of a monopoly. It will be noted that the trend of the price margin is just the opposite to that of the price: the price rises with the growing number of competitors but the margin of price is significantly reduced (for the monopoly the price is over 2,000 times the unit cost, and for ten firms the price is only 35% higher). But partition of the industry into a number of equal-sized firms in the presence of economies of scale creates a very unstable situation, and even a small deviation of the firms' size starts the process of increasing concentration. The rate of concentration growth increases with the rate of changes of the economies of scale (that is, *a* in equation (6.3)) and with growing variability of the firms' size distribution. It may be said that, in contrast to the case of uniform distribution, in the case of non-uniform firms' size distribution we move not only along one curve (for constant industry concentration), as in Figure 6.9 from right to left, but at the same time, we also jump from the curves of smaller to those of greater concentrations up to the point where monopoly, or, in some situations, oligopoly is reached. The result is that for sufficiently large *a* (in our simulations for *a* greater than three), independently of the value of the initial concentration, the largest firm eliminates all other competitors. The growth of industry concentration for two values of initial concentrations is presented in Figure 6.12. An evolution of industry concentration for a very small variation in firms' size is shown in the upper chart of Figure 6.12. The Herfindahl index of concentration at the beginning of the simulation is equal to 15.97, that is, very close to the equi-partition of the market, but even this small deviation causes the growth of concentration. The economies of scale act endlessly. In the first phase of the industrial development, the rate of concentration growth is rather small, but at about $t = 50$ the changes accelerate and within 20 years the market becomes dominated by one firm, and by the end of the simulation almost all firms are eliminated from the

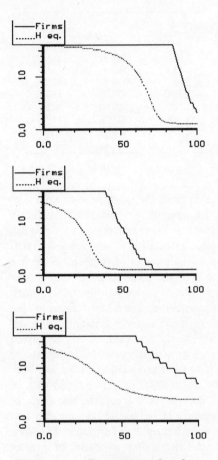

market. For the same simulation conditions but for greater initial asymmetry of industry structure the growth of concentration is much quicker. In the middle chart of Figure 6.12, the initial Herfindahl firms' number equivalent is equal to 14 firms. The mode of concentration evolution is similar to that of the previous experiment but the shift towards monopoly occurs much earlier. If we assume a more realistic assumption that diseconomies of scale act, then from some level of production the growth of concentration is not so quick, and at the end of the simulation the market is dominated by a few large firms (oligopoly) instead of the pure monopoly of the two former simulation runs. The evolution of concentration in such an experiment (for a and b equal to five) is shown in the bottom chart of Figure 6.12. The initial concentration is relatively high (as in the previous experiment, the n_H index is equal to 14 firms) but, contrary to the behaviour of firms in the former two runs, in this run, by the end of the simulation, the market is dominated by four almost equal

Figure 6.12. Economies of scale and the industry concentration

firms. So, under the more realistic assumption of the shape of economies of scale, we may expect the emergence of an oligopoly in which at equilibrium the market is partitioned into a few more or less similar firms.

But as the simulation results reveal, the oligopoly in equilibrium for non-uniform firms' distribution is formed not only in the presence of diseconomies of scale. Even if the diseconomies of scale are absent, or far placed, but the rate of change of economies of scale (controlled by the value of a) is relatively low, is it observed that in equilibrium the market is dominated by a few large firms. It transpires that for low rates of economies of scale small handicapped firms are able to compete with the largest firms by accepting smaller profits as a result of lower price and making their products as competitive as, or even more than, those of the largest firm. Obviously, this strategy of catching up is not applicable for very small firms. For our simulation conditions this situation of catching up is observed for a smaller than three, for example, for $a = 2$, and $b = 0$; out of 16 firms of the initial concentration equal to 14 firms only four large firms are able to compete with the largest one, and at the end of the simulation the market is dominated by five firms, the remaining 11 firms being eliminated from the market.[16] For smaller values of a more firms are able to catch up (for example, for $a = 1.5$ six firms dominate the market). A similar effect of catching up is observed for larger (for example, 25 and 35) and smaller (for example, 12 and 8) numbers of competitors. So, it may be said that in some circumstances the final outcome of economies, and diseconomies, of scale is the presence of oligopoly, not monopoly. A more detailed study of oligopoly with the presence of economies and diseconomies of scale will be presented later on in this section, but before that a few words will be said on the modes of development of some other characteristics of industry development in the presence of economies of scale. The growth of industry concentration in the case of non-uniform firms' size distribution may mean that in some periods of industry development the profit is not reduced but even increases; this happens if the jumps from one curve of constant concentration (Figure 6.9) to the succeeding one are quicker than the move along the same curve for a given industry concentration. As an example, the evolution of the profit/capital ratio is shown in Figure 6.13. The upper chart in Figure 6.13 corresponds to the middle chart of Figure 6.12. When there are no limits on the reduction of the unit cost because of the economies of scale, the profit diminishes in the first phase of development. The movement along the curve (see Figure 6.9) of the constant concentration is quicker than shifting (jumping) from one curve to the next one, that is, to that of greater industry concentration. At the beginning of the second phase the growth of concentration is faster and the jumps from one curve to the next one are much quicker than moving along the curve of constant concentration, so the build-up of profit (up to 6%) is observed. From that moment the industry is very close to the monopoly state and evolves along the curve of constant

---

[16] The initial shares of the five largest firms in this run are equal to 12%, 11.2%, 10.5%, 9.7% and 8.2%, respectively; the initial shares of the remaining 11 firms decrease almost uniformly from 7.4% down to 0.5%.

concentration. There is no limit to the cost reduction, so the cost ratio is also constantly reduced. Reduction of the cost ratio causes the diminishing of the profit/capital ratio (to be very close to zero when equilibrium has been established for a sufficiently long time).

When there exists an 'optimal' value of the unit costs because of the presence of economies and diseconomies of scale the first phase of development is similar to the former run – the movement along the curve dominates the shifts from one curve to the ensuing one (the bottom chart of Figure 6.13 corresponds to the bottom chart of Figure 6.12). During the phase of a relatively quick growth of concentration the movement process along the curve and the shift process (jumping) from one curve to the ensuing one are more balanced and the rate of profit growth is not so high as in the former simulation run; but reduction of the unit cost of production is exhausted at a certain time, and the industry stops its development at some point of the curve of constant concentration (oligopoly) – the profit is kept almost at the same level (in our simulation the limit has been reached in the last five years of the simulation – see the bottom chart of Figure 6.13).

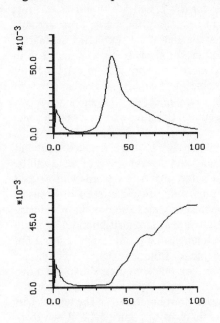

Figure 6.13. Profit/capital ratio for different modes of economies of scale

All simulation results presented in this section suggest that in the presence of economies and diseconomies of scale the industry tends to an oligopolist structure. To investigate how different modes of economies and diseconomies of scale influence the behaviour of industries composed of oligopolist firms, the following series of experiments with the four types of economies of scale presented in Figure 6.11 (for $b > 0$) and a different number of firms, from full monopoly up to ten competitors, were prepared. The results are summarized in Figure 6.14 and in Figure 6.15. If diseconomies of scale are absent ($a = 5$, $b = 0$; see Table 6.7), the 'optimal' behaviour of the industry, from the market's (buyers') point of view, is full monopoly. Only the monopolist is able to fully utilize the abilities of economies of scale and supply the market with the highest production at the lowest prices. The situation is essentially different if diseconomies of scale are present. There emerges the 'optimal' structure of the market, other than the monopolist's one, for which the market is supplied with the highest production at the lowest price. It is important to note that the 'optimal' production, from the market point of view, differs from that expected by the industry (firms) – the maximum profit in all cases is still the highest for the monopolist. The earlier the diseconomies of scale emerge, the more firms are involved in forming the optimal industry structure (see the two upper charts of Figure 6.14 and Figure 6.15); for $a = 15$, $b = 10$, when diseconomies of scale dominate for production greater than 60 units, the optimal number of firms is equal to six, and similarly for $a = b = 5$ (the minimum unit cost is for production equal to 150 units) the optimal number of firms is 5. For belated diseconomies of scale the optimal number of firms is significantly smaller: for $a = 5$, and $b = 2$ (the minimum costs for production of 250 units) the best performance is for three competitors, and for $a = 5$, $b = 0.5$ (the minimum costs for 450 units) the best performance is for a duopoly. If we look at the charts of price and global production we see that the optimum is very sharp and clearly distinguishable for

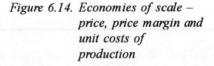

Figure 6.14. Economies of scale – price, price margin and unit costs of production

belated diseconomies of scale ($a = 5$, $b = 0.5$; and $a = 5$, $b = 2$) and very flat for the case where diseconomies of scale emerge very early – for

$a = b = 5$, and $a = 15$, $b = 10$ the industry behaviour is very similar for the number of competitors between four and eight (variability of price and global production for that number of firms is smaller than 5%). The 'optimal' industry structure results from the compromise between the exploitation of the capabilities of the economies of scale (better for a small number of firms) and the competitive conditions (more severe for a greater number of firms). As a result of the compromise there appear significant discrepancies between: (1) the firm's production for optimal industry structure[17] (equal in our four cases to 65, 137, 356 and 64), and (2) the production which allows minimization of the unit costs (equal to 102, 167, 408 and 64), and (3) the optimal production of the economies of scale (equal to 150, 250, 450 and 60, respectively for the four cases). For very early emergence of diseconomies of scale ($a = 15$, $b = 10$, and $a = b = 5$) the differences in the unit costs of production for the monopolist and for larger number of firms are not so big (see the bottom chart in Figure 6.14) but differences in equilibrium price are significant (the upper chart of the same figure). The changes in the price margin and profit to capital ratio are very similar for different modes of economies–diseconomies of scale (the middle chart in

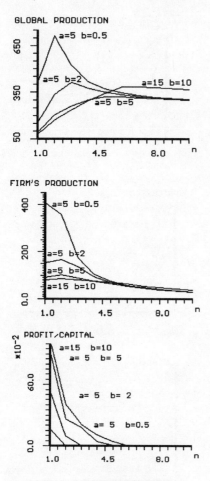

Figure 6.15. Economies of scale –
global production,
firm's production and
profit to capital ratio

---

[17] The structure for which the global production sold on the market is maximal and the product price is the lowest.

Figure 6.14, and the lowest chart of Figure 6.15). The more competitive conditions cause the reduction of the price margin up to 30–40% and a zero profit. For greater industry concentration, the sooner the diseconomies of scale take effect, the larger are the price margin and the profit. For belated diseconomies of scale ($a = 5$, $b = 0.5$) the maximal reduction of the costs is made by the monopolist (the bottom chart of Figure 6.14), but the monopolist forces much larger margins in price, and the best performance is for those two competitors whose unit cost of production is only slightly higher than that of the monopolist but whose price margin is significantly smaller. A similar discrepancy is observed for two other curves (for $a = 5$, $b = 2$, and $a = b = 5$) – the minimum unit cost is for two competitors and the best industry performance is for five and six competitors. Each duopoly firm produces less than the monopolist (see the middle chart in Figure 6.15) but the total production of these two firms is much higher (the upper chart of the same figure). If we compare the total production (the upper chart in Figure 6.15) with the average firm's production (the middle chart in Figure 6.15), we note that there are discrepancies between the maximum total production and the maximum firm's production. The latter is for the monopolist or duopolist structures of the industry, and the former is for two, three, five, and six competing firms.

As we have said, the three curves of economies of scale for which $a = 5$ and b differs represent a family of curves, in the sense that the shape of the economies of scale is the same and only the moments of emergence of the diseconomies of scale are different. The fourth curve (for $a = 15$, $b = 10$) differs but is very similar to the curve for $a = b = 5$. It allows us to notice regular changes in the mode of industry development for the family of curves, for example, with the growing value of b, a regular shift of the optimal structure of the market towards less concentrated industries is observed (Figure 6.14 and Figure 6.15). The earlier presence of diseconomies of scale ($a = 15$, $b = 10$) causes only small differences in the mode of the development of price margin (the middle chart of Figure 6.14), firms' production and profit (Figure 6.15) but significant differences are observed in the mode of unit costs reduction (the bottom chart of Figure 6.14) – a greater rate of economies of scale (controlled by a) and the earlier emergence of diseconomies of scale (controlled by b) cause a greater reduction of unit costs and shift the minimum costs towards less concentrated industries.

DEMAND FUNCTION

Neoclassical demand curves are frequently drawn as downward-sloping curves representing the inverse relationship between the price and the production. Analysis of the demand curve rarely concerns the influence of the shape of the curve on industry development. Two parameters control the shape of our demand function (equations (5.4) and (5.5)), namely the growth rate of the market size γ and the average price elasticity[18] β of money which the market is inclined to spend to buy products at the average price $p^e(t)$. In this section the results of the simulation of the model for different rates of expansion of the market γ and variety of price elasticity β are presented.

Rate of the Market Size Growth

As has been seen in the previous experiments, the positive growth rate γ for pure competition causes positive profit at equilibrium even if we diminish the overall profit by the amount of investment related to the expanding market, that is, the positive rate of growth also causes the positive values of the discounted profit. The results of more systematic simulation for diversified values of the growth rate γ are presented in Figure 6.16. For highly concentrated industries the positive growth rate γ does not significantly influence the equilibrium values of profit and price; the relevant curves are almost horizontal. On the contrary, for less concentrated industries, close to pure competition, the equilibrium values of the basic characteristics of development are greatly affected by positive γ; relevant curves are not horizontal, as for high industry concentration, but upwardly sloping. The differences are caused by different sources of investment required by positive γ. Large firms finance the extra investment from their own sources collected in the past and related to much higher profit gained as a result of their monopoly or oligopoly position. Small firms have no such funds and are forced to take credits and increase the price of their products. For four or less competitors no firm takes credit, their own sources allow them to finance the expansionary investment. But their savings decline for high rates of market growth (for example, for γ equal to zero, at the end of the simulation the savings for four competitors are equal to 650% of capital, and for 10% growth rate the savings are only 48%). Small firms (for example, in our simulations, for an industry with eight and sixteen competitors) are forced to take credit and raise the price of their products. For a constant market size, all firms have at equilibrium no debt and no savings, but for an expanding market both debt and savings increase, for example, for eight firms and for 10% annual market growth the savings at equilibrium are almost 6% and the debt is over 32%. To make the pictures readable, in some of the charts of Figure 6.16, there are no curves for high industry concentration (i.e. for duopoly and monopoly) – but from a qualitative point of view the behaviour of these industries is similar to that for four competitors, although values of equilibrium profit and price are

---

[18] The overall price elasticity of the demand function is equal to $\beta - 1$, and is always negative.

much higher. Looking at the diagrams in Figure 6.16 we see a kind of convergence of development of industries in the course of high rates of market-size growth. Due to larger slopes of curves for small industry concentration, the curves of medium and small concentrated industries converge for relatively small values of the growth rate; for example, for γ greater than 2% the development of industries with eight and sixteen competitors is exactly the same. For four competitors the rise of the profit/capital rate is almost linear and grows from 17% for constant market size to almost 22% for 10% growth of the market; concurrently the price margin grows from 1.64 to 1.69. The rise of the profit rate and price margin for less concentrated industries is higher, and relevant values are: for eight competitors, the profit rate grows from 1% for the constant market size to over 9% for γ = 10%, and the price margin increases from 1.32 to 1.47.

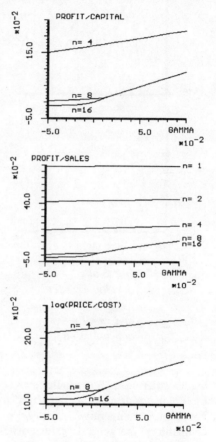

So, it may said that an expanding market creates more competitive conditions and even an industry with a relatively small number of competitors behaves very similarly to an industry with pure competition (theoretically with an infinite number of competitors).

Figure 6.16. Growth of the market size

Astonishingly for a relatively large number of competitors and for the negative growth rate γ we observe a wave-like mode of development. In our simulations the fluctuations are observed for 16 (and more) competitors. As an example Figure 6.17 presents the development of the price margin for two rates of declining market, the upper chart for γ = −1% and the lower one for γ = −5%. For the 5% collapsing market the amplitude is higher and the period is longer. In contrast to the case of the 1% collapsing market, where the amplitude is steadily reduced, the

amplitude of fluctuations is constant for the 5% collapsing market; (for
$t > 100$ the development is similar to that in the period 50–100). For a

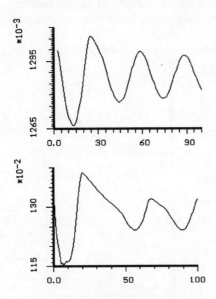

highly collapsing market (for
example, for $\gamma = -10\%$)
fluctuations disappear, but
instability occurs – small firms
choose the strategy of raising the
price and keeping the positive
profit; this strategy causes much
quicker reduction of the
production and destruction of the
market.

Price Elasticity

Statistical analysis and
consumption theory suggest that
almost all price elasticities of
demand are negative: for primary
needs (or necessities, for
example, flats and houses, food,
clothing) elasticities are between
0 and –1, that of secondary
needs (or luxuries) are below –1.
So, it may be expected that for
commodities fulfilling primary
needs β is greater than zero and
smaller than one, and for
commodities fulfilling

*Figure 6.17. Wave-like
development for
negative growth rate
and small industry
concentration*

higher-order needs β is smaller than zero.[19] Influence of the price elasticity
β on industry development depends strongly on the industry concentration.
For a pure competitive industry (in our simulations, for 16 and more
competitors) the general characteristics are exactly the same in the whole
plausible range of variability of β (for example, the profit is equal to zero,
the price is kept at the same equilibrium level). But for more concentrated
industries the behaviour of the model greatly depends on the value of β, and
the more concentrated the industry is, the greater the impact of β. The
results of the simulation for β varying from –1 to 1 are presented in
Figure 6.18. The diversity of values of the characteristics of industry
development for different β and different concentration of industry are very

---

[19] Selected price elasticities of demand (relevant values of β in parentheses): electricity 0.13
($\beta = 0.87$), bread –0.15 (0.85), tobacco products 0.46 (0.54), beef 0.64 (0.36), restaurant meals
–2.27 (–1.27), (McConnell, 1984, p. 415).

high, so logarithmic scales are used for all three characteristics presented in Figure 6.18. As may be expected for the same value of β the values of profits and prices are the greater the larger the industry concentration. For medium concentrated industries (for example, for eight firms) the rate of change in the course of increasing values of β is relatively low, for example, the profit/capital increases from 0.14% for β = −1 to 3.1% for β = 1, and

relevant values of the price/cost ratio are 1.30 and 1.36. It may be said that for medium concentrated industries, small values of β create more competitive conditions for the behaviour of firms. It is understandable because small β are characteristic of markets of secondary goods. For the medium industry concentration and for β close to −1 the profit drops very quickly (see Figure 6.18). For sufficiently small β the behaviour of oligopolist industries is very close to pure competition, for example, for eight firms and for β smaller than −1.1 the profit is equal to zero and the price margin is equal to the equilibrium value for pure competition. But cutting down β in the case of large concentration does not lead to the creation of pure competition conditions. It is possible to reduce β up to some threshold value, which leads to further diminishing of profit and price (for example, for four competitors the threshold value of β is −2.1, for this value the profit/capital ratio is equal to

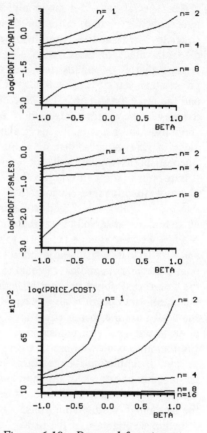

Figure 6.18. Demand function;
price elasticity (β)

7.8% and the price/cost ratio is 1.46). For β below the threshold value the behaviour of the model is unstable, firms choose the strategy of endless price rises and steady reduction of production.

For high industry concentrations the behaviour is much more sensitive to changes of β. For medium industry concentrations the basic characteristics of industry development are almost linear functions of β but for the large concentrations the relationship becomes exponential; for example, for four firms the profit/capital grows from 12.7% for $\beta = -1$ to 19.4% for $\beta = 0$, and to 30.4% for $\beta = 1$; for a duopoly the profit rate is 27.4%, 63.8%, and 544% for β equal to -1, 0 and 1, respectively; the price/cost ratio rises from 1.55 for $\beta = -1$, to 1.69 for $\beta = 0$, and to 1.91 for $\beta = 1$, for a duopoly the price margin is 1.85, 2.58 and 12.2 for β equal to -1, 0 and 1, respectively.

The special case is a monopoly; for negative values of β we observe hyperbolical growth of profit and price; for $\beta = -1$ the profit/capital ratio is equal to 34.3% and the price margin is equal to 1.99, but for $\beta = 0$ the relevant values of these ratios are 7,355% and 148.4. It is possible to assume that β is slightly positive, and the asymptotic value is slightly greater than 0.005; for $\beta = 0.005$ the profit rate at equilibrium is 28,198% and the price margin 565. The case of greater β corresponds to an unstable industry, where firms raise their prices endlessly. The results of the simulation for a monopoly, particularly the value of the threshold of β so close to zero, suggest that for some values of the model parameters the 'theoretical' asymptotic value of β for a monopoly ought to be exactly zero. It transpires that the threshold value depends on parameters a_4 and a_5 in the objective function (see equation (5.12)). In all our simulations it is assumed that $a_4 = 1.0$ and $a_5 = 5$, and it seems that these are plausible values, very close to those observed in real industrial processes. From a theoretical point of view we may assume the extreme situations, and decree that (1) $a_4 = 1.0$ and $a_5 = 0$ (that is, rising production is the sole firms' objective) and that (2) both parameters a_4 and a_5 are equal to zero (that is, income maximization is the sole firms' objective). For all industry concentrations, in the first case, the equilibrium profit is always equal to zero and the price/cost ratio is the same all the time, being equal to 1.30.[20] The sole difference is that for β close to one and high industry concentrations, only in the initial phase of simulation runs do we observe fluctuations of industry development, but at the end of simulation runs the firms steadily approach equilibrium. There is no unstable behaviour of the monopolist for β greater than zero. For small industry concentrations all firms steadily approach to the equilibrium from the beginning of simulation runs.

In the second case, if the firms' only objective is income maximization, the industry behaviour depends on the concentration rate, and as might be expected the profit and the price for the same values of β are greater for greater industry concentration; but what is interesting for $\beta = -1$ and for all values of industry concentration is that the profit rate at equilibrium is

---

[20] The value of the equilibrium price depends mainly on the values of the normal rate of return ρ and the capital physical depreciation rate δ; for example, if we assume quite a theoretical situation in which both parameters are equal to zero, then the equilibrium price is equal to the unit cost of production and the price/cost ratio 1.0.

always the same (equal to 35%) and the price/capital rate is always equal to 2.0. The behaviour of the monopolist is very similar to that observed in the previous series of experiments (that is, for $a_4 = 1$ and $a_5 = 5$). But as we expected, for both parameters equal to zero, when the only objective of the monopolist is raising its income, the asymptotic value of β equals exactly zero. If we increase β to become closer and closer to zero, the profit and price rise hyperbolically to infinity.

For a_4 and a_5 equal to zero the rise of the profit and price for small concentration is moderate,[21] for example, for 16 firms the profit rises from 35% for $\beta = -1$ to 48% for $\beta = 1$, concurrently the price margin rises from 2 to 2.04. For high concentration the rise of profit and price is very close to the exponential, for example, for four competitors the profit rises from 35% for $\beta = -1$ to 51% for $\beta = 0$, and to 85% for $\beta = 1$. What is interesting for such conditions is that the unstable behaviour is observed not only for a monopoly (as in Figure 6.18) but also for a duopoly. For $\beta = 1$ both firms in the case of a duopoly choose the strategy of endless price rises. For β very close to one we observe a hyperbolical mode of development similar to that in Figure 6.18 for the monopoly and β close to zero; the values of profit for β equal to 0.9, 0.95 and 0.99 are: 985%, 1,985%, and 9,985% respectively. Such huge values of profits and prices in all our simulations in this section for high industry concentrations are purely theoretical. We do not observe such kinds of behaviour in real industrial processes, as other factors, not included in our model (for example, socio-political ones) prohibit such almost boundless behaviour.

In concluding this section we may say that the secondary markets (that is, those characterized by negative values of price elasticity β) create relatively high competitive conditions for oligopoly, and even for monopoly and duopoly – the equilibrium prices and profits are kept by the firms at a moderate level. But this is not the case for markets of primary goods (for positive β), high industry concentration leads to enormous growth of price and firm's profit. The only solution in such a case is to create proper conditions for the free entry of new firms, making the industry more competitive and in this way providing for prices and profits to be kept at moderate levels.

ECONOMY IS A DYNAMIC SYSTEM

So far we have investigated the behaviour of the industry in the equilibrium state, but there are at least two reasons to treat the dynamic processes of

---

[21] But it is necessary to point out, even for small concentrations, that is, from the neoclassical point of view for pure competition, that the equilibrium profit is positive for the whole assumed range of variability of price elasticity β (that is, from -1 to 1).

economy as being much more important. First, the real process of economic development is vigorous and dynamic all the time, so being in equilibrium is a very rare state, and second, as we have seen in the previous experiments, the changes are frequently so slow that even if nothing has happened in the economic life, such as exogenous influences from other spheres of life (for example, politics), or endogenous influences (for example, innovation), the time span for reaching an equilibrium is to be counted in decades.

In this section, the preliminary results of a dynamic view of economy are presented. First, we consider the response of the industry to discontinuous changes of the unit cost of production. Similar investigations on discontinuous changes of some other variables (for example, size of the market) were made; there is no room to present them in detail, but it may be said that the mode of the industry response in these experiments is similar to that of discontinuous changes of the unit cost of production. An example of development of the industry in the case of the emergence of innovations is presented at the end of this section. The essence of dynamics in economy lies in the appearances of innovations, and the problems related to their emergence will be discussed in the following chapter; the results of one experiment will be presented here, mainly to show how positive profit originates following the emergence of innovations.

Disruptive Cost of Production

In two experiments presented in this section, the following mode of changes in the cost of production is assumed: up to the 10th year the industry is in equilibrium, the unit cost of production is constant and equal to 5.0, in the 10th year an external price shock is assumed, and the cost increases to 6.0 (that is, 20% rise), up to the 40th year the cost remains constant (the system by this year is very close to the equilibrium state), and in the 40th year the cost goes back to the initial value, 5.0; all the other parameters of the model remain constant (particularly the size of the market, measured in terms of money N which the market is inclined to spend on buying the products).

After the jump of the unit cost of production the price grows but not quickly enough to keep positive profit (the average profit within the industry is below zero during three years after the shock – see Figure 6.19(a)); 20% growth of the unit cost of production leads to a reduction in the profit/capital ratio to −7%. The negative profit and the higher price cause significant reductions in investment and global production (Figure 6.19(c) and (e)). After a period of readjustment the system goes to the new equilibrium and within 30 years the values of the basic characteristics are very close to the equilibrium values: profit and production growth rates are very close to zero, investment to capital ratio is equal to 10% (that is, equal to the capital physical depreciation). Because of a higher equilibrium price the equilibrium level of global production is smaller than before the shock (Figure 6.19(e)). In the 40th year the cost goes back to its former value, and the system reverts to the initial values. Greater production (Figure 6.19(e)) requires new investment, and to find new capital firms raise prices to make the profit positive (maximum value is equal to 10% of the capital). The average profit/capital ratio in the period 0–70 is equal to 0.634%, but the average investment/capital ratio in that period is 10.446%, so the discounted profit is equal to 0.188% (instead of zero for development without the cost shocks).

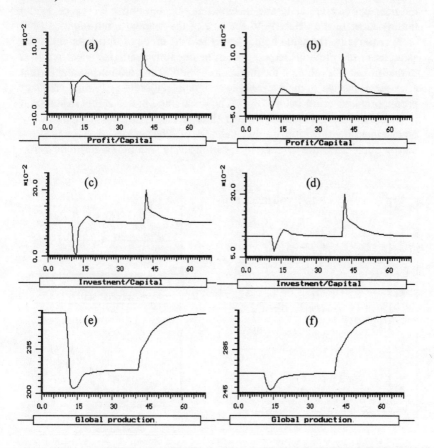

Figure 6.19. Long-run development and the disruptive unit cost of production

To check to what extent it is possible to control the crises after the jump in the unit cost, an experiment was made in which at the moment of raising the cost the amount of money N, which the market is inclined to spend on buying, also increases to keep the production at the same equilibrium level (that is, the purchasing power of the market is artificially stimulated). In spite of this 'effort' we observe a similar mode of development as in the previous experiment (the results of this experiment are presented in Figure 6.19(b), (d) and (f)), although the cutting of the profit and investment is not so significant as in the previous experiment, and the crisis in production is not as deep (reduction of production is about 15%, compared to a 25% reduction in the former experiment). As before, the system reaches the near-equilibrium state and in the 40th year the unit cost reverts to the initial value. In the year $t = 40$ the size of the market is not reduced (that is, N remains on the same higher level) and the mode of development is the same as in the previous experiment after the 40th year. If N were reduced to the 'normal' level, then the mode of development would be similar to that after the 10th year in the previous experiment (with relatively high crises of production and profit below zero). The discounted profit in this experiment is 0.211%, that is, is slightly higher than in the former experiment. Many other experiments with disruptive changes of other model parameters show that in such cases the average long-run profit is slightly greater than zero.

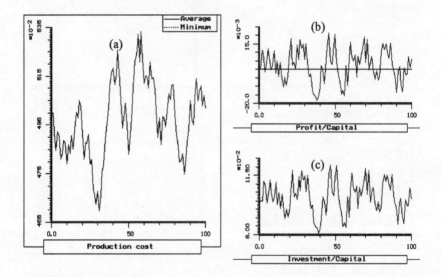

Figure 6.20. Long-run profit and random fluctuations of the unit cost of production

Iwai (1984a, b) shows that in the presence of technical change in the long-run the system reaches at best a statistical steady state due to the 'offsetting motions of a large number of firms alternately winning and losing the competitive struggles for technological superiority' (Iwai, 1991). But the technological change is not the only cause for the existence of the statistical steady state. I would like to point out that the statistical steady state is in fact the normal state of the economy, and there are so many endogenous as well as exogenous factors influencing the development of the economy that being in the equilibrium state (in the sense of classical or neoclassical theory) is a very improbable event. As will be seen in the following section, the fluctuations of industry development are frequently observed as a result of natural finite 'computing power' of decision-makers (bounded rationality).

In the following experiment it is assumed that the cost of production randomly fluctuates,

$$V(t+1) = V(t) + \xi,$$

where ξ is a random variable uniformly distributed within the range $(0.95V(t), 1.05V(t))$, that is, we assume up to 5% yearly fluctuations of the unit cost of production.

The results of such a 'random walk' of the cost of production are presented in Figure 6.20(a); the production cost fluctuates around the equilibrium value (5.0) and maximum fluctuations are about 8% of the equilibrium value. The fluctuations of the unit cost lead to significant fluctuations of the whole system – as an example the behaviour of profit/capital and investment/capital ratios are shown in Figure 6.20(b) and (c). The average value of the unit cost of production is equal to 4.97 (that is, very close to the theoretical value equal to 5.0), the average rate of production growth is slightly below zero (−0.013%), and also the discounted profit is very close to zero (0.01%). It may be said that the average picture of the long-run development is very similar to the theoretical

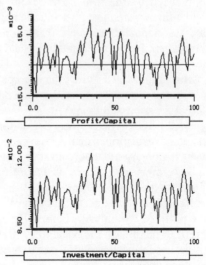

Figure 6.21. Long-run profit and random fluctuations of the market size

prediction of classical (or neoclassical) theory – the long-run profit is equal to zero. But the dynamic view (as shown in Figure 6.20(b)) is far from the static view of equilibrium theory.

Similar steady-state fluctuations are observed with random influences of many other model parameters. As an example, in Figure 6.21 the development of the profit and investment ratios under the 'random walk' of the size of the market with 5% yearly uniform distribution is presented. As before, the average values of some characteristics of industry development are very close to the equilibrium values of neoclassical expectations, but the dynamic picture of the industry development is far from the neoclassical view.

Supernormal Profit and Innovation

A full description of the model with the possibility of innovation emergence and results of its simulations are presented in the following chapters; here we present only the results of one experiment simply to check to what extent 'supernormal profit' emerges in our model's behaviour in the case of introducing innovation. Up to the 10th year the system is in the equilibrium state (for example, the profit is equal to zero), since then the R&D process acts and innovations, reducing the cost of production, increasing the productivity of capital and increasing the technical competitiveness, are introduced by the firms. The results are presented in Figure 6.22. In the initial three years, just after introducing the first innovations, the conditions for development are very hard for all firms (profit below zero and investment below the capital physical depreciation, see Figure 6.22(a) and (c)).

But in the next 15 years the average profit grows to reach a maximum in $t = 28$ (almost 12%); since this time the innovation rate is not so high as in the first period and the profit is reduced over the time (see Figure 6.22(a), years 30–100). The profit is not uniformly distributed within the industry, the successful firms (that is, the leaders in introducing innovations) utilize their temporary monopoly positions and make a much higher profit than the followers; as an example, in Figure 6.22b, the profit/capital ratio for two firms – the leader (firm No. 9) and the follower (firm No. 2) – are presented. It can be seen that the profit of the innovator is much higher than the profit of the imitator. Let us also note that while the average maximum profit in the industry is equal to 12% and is for $t = 28$, the maximum profit of the leader occurs eight years earlier and is significantly greater than the average one (that is, around 20%). Most of the profit goes to the investment (for replacement of old capital and for expansion of production) – the average rate of the production growth within the period of simulation is 0.74% and the discounted profit is only 0.166% (the average profit/capital is equal to 2.292% and investment/capital is 12.626%).

In his publications, Joseph Schumpeter stressed the importance of radical innovation as the main driving force underlying economic growth and as the major source of supernormal profit. In Schumpeter's opinion, such profit arises from the temporary monopoly position of a successful entrepreneur until successful imitators are able to enter the market. Our simulations confirm fully the opinion that innovations are the most important source of supernormal profit.

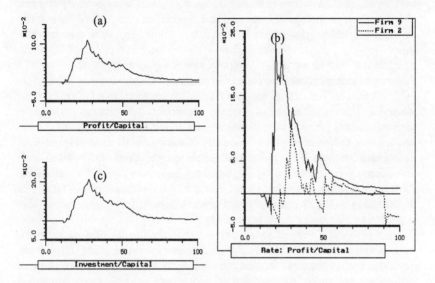

Figure 6.22. Long-run profit and innovation

Neoclassical economists think of equilibrium as the state or condition that the economy is normally in. This is not true – there are so many forces influencing the development that the probability of staying in the equilibrium state is of the zero order. It seems that besides the equilibrium analysis, which has been in the centre of research since Léon Walras, we should pay much greater attention to the dynamic perspective, as it was correctly pinpointed by J.A. Schumpeter.

BOUNDED RATIONALITY AND FLUCTUATIONS IN INDUSTRY DEVELOPMENT

The main aim of this section is to show that fluctuations in industry development, as observed in the behaviour of our model, may occur because of the limited firms' computational ability (bounded rationality). Fluctuations in our model could not be the effect of altering interest rate because of our assumption that the interest rate is constant during the simulation. In a real economic system the interest rate changes according to banks' fiscal policy and the current situation of industry. A modified interest rate causes the emergence of fluctuations or periodic development, as is explained by the monetary cycle theories (formulated by Knut Wicksell, Ludwig von Mises and Friedrich A. von Hayek). Broadly speaking, they may be considered as the interplay of loans, interest rates and investment. To expand their loans banks have to stimulate demand for loans by lowering their interest rates (they do so to the level where their rates are below the Wicksellian real rate). Firms will invest until the money rate is higher than the real rate. The process of cumulative inflation sets in and the time structure of production is distorted. Banks run up against the limits set to their lending by their reserves. The end of boom occurs and the interest rate grows.

There is no problem about making the interest rate changeable in our model, as proposed by the monetary theories, and observing how it influences the model's behaviour; anyhow we keep the interest rate intentionally constant to filter the monetary causes of the periodical modes of development. For the same reasons we discuss the problem of fluctuations in the absence of innovation, which, as is well known, is also a source of fluctuations in the economy.[22]

It is not denied that monetary factors and innovations play an essential role in fluctuations of economic processes but I want to point out that the primary factor causing fluctuations ought to be sought in the limited computational ability of man, and related to this natural human proneness to make errors, lapses, fallacies, and so on. As Mises (1957, p. 268) writes:

> To make mistakes in pursuing one's ends is a wide-spread human weakness. Some err less often than others, but no mortal man is omniscient and infallible. Error, inefficiency, and failure must not be confused with irrationality. He who shoots wants, as a rule, to hit the mark. If he misses it, he is not 'irrational'; he is a poor marksman. The doctor who chooses the wrong method to treat a patient is not irrational; he may be an incompetent physician. The farmer who in earlier ages tried to increase his crop by resorting to magic rites acted no less rationally than the modern farmer who applies

---

[22] 'Most economists today believe in a combination of external and internal theories. To explain major cycles, they place crucial emphasis on fluctuations in *investment* or *capital* goods. Primary causes of these capricious and volatile investment fluctuations are found in such external factors as (1) technological innovation, (2) dynamic growth of population and of territory, and even in some economists' view, (3) fluctuations in business confidence and "animal spirit".

With these external factors we must combine the internal factors that cause any initial change in investment to be *amplified* in a cumulative multiplied fashion – as people who are given work in the capital goods industries respend part of their new income on consumption goods, and as an air of optimism begins to pervade the business community, causing firms to go to the banks and the securities market for new credit accommodation.

Also, it is necessary to point out that the general business situation definitely reacts in turns on investment. ...

Therefore especially in the short run, investment is in part an *effect* as well as a *cause* of income movements' (Samuelson, 1980, p. 246).

more fertilizer. He did what according to his – erroneous – opinion was appropriate to his purpose.

Reason dictates man's actions and from this point of view man may be called a rational being. Rethinking human development from an evolutionary and historical perspective supports the view that man's actions are directed towards the search for a state of affairs that suits him (her) better. But as Herbert Simon observed: 'The capacity of the human mind for formulating and solving complex problems is very small compared to the size of the problems whose solution is required for objectively rational behaviour in the world – or even for a reasonable approximation to such objective rationality' (Simon, 1955). It seems almost impossible that human beings are able to make rational decisions under severe time constraints, huge numbers of variables, and a vast volume of information to be considered in almost every life situation. Human beings manage in such complex situations by considering only a small part of the complexity, making simplifications and idealizations of life situations. To proceed with these complex problems each of us builds a highly simplified mental model of the world. In the end our decisions are made in terms of that model (Simon, 1986 p. 34). To describe our cognitive situation Simon advanced the hypothesis of bounded rationality (Simon, 1955).

> The term 'rational' denotes behaviour that is appropriate to specific goals in the context of a given situation. If the characteristics of the choosing organism are ignored, and we consider only those constraints that arise from the external situation, then we may speak of substantive or objective rationality – that is, behaviour that can be adjudged objectively to be optimally adapted to the situation. On the other hand, if we take into account the limitations of knowledge and computing power of the choosing organisms, then we may find it incapable of making optimal choices. If, however, it uses methods of choice that are as effective as its decision-making and problem-solving means permit, we may speak of procedural or bounded rationality. (Simon, 1988)

Although in a very stylized form, the concept of bounded rationality is incorporated into our model. Through controlling some parameters of the decision-making procedure we are able to imitate diversified levels of skill ('knowledge and computing power') of the firms to make correct evaluations of investment, price, profit, and so on.

In the decision-making procedure (presented in Chapter 5) the price, investment, profit and production are established by applying some local optimization procedure. In all experiments up to now it was assumed that firms are able to reach the optimum (that is, maximum of the firm's objective) and it was not important what kind of optimization algorithm firms apply. In this section the way of reaching the optimum, or near optimum state, becomes important. It seems that as the first approximation to what firms (decision-makers) do, the following reasoning may be assumed: let us say that the proper decision, in the sense of the assumed objective of action, ought to be adopted within an assumed, relatively short, period of time, and the computational ability of the decision-maker is finite.[23]

The decision-maker chooses first of all a set of crucial (primary) variables influencing the objective and on the basis of which it is possible to estimate all other characteristics of the economic process (for example, the product price plays the role of the primary variable in our decision-making procedure). Next, variability of the primary variables is assumed and within the domain defined by the variability scope an optimal decision is sought. In principle, it is not possible to present the analytical form of the objective as a function of the primary variables. Therefore, there is no possibility of calculating (estimating) the objective's derivatives and directly determining the optimum (in which the derivatives are equal to zero). At best it is possible to calculate the values of the objective for discrete sets of values of the primary variables. The decision-maker makes such calculations for a finite number of values of the primary variables. The number of such trials depends directly on the computational ability of the decision-maker.

From all the trials the best value is chosen and the values of the primary variables for which the objective reaches maximum (or minimum) are assumed by the decision-maker as his (her) final decision. The distance of that decision from the objectively optimal decision depends directly on the number of trials and the way of choosing the successive values of primary variables (that is, on the optimization algorithm). Theoretically, to reach the optimum it is necessary to make an infinite number of trials. Something similar is done by the firms in our model. The price is the only primary variable (all others, such as investment and production, are an outcome of the price – as proposed in the decision procedure). The scope of variability of the price is controlled by the model parameter (λ). The scope of search for the optimal price (that is, the minimum and maximum of the price) depends on the actual value of the firm's product price, namely we assume that $\mathrm{Min}\,P_i = p_i/\lambda$, and $\mathrm{Max}\,P_i = p_i\lambda$ (where p_i is the actual product price of firm i).

To make the search for optimal price effective, one of the best algorithms of single variable optimization was chosen, namely, the so-called golden division algorithm. Making L trials[24] the firm is able to reduce the initial scope of search ($\mathrm{Min}\,P$, $\mathrm{Max}\,P$) about $(1.62)^L$ times. It means that after making, for example, 25 trials, the distance to the optimal price is not greater than $(\mathrm{Max}\,P - \mathrm{Min}\,P)/103{,}680$, that is, about 10^{-5} of the initial price range; after making ten trials the reduction is only by a factor of 76.[25] Many

---

[23] In our understanding the notion of computational ability parallels Simon's 'limitations of knowledge and computing power' of the decision-maker. Later on computational ability will be shortened to 'computability'.

[24] It means that the best value (assumed as the optimal one) is chosen from the set of L values.

[25] To reach the same reduction of the initial scope in other commonly known single variable

simulations were done for other optimization algorithms such as dichotomy, and random search. If we assume a sufficiently large number of trials (that is, to simulate the infinite computational ability of each firm) the behaviour of the model is exactly the same for each optimization algorithm applied. In all the simulation runs the results of which are presented below in this section, the golden division algorithm is applied, but very similar behaviour of the model is observed for two other algorithms applied, namely dichotomy and random search.

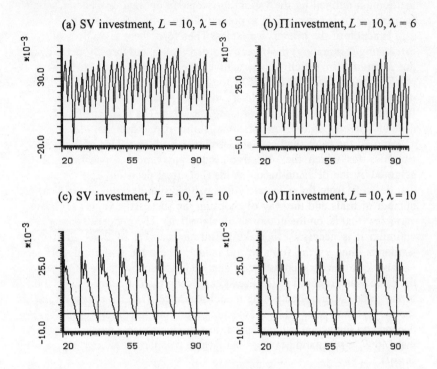

Figure 6.23. Profit to capital ratio; SV and Π strategies and two levels of computability: λ = 6 and λ = 10 (L = 10)

By assuming different values of the number of trials (L) in the optimization algorithm and the price scope of search (λ) we are able to control the level of the firms' computational ability (computability); the larger the number of trials and the smaller the scope of search for the

_____

optimization algorithms, for example, the dichotomy and random search, it is necessary to make a much greater number of trials, for example, instead of 25 trials in the golden division it is necessary to make 36 trials when applying dichotomy.

optimal price,[26] the greater the firm's computability, that is, the firm's
decisions may be closer to the optimal ones. Thanks to this property of the
optimization algorithm we are able to simulate the influences of bounded
rationality on the model's behaviour. We correlate the firm's computability
with bounded rationality, and we use the values of the number of trials (L)
and the price scope of search (λ) as a measure of the firm's rationality.

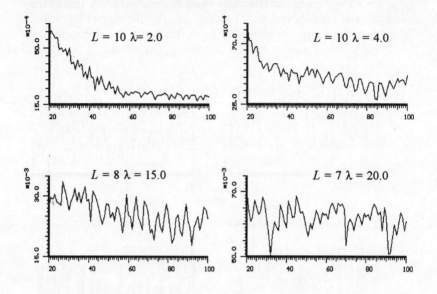

*Figure 6.24. Profit to capital ratio for the selected values of firms'
              computability*

Quite accidentally, during the preliminary simulations for a small number
of trials in the optimization algorithm, fluctuations were observed in the
model's behaviour. Further study confirmed these preliminary observations.
I guess that these observations may be related to Simon's concept of
bounded rationality. Before a fuller discussion of the influence of the limited
firms' computability on the model's behaviour, I would like to show that
there are no qualitative differences in the model's behaviour due to the
bounded rationality for different strategies of the firms' investment. Very
similar fluctuations are observed for the same simulation conditions for
firms applying either the SV investment strategy or the Π investment
strategy.[27]

---

[26] Providing that the optimal price belongs to the assumed scope of search.
[27] See page 91 for comments on the investment strategies applied in the model.

As an example, the fluctuations of profit/capital ratio are presented in Figure 6.23. In all four runs the number of iterations is equal to ten, and the level of the firms' computability is controlled by the scope of search λ. For a given level of the computability (that is, for λ equal either to six or to ten) the fluctuations look very similar for both strategies, although there are differences in average values of the profit/capital ratio (for example, for $\lambda = 6$ the average profit/capital ratio is equal to 2.6% and 1.9%, respectively for the SV and the Π investments). Let us note that the type of fluctuations depends on the firms' computability level, for $\lambda = 6$ the fluctuations are significantly more frequent than for $\lambda = 10$.

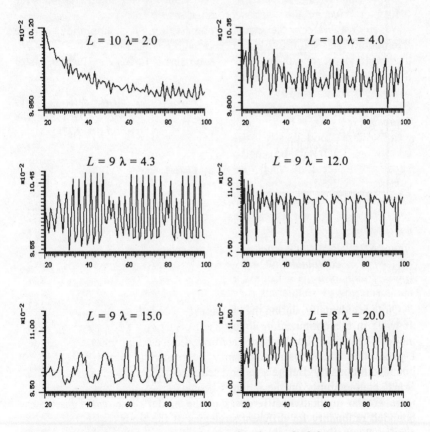

Figure 6.25. Investment to capital ratio for diversified firms'
computability

These observations are confirmed by the results of more systematic research related to different levels of computability. If computability is high, the firms are able to find optimal, or very near to optimal, decisions, and the industry moves steadily to the equilibrium state (as in Figure 6.6(e) and (f). In the case of poor computability, firms' decisions deviate from the optimal ones, which causes fluctuations in the industry behaviour. Great diversity in the modes of industry development due to different levels of firms' computability is observed. It is impossible to show all types of fluctuations, and therefore only a selection of the simulation results is presented, being only a small part of the observed diversity in the model's behaviour, in Figure 6.24 (the profit/capital ratio), and in Figure 6.25 (the investment/capital ratio). For relatively high firms' computability (for example, for $L = 10$, $\lambda = 2.0$) the fluctuations are not significant, and the industry reaches an almost stable equilibrium.

When we reduce the firms' computability the amplitude of the fluctuations rises significantly. For very poor computability ($L = 7$, $\lambda = 20$) the amplitude of investment/capital ratio rises to 1.5%. The fluctuations of investment are about the equilibrium value of 10% (that is, the value of the physical capital depreciation $\delta = 0.1$), which means that periodically the investment is below the capital physical depreciation and we observe cyclical slumps in production. The smaller the firms' computability, the deeper are the depressions.

The results presented above are for small concentrated industry (pure competition, 12 firms); a similar series of simulation runs were done for high concentrated industry (oligopoly). From a qualitative point of view the results are very similar to those for the pure competition, besides differences in the values of the characteristics of industry the fluctuation modes of the industry development are very similar to those in the above figures. The significant differences, which needs to be mentioned, are in the values of the average profit. It turns out that, in general, for pure competition the average profit grows with the diminishing firms'

Table 6.8. Computability and average profit (in the period 60–100)

Computability		12 firms	4 firms
L	λ	Π/K [%]	Π/K [%]
25	1.5	0.029	17.11
15	2.0	0.059	17.43
10	2.0	0.207	16.92
10	3.0	0.289	17.74
10	4.0	0.405	18.69
9	4.0	0.967	16.94
9	4.3	0.788	18.65
9	4.7	0.658	17.52
9	5.0	0.786	16.91
9	7.0	1.100	17.35
9	10.0	1.497	17.46
9	10.3	1.430	18.38
9	10.7	2.098	17.43
9	11.0	1.933	17.97
9	12.0	1.642	14.21
9	15.0	2.622	17.61
8	15.0	2.376	15.56
8	20.0	3.142	16.81
7	20.0	6.156	18.31

computability, and for highly concentrated industry no such trend is observed. As an example, the values of profit/capital rate for small concentrated industry (12 firms) and oligopoly (four firms) are presented in Table 6.8. For high computability ($L = 25$, $\lambda = 1.5$) the industry moves steadily to the equilibrium; the average value of profit at the end of the simulation is equal to zero for pure competition, and stabilizes on the level of 17% for four firms. The equilibrium investment/capital rate is equal to 10% in both runs. The data in Table 6.8 are presented in decreasing order of the values of the firms' computability. As can be seen, the profit to capital ratio for 12 firms increases almost steadily with decreasing computability, only in a few cases (for example, for $L = 9$, and $\lambda = 4.3$, $\lambda = 4.7$) does the profit to capital ratio drop. For oligopoly the profit is always relatively high and frequently drops and rises for different values of computability.

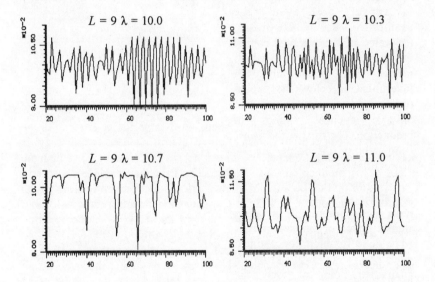

*Figure 6.26.   Investment to capital ratio for small deviations of the firms'
computability*

It seems obvious that for pure competition we observe an increase in profit due to decreasing firms' computability. The equilibrium profit for high computability (perfect knowledge and infinite computational power) for pure competition is equal to zero. For small computability the firms make their evaluations of the objective values for a limited number of trials. As may be expected, the values of the firm's objective and profit in all trials are

greatly diversified, and very rarely the best trial is close to the maximal
value of the objective. In the whole set of trials there are cases with positive
and negative profits, and it seems natural that the firm chooses the case
(trial) which is closest to the optimum and yielding the positive profit. As
we may expect, the distance of the best trial from the optimal decision is the
farther the poorer the firms' computability. The positive profit provides for
larger investment capabilities and allows for the firm's future development.
Achieving the highest profit is not so crucial for oligopolist's firms, so the
profit rises and drops in our simulation experiments.

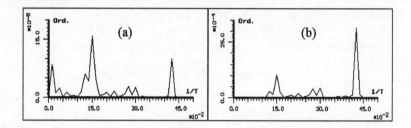

*Figure 6.27.   Spectral density of profit/capital (a), and investment/capital
          ratios (b)*

One may say that making poor estimations is a profitable strategy in the
case of pure competitive industry, but if a firm chooses the strategy of
making higher 'intentional error estimations' (to gain higher profit), then the
prices of its products are also higher. The firm may achieve short-term
positive profit, but because of higher prices the competitiveness of its
products is smaller and as a direct consequence its market share will drop;
in the end the firm will be eliminated from the market. The competition
process and free entry of firms ensure that the quality of estimations will be
kept at the lowest possible level, which may be called a natural level. In all
experiments presented the computability was constant and the same for all
firms operating on the market. Later on in this section, the results of an
experiment with varying computability of each firm will be presented. To
check to what extent firms with small (intentional) computability are
eliminated from the market a series of experiments were made in which
values of the firms' computability were diversified, but were constant during
the simulation (for each firm the values of L and λ were drawn randomly
at the beginning of the simulation). Some 'clever' firms were able to make
good estimations, or even optimal decisions, while many others made
considerable errors. The results of experiments confirm our conjecture that
the firms with 'poor' computability are superseded from the market and that
at the end of the simulations only the 'cleverest' firms remain.
    Spectral analysis of the periods of fluctuations does not enable us to find

any regular relationship between the period of fluctuations and the level of computability. Great diversity of the modes of fluctuation is evident in the figures presented earlier in this section, but even small deviations of computability lead to significant changes of the basic periods of fluctuations. As an example, the fluctuations of the investment/capital ratio in one series of experiments with small deviations of computability are presented in Figure 6.26 (the number of trials (L) is constant and only the scope of search λ deviates slightly). Significant changes in the mode of fluctuations are clearly visible, even without making any spectral analysis.

Table 6.9. The basic Fourier periods (in years)

Computability		profit/capital			investment/capital		
L	λ	1st	2nd	3rd	1st	2nd	3rd
10	3.0	4.2	2.7		4.2	2.7	
10	4.0	5.0	11.4		4.8	2.6	25.0
9	4.0	10.0			10.0	5.3	
9	4.3	25.0	2.9	11.4	2.9	3.2	
9	4.7	5.0	20.0	2.5		5.0	2.5
9	5.0	3.1			2.9		
9	7.0	2.7	10.0		2.7	2.1	
9	10.0	3.6	2.8	4.2	2.8	3.4	4.2
9	10.3	16.4	11.1	9.1	9.1	11.1	16.4
9	10.7	16.4	6.7	4.3	6.7	3.7	4.2
9	11.0	6.7	3.2		5.0	3.2	
9	12.0	6.7	2.4	3.6	2.4	6.7	3.4
9	15.0	11.4	6.7		6.7	11.4	
8	15.0	5.0			5.0	3.4	2.4
8	20.0	5.0	11.4	3.5	5.0	3.5	
7	20.0	20.0	10.0	3.5	3.5	4.2	10.0

Based on the Fast Fourier Transformation, spectral analyses of all simulation runs were carried out. As a result of such analyses, spectral densities are obtained for each run, similar to that presented in Figure 6.27 (the run for $L = 9$, and $\lambda = 12$). From the analysis of the spectral densities of either the profit/capital ratio or the investment/capital ratio it is possible to identify the basic periods of fluctuations (those with the highest densities). For example, the analysis of the spectral density in Figure 6.27 allows us to identify the following basic periods (T) of the profit/capital rate: 6.7 years (the highest ordinate), 2.4 years (the second ordinate) and 3.6 years (the 3rd ordinate). The period of 80 years (the first peak on the left side of Figure 6.27(a)) is not considered because, in fact, it represents the trend in the 80-element sample. Much-correlated basic periods are for the investment/capital ratio (Figure 6.27(b)), but the highest ordinate has a frequency with a period of 2.4 years, the second one is with a period of 6.7

years, and the third one with the period of 3.6 years. It means that the basic periods of the profit and of the investment are the same but the order is slightly different. Very similar pictures are obtained for all other runs. The basic periods of the fluctuations observed in different runs are presented in Table 6.9.

As we have said, there is no clear relationship between the computability and the basic periods of fluctuations. A thorough study of fluctuations (based, for example, on the Lyapunov exponents) due to the finite firms' computability is needed, but for our preliminary analysis it is enough to note

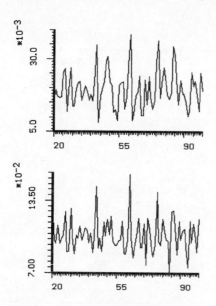

that the distribution of the basic periods is far from being uniform. The rough cluster analysis of the basic periods presented in Table 6.9 shows that there are two clusters: (1) within three to seven years, and (2) about 10 years, and also a few scattered oscillations of longer periods of 16, 20 and 25 years.

In most of the simulation runs presented in this section it was assumed that computability is constant during simulation and identical for all firms. This assumption allowed a systematic study of the influence of different values of computability on the industry behaviour to be undertaken. Naturally it makes some features of the model's behaviour quite artificial – no two firms have the same computational ability, and even the same firm is not able to make calculations of the same quality in different periods and

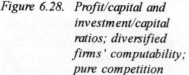

Figure 6.28. Profit/capital and investment/capital ratios; diversified firms' computability; pure competition

for diversified external influences (from other industries, and from other spheres of social life) as well as internal influences (for example, emerging innovations). The unnatural behaviour of the model in the case of constant and uniform value of the firms' computability is clearly visible in some of the figures presented, for example, sharp jumps and very regular, saw-like charts of the profit/capital or the investment/capital ratios. As may be expected, computability is firm specific and embedded in its routines. In general, the firm's computability ought to be described as a stochastic process coupled with the evolution of the firm's routines. Pure random factors may influence the firm's computability, for example, innovation emergence may cause the future industry development to be highly non-deterministic and unpredictable, and the probability of correct expectation to be especially small in the first phase of the innovation diffusion. To get closer to a real situation, in the following series of experiments random changes of either the number of trials L or the scope of search λ are assumed.[28] This assumption causes a stochastic behaviour of the model. Simulation results of two such experiments are presented in Figure 6.28 (pure competition – 12 firms) and in Figure 6.29 (oligopoly – four firms). It may be said that the behaviour of the model is a 'sum of the elementary behaviours' observed in earlier simulation runs. Statistical analysis of numerous simulation runs for diversified firms' computability shows that for such created simulation conditions the emergence of basic fluctuations with periods between three to seven years, and about 10 years can still be observed. In contrast to the former simulation runs where on account of the assumption of constant firms' computability all firms are equal and their market shares do not change during simulations, in this series of simulation runs we observe

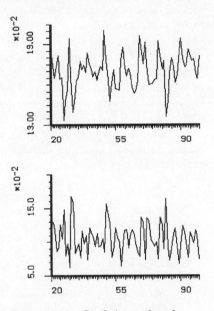

Figure 6.29. Profit/capital and investment/capital ratios; diversified firms' computability; oligopoly

diversity of firms' size, that is, shares of firms fluctuate around the equilibrium values (8.33% for 12 firms and 25% for four firms). The firms do not choose the same price of products so we also observe relatively high diversity of prices, diversity of investment and diversities of all other firms' characteristics. It may be said that for stochastic firms' computability all

---

[28] It is assumed that values of L and λ are drawn for each firm every year using the uniform distributions, for L within the range 5 to 15, and for λ within 1.5 to 10.

industry characteristics fluctuate about their equilibrium values and the industry is in the steady state.

Results of many other simulation experiments with the model (presented not only in this section) suggest that fluctuations are the natural mode of development of the economy. There are so many endogenous (for example, innovation) as well as exogenous (from other spheres of social life, such as politics and demography) factors causing the fluctuations that there is no escape from this mode of economy development. Results presented in this section demonstrate that fluctuations in industry development may be due to the decision-making process of economic agents caused by the lack of knowledge of current and future development of the system and inaccurate predictions of the behaviour of its competitors. A similar conclusion that 'chaos can in fact be produced by the decision-making process of real people' is expressed by Sterman (1988) on the basis of experiments with two models: the economic long-wave model and the Beer Distribution Game (the production–distribution system). But while in our model fluctuations are caused by the lack of knowledge and limited 'computing power', in Sterman's models these fluctuations and periodic development are caused primarily by lags between action and effect. As Sterman writes (1988, p. 149):

> The regulation of a stock or system state is one of the most common dynamic decision-making tasks. ... Typically, a manager must set the inflow rate to compensate for losses from the stock and to counteract environmental disturbances that may push the stock away from its desired value. There are frequently lags between the initiation of a control action and its effect on the stock, or lags between a change in stock and the perception of that change by the decision maker.

The main aim of this section is to point out that the lack of knowledge, finite 'computing power', and natural human proneness to make errors may cause fluctuations of the industry development. Naturally there are many other causes of industry fluctuations (for example, 'lags between the initiation of a control action and its effect on the stock, or lags between a change in stock and the perception of that change by the decision maker'). The other problem which pleads for deep and systematic study is how fluctuations within a number of separated industries may be correlated with the macroeconomic fluctuations. Analysis of statistical records suggests diversified modes of development of macroeconomic systems including short-term business (Kitchin) cycles with periods of about three years (for example, Gordon 1951; Mitchell 1927), the 9 to 25 years construction (Juglar, Kuznets) cycles (for example, Riggleman 1933; Kuznets 1973), and 45 to 60 years economic long waves, the so-called Kondratieff cycles (for example, Kondratieff 1935; van Duijn 1983; Freeman 1983). Some observations indicate that different modes of economic development interact with one another such that each long wave spans a full number of Kuznets

(Juglar) cycles, and each construction cycle a full number of business cycles. Joseph Schumpeter, who was a proponent of such a view (Schumpeter, 1939), opted for three cycles: three Kitchins equalled a Juglar, six Juglars a Kondratieff.

7. Innovation and Economic Development

The essence of cultural development in general, and socio-economic evolution in particular, lies in the creative process of human beings. The real tissue of creative processes is almost impossible to observe. The collection of relevant quantitative data on innovation processes is mostly confined to such data as number of researchers, R&D funds, number of patents, and so on. Estimation of some essential parameters and characteristics (for example, probability of the emergence of innovation within an assumed period of time) on the basis of such aggregate data is almost impossible. The most important, and the most interesting, phenomena of creative/cognitive processes occur in the minds of researchers, and these kinds of processes are, in general, out of reach of any observations. The only way to deal with the creative processes and dare to describe them in a more or less formal way is to make some arbitrary assumptions, incorporate them into the economic model and observe if the development of the model resembles the development of real processes. In some sense, it is a combination of quantitative modelling (based on hard economic data) and qualitative modelling (based on heuristics, analogies and metaphors). This kind of approach is proposed in this chapter, where the extension of the basic model with innovative processes embedded is presented. This proposition is treated as the first approximation being the subject of further development ('stepwise concretization').

The creative process is evolutionary by nature, and as such its description ought to be based on a proper understanding of the hereditary information (see Chapter 2). According to the tradition established by J.A. Schumpeter, and S. Winter and R. Nelson we use the term 'routine' to name the basic unit of the hereditary information of a firm.[1] The set of routines applied by

---

[1] In Chapter 2, the term paragon was used to describe the cultural heritage information of a human being. It might be argued that the same term ought to be used to describe firms' behaviour. Use of 'routine' to name the hereditary information is sanctioned by the just-mentioned Schumpeterian tradition. The other reason is that the behaviour of a firm is an 'outcome' of habits (paragons) of all individuals engaged in the firm's activity. A full description of the firms ought to consist of the descriptions of modes of behaviour of all the individuals engaged. For practical reasons it is almost impossible to do it because of the great diversity of individualities. Therefore to model a firm's behaviour properly it is necessary to apply an abstraction and construct artificial entities, such as routines, being an effect of cooperation of all individuals. As we have already said, paragons play the role of an ideal pattern of behavior; they are related in some way to the judgement values of human beings. Any artificial entity, for example, a firm, has no mind and has no judgmental value system, so paragons may be considered as the exclusive property of the

the firm is one of the basic characteristics describing the firm. Each firm searches for new routines and new combinations of routines. Nelson and Winter (1982, p. 14) define routines as 'regular and predictable behavioral patterns of firms' and include in this term such characteristics of firms as 'technical routines for producing things ... procedures of hiring and firing, ordering new inventory, stepping up production of items in high demand, policies regarding investment, research and development, advertising, business strategies about product diversification and overseas investment'. A large part of research activity is also governed by routines. 'Routines govern choices as well as describe methods, and reflect the facts of management practice and organizational sociology as well as those of technology' (Winter, 1984).

Each firm tends to improve its situation within the industry and in the market by introducing new combinations of routines in order to minimize the unit cost of production, maximize the productivity of capital, and maximize the competitiveness of its products in the market. Productivity of capital, unit cost of production, and characteristics of products manufactured by a firm depend on the routines employed by the firm (examples of the product characteristics are: reliability, convenience, lifetime, safety of use, cost of use, quality and aesthetic values). The search activities of firms 'involve the manipulation and recombination of the actual technological and organizational ideas and skills associated with a particular economic context' (Winter, 1984), while the market decisions depend on the product characteristics and prices. We may speak about the existence of two spaces: the space of routines and the space of product characteristics.[2] Distinguishing these two spaces enables us to separate firms' decisions from the market's decisions. As in the basic model discrete time, for example, a year or a quarter, is assumed, and the firms' decisions relating to investment, production, research funds, and so on, are taken simultaneously and independently by all firms at the beginning of each period. After the decisions are made the firms undertake production and put the products on the market. The products are evaluated by the market, and the quantities of different firms' products sold in the market depend on the relative prices,

human being as an individual. To distinguish these two connotations, the use of both terms is preferred, paragons and routines, being specific in both situations.

[2] A space of routines and a space of characteristics play in our model an analogous role to a space of genotypes and a space of phenotypes in biology. The existence of these two types of spaces is a general property of evolutionary processes (Kwaśnicka and Kwaśnicki, 1986a). Probably the search spaces (that is, spaces of routines and spaces of genotypes) are discrete spaces in contrast to the evaluation spaces (that is, space of characteristics and space of phenotypes) which are continuous spaces. The dimension of the space of routines (space of genotypes) is much greater than the dimension of the space of characteristics (space of phenotypes). As some simulation experiments reveal, big differences in the dimensions of the two spaces play an important role in long-term evolution and enables escape from so-called evolutionary traps (see also Chapter 2).

the relative value of product characteristics and the level of saturation of the market. Because of imbalances of global supply and demand as well as 'local' imbalances of demand and supply of products of a specific firm it may happen that the products evaluated as the best are not sold in the full quantity offered, and conversely, the inferior products are frequently sold in spite of the possibility of selling the better ones. But during long periods the preference for better products, that is, those with a lower price and better characteristics, prevails.

In the model presented below each firm may simultaneously produce products with different prices and different values of the characteristics, that is, the firm may be a multi-unit operation. Different units of the same firm manufacture products by employing different sets of routines. Multi-unit firms exist because of the searching activity. New technical or organizational solutions (that is, a new set of routines) may be much better than the actual ones but full modernization of production is not possible because of investment constraints on the firm. In such situations the firm continues production employing the old routines and tries to open a new unit where production, on a lesser scale, employing the new set of routines is started. Subsequently the 'old' production may be reduced and after some time superseded by the 'new' production.

In the model, a simulation of industry development is made in discrete time in four steps:

1.	Search for the new sets of routines which potentially may replace the 'old' set currently employed by a firm.
2.	Calculation and comparison of the investment, production, net income, profit and some other characteristics of development which may be obtained by employing the 'old' and the 'new' sets of routines. Decisions of each firm on: (a) continuation of production by employing old routines or making modernization of production, and (b) opening (or not) of new units.
3.	Entry of new firms.
4.	Market evaluation of the offered pool of products. Calculation of firms' characteristics: production sold, shares in global production and global sales, total profits, profit rates, research funds, and so on.

Apart from the first step, the three others are almost exactly the same as in the basic model described in Chapter 5. The only difference is that the productivity of capital A, the unit cost of production V, and technical competitiveness q are now the functions of routines applied by each firm, and may vary according to discovered inventions and introduced innovations. Because of innovation and new technologies introduced by firms the modernization investment is also taken into account in the decision-making process (that is, besides the expansionary investment related to the growth of production we have the modernization investment related to adjusting the 'old' capital to 'new' technology).

SEARCH PROCESS

We assume that at time t a firm unit is characterized by a set of routines actually employed by the firm. There are two types of routines: *active*, that is, routines employed by this firm in its everyday practice, and *latent*, that is, routines which are stored by a firm but not actually applied. Latent routines may be included in the active set of routines at a future time. The set of routines is divided into separate subsets, called segments, consisting of similar routines employed by the firm in different domains of the firm's activity. Examples are segments relating to productive activity, managerial and organizational activity, marketing, and so on. In each segment, either active or latent routines may exist. The set of routines employed by a firm may evolve. There are four basic mechanisms for generating new sets of routines, namely: *mutation, recombination, transition* and *transposition*.

The probability of discovering a new routine (mutation) depends on the research funds allocated by the firm for autonomous research, that is, in-house development. The firm may also allocate some funds for gaining knowledge of other competing firms and try to imitate (recombination) some routines employed by competitors. It is assumed that recombination may occur only between segments, not between individual routines, that is, a firm may gain knowledge about the whole domain of activity of another firm, for example, by licensing. A single routine may be transmitted (transition) with some probability from firm to firm. It is assumed that after transition a routine belongs to a subset of latent routines. At any time a random transposition of a latent routine to a subset of active routines may occur. A more detailed description of the four basic mechanisms of evolution of routines is presented in the following sections.

Research Funds

It is assumed that R&D funds (R_i) allocated by a firm into research (innovation and imitation) are a function of actual capital (K_i) of the firm.

$$R_i = (h_2 \exp(-h_1 K_i) + h_0) K_i. \tag{7.1}$$

Research funds are proportional to a firm's capital if h_1 and h_2 are equal to zero. If h_1 and h_2 are greater than zero, small firms allocate a greater percentage of their capital into research and a local maximum of R&D funds will appear near $K_i = 1/h_1$. Total R&D funds are partitioned into funds (R_i^m) for innovation (mutation) and funds (R_i^r) for imitation (recombination). The strategy of research of firm i in year t is described by the coefficient (g_i) of partition of the total R&D expenditure into innovation and imitation.

$$R_i^m = g_i R_i, \qquad R_i^r = (1 - g_i) R_i. \tag{7.2}$$

The strategy of research changes from year to year and depends on the actual state of affairs of a firm. It is assumed that the share of research on innovation increases if the firm's share in global production is increasing (that is, if the assumed position of the firm against a background of other competing firms is good). If the firm's share decreases, more funds are allocated to imitation, that is, the firm supposes that there are other firms applying better technology and it is better and safer to search for these technologies. The rate of changes of coefficient g_i depends on the size of a firm, and it is the smaller, the larger the firm is.

$$g_i(t+1) = \left(1 + \frac{G}{K_i} \frac{f_i(t) - f_i(t-1)}{f_i(t-1)}\right) g_i(t), \tag{7.3}$$

where $g_i(t)$ is the coefficient of R&D funds partition at time t, G is the constant parameter controlling the rate of changes of g_i, and $f_i(t)$ is the share of firm i in global production at time t.

During any year of searching activity more than one set of new routines r^* may be found. The number of such alternative sets of routines, the so-called number of experiments, is a function of research funds,

$$NoExp_i = \text{round}(e(R_i)^\psi) + E_0, \tag{7.4}$$

where $NoExp$ is the number of experiments of firm i, e, ψ, and E_0 are coefficients with the same values for all firms, R_i is the R&D expenditure of firm i, and round (x) is a function producing the closest integer number to x.

Mutation

It is assumed that routines mutate independently of each other. Since the range of the routines is bounded, all possible routines are enumerated and it is assumed that the range is from $MinRut$ to $MaxRut$. Let r_{lk} denote the l-th routine in the k-th segment employed by a firm in period $(t-1, t)$. After mutation routine r_{lk}:

1. is not changed, that is, $r_{lk}^* = r_{lk}$, with probability $(1 - PrMut)$, or
2. is changed and is equal to

$$r_{ik}^* = r_{ik} + x; \qquad x \in (-MaxMut, \ MaxMut),$$

with probability $PrMut/(2MaxMut)$ for every x. The probability of mutation of a routine depends on R&D funds allocated by firm i to search for innovations,

$$PrMut_i = a^m (R_i^m)^\zeta + b^m, \tag{7.5}$$

where a^m, ζ are coefficients controlling probability of mutation, and b^m is the probability of mutation related to the public knowledge. Maximum scope of search depends also on the funds allocated to autonomous research, and it is assumed that,

$$MaxMut_i = a^u (R_i^m)^\vartheta + b^u, \tag{7.6}$$

where a^u, ϑ are coefficients controlling the scope of mutation, and b^u is the scope of mutation related to the public knowledge.

Recombination

A firm i may get knowledge about the routines of a single segment of a firm j with probability $PrRec$. At the same time the firm i may get knowledge employed by different firms, so new sets of routines may consist of routines of different firms. In the model the firm i may apply one of three strategies of recombination:

1. conditional probability of recombination of segment k of firm-unit i with segment k of firm-unit j is proportional to the share of firm-unit j in global production;
2. conditional probability of recombination of segment k of firm-unit i with segment k of firm-unit j is proportional to the rate of expansion of firm-unit j, that is, is proportional to the derivative of the share of firm-unit j;
3. conditional probability of recombination of segment k of firm-unit i with segment k of firm-unit j is reciprocal to the number of firms existing in the market, that is, is equal for each firm-unit j.

The probability of recombination of a segment is a function of R&D funds allocated to imitation:

$$PrRec_i = a^r (R_i^r)^\xi + b^r, \tag{7.7}$$

where a^r, ξ are coefficients controlling probability of recombination, b^r is the probability of recombination related to the public knowledge.

Transition, Transposition and Recrudescence

It is assumed that the probabilities of transition of a routine from one firm to another and the probabilities of transposition of a routine (from a latent to an active routine) are independent of R&D funds, and have the same constant value for all routines. In general, the probability of transposition of a routine for any firm is rather small. But randomly, from time to time, the value of this probability may abruptly increase and very active processes of search for a new combination of routines are observed. This phenomenon is called recrudescence (see Chapter 2, page 26). Recrudescence is viewed as an intrinsic ability of a firm's research staff to search for original, radical innovations by employing some daring, sometimes apparently insane, ideas. This ability is connected mainly with the personalities of the researchers and random factors play an essential role in the search for innovations by recrudescence, so the probability of recrudescence is not related to R&D funds allocated by a firm to 'normal' research.

It is assumed that recrudescence is more probable in small firms than in large ones which spend huge quantities on R&D, although by assuming that u_2 is equal to zero in the equation below, then the probability of recrudescence does not depend on the firm's size and is constant (equal to u_1). The probability of recrudescence in firm i is equal to,

$$PrRence_i = u_1 \exp(-u_2 K_i). \tag{7.8}$$

As a rule, mutation, recombination and transposition on a normal level (that is, with low probabilities in long periods) are responsible for small improvements and in short periods of recrudescence for the emergence of radical innovations.

DIFFERENTIATION AND COMPETITION OF PRODUCTS

Productivity of capital, variable cost of production and product characteristics are the functions of routines employed by a firm. Each routine has multiple, pleiotropic effects, that is, may affect many characteristics of products, as well as productivity, and the variable cost of production. We assume that the transformation of the set of routines into the set of product characteristics is described by m functions F_d,

$$z_d = F_d(r), \quad d = 1, 2, 3, ..., m, \tag{7.9}$$

where z_d is the value of d characteristic, m the number of product characteristics, and r the set of routines.

Attractiveness of the product on the market depends on the values of the product characteristics and its price. In Chapter 5, the product competitiveness (see equation (5.1)) is a function of constant technical competitiveness and varying product price. In the presence of innovation, the technical competitiveness varies according to the modification of routines made by each firm, or because of introducing essentially new routines. Technical competitiveness is an explicit function of product characteristics. As we have said, each routine does not influence directly the product's performance but indirectly through the influences of its characteristics. We assume the existence of a function q enabling calculation of technical competitiveness of products manufactured by different firms. We say that function q describes the adaptive landscape in the space of product characteristics. In general, this function depends also on some external factors, varies in time, and is the result of co-evolution of many related industries. We say that the shape of the adaptive landscape is dynamic, with many adaptive peaks of varying altitudes. In the course of time some adaptive peaks lose their relevant importance, some become higher.

Similar to equation (5.1), the competitiveness of products with characteristics z and price p is equal to,

$$c(p,z) = \frac{q(z)}{p^{\alpha}}, \quad z = (z_1, z_2, z_3,..., z_m), \tag{7.10}$$

where $q(z)$ is the technical competitiveness, z a vector of product characteristics, and α the elasticity of price in the competitiveness.

Due to the ongoing search process, at any moment each firm may find a number of alternative sets of routines. Let us denote by r the set of routines actually applied by a firm and by r^* an alternative set of routines. Each firm evaluates all potential sets of routines r^* as well as the old routines r by applying the decision-making procedure presented in Chapter 5. The only difference is that values of productivity of capital A, the unit cost of production V, and technical competitiveness q are not constant but are modified according to an actually considered set of routines, either r or r^*. For each alternative set of routines the price, production, investment (including the modernization investment), and value of objective function are calculated. The decision of firm i on making modernization (that is, replacing the r routines by r^* routines) depends on the expected value of the firm's objective and its investment capabilities. Modernization is made if the maximum value of the objective distinguished from all considered alternative sets of routines r^* is greater than the value of objective possible to get by continuing the actually applied routines r, and if the investment capability of the firm permits such modernization. If the investment capability does not allow us to make modernization, then the firm:

1. continues production employing the 'old' routines r, and
2. tries to open a new small unit where routines r^* are employed; production is started with an assumed value of the capital, *InitCapital*.

It is assumed that the productivity function $A(r)$, the cost functions $V(r)$ and $v(Q)$ are not firm specific and have the same function form for all firms (presented in the Appendix).

To modernize production it is necessary to incur an extra investment. The modernization investment depends on the discrepancy between the 'old' routines r and the 'new' routines r^*. For simplicity of calculation, it is assumed that the modernization investment *IM* is a non-decreasing function of distance between the old routines r actually applied by a firm and the new set of routines r^*.

$$IM_i(t) = K_i(t) \| r - r^* \|, \tag{7.11}$$

where $\| .. \|$ is the distance function.

The research is financed from the current firm's income, so the relevant equations (5.30) and (5.31) for the firm's profit Π_i and income Γ_i ought to be modified.

$$\Gamma_i = QS_i(t)(p_i(t) - V(r)v(Q_i(t)) - \eta), \tag{7.12}$$

$$\Pi_i = \Gamma_i - K_i(t)(\rho + \delta) - D_i(t)/\mu_1 - R_i(t), \tag{7.13}$$

where Q_i^s is the current production of firm i, QS_i the production of firm i sold on the market, p_i the product price, $V(r)$ the unit cost of production when routines r are applied, K_i the capital, D_i the debt of firm i, and R_i the research funds of firm i.

Our model does not include explicitly the notion of labour, considered in economic analysis as the classical factor of production. Such important economic characteristics as labour and wages ought to be present in any model, and are present in our model, although indirectly, namely they are present in the cost functions $V(r)$ and $v(Q)$. At the current stage of the model's development it is not necessary to disaggregate the cost functions, although the possibility still exists to isolate labour and wages and build them explicitly into the model. This will be done in the future development of the model as a natural process of the model's stepwise concretization.

It is a kind of tradition that if economists speak of technological progress and innovation they distinguish two kinds of innovation, namely product and process innovation. The discrimination of such types of innovation is not relevant to our approach. Our interest is focused on innovation which influences some operationally defined economic variables, such as cost of production, productivity of capital or technical product's performance. But, although in hidden form, process and product innovation are present in our model – we may say that innovation focused on the reduction of the cost of production, and to a degree on productivity of capital, is related to process innovation, and innovation aiming at better technical performance of products is related mainly to the product innovation.

INNOVATION – GROPING IN THE DARK

In all simulation experiments presented below the number of firms is constant, equal to 12. No entry of new firms is assumed in this section, mainly to provide the comparability of results in different runs under the same simulation conditions. There is no possibility of abstaining from the randomness of the development in the presence of innovation; the search process is by its nature a stochastic one. Also the entry of new firms is a stochastic process. Involving two stochastic processes causes problems in the proper interpretation of results, so without losing the generality of consideration it is reasonable to assume that no new firm may enter the market. But in some specific experiments, entry will be allowed.

The search for innovation is a result of the interplay of different mechanisms of novelty generation, that is, different strategies of search. Dichotomously the firms' strategies may be partitioned into: innovation search (that is, an attempt to search for real novelty through the autonomous, in-house research of a firm) and imitation (that is, a search for innovation through the recombination of some existing solutions). But within the innovation strategy two mechanisms ought to be distinguished: search for novelty through the relatively small modification of current solutions and search for radical novelty through the essential rebuilding (reshaping) of existing solutions. Let us call the innovation strategy through moderate modifications 'mutation' and the search strategy for a radical novelty 'recrudescence'. All these three mechanisms of novelty generation are crucial for long-range economic development, and for all evolutionary processes in general. Mutations enable us to adjust current solutions (technologies) to local environments, to ongoing changes of exogenous conditions, and also to temporal changes of markets' preferences on which the firms operate.

Recombination (imitation) enables relatively quick dissemination (diffusion) of innovations and also enables new solutions to be found through the search for new combinations of existing routines. Collaboration of mutation and imitation enables much quicker development, and provides competitive conditions within the industry, being important forces prohibiting a tendency towards market monopolization. Mutation and imitation act all the time on the same relatively high level, they are vigorous forces allowing each individual firm to keep its position on the market or, with a bit of luck, to reach a temporary superior position.[3] It seems that the practice of recrudescence is different. As has been said before, recrudescence reflects phenomena frequently observed in creative processes and described as revelation, vision, bisociation (Arthur Koestler), or gestalt–switch (Karl Popper).

Table 7.1.   The innovation strategies

	n_H	Π/K %	Price	Price st.dev. %	A (100)	q (100)	V (100)
Innovation (mutation)							
normal	7.55	5.09	6.82	5.56	0.106	0.83	4.91
high	5.85	7.13	7.05	6.05	0.100	0.96	4.74
Innovation and Imitation (private knowledge only)							
normal	9.82	0.53	6.41	2.00	0.106	0.97	4.87
high	10.00	0.48	6.40	1.69	0.114	0.99	4.84
Innovation and Imitation (public knowledge only)							
normal	10.31	0.77	6.40	1.57	0.109	0.95	4.83
high	10.72	0.12	6.36	1.42	0.100	0.97	4.85
Innovation, Imitation and Recrudescence							
	6.04	0.33	6.18	5.41	0.155	1.14	4.91

In contrast to imitation and mutation, recrudescence is hardly detectable during 'normal' research, and may be called a dormant mechanism, but it is highly active during the periods of stagnation, when prospects of current technologies seem to be exhausted. During these relatively short periods, large numbers of inventions are generated, most of which are useless but some of them open the way for the emergence of radical innovation which focuses the attention of the majority of researchers; in effect the ratio of

---

[3] The evolutionary development (with the presence of innovation) resembles Alice's trip with the Red Queen from 'the Second Square' to 'the Eighth Square' in 'The Garden of Live Flowers'. The Queen and Alice 'went so fast that at last they seemed to skim through the air, hardly touching the ground with their feet. ... The most curious part of the thing was, that the trees and the other things round them never changed their places at all: however fast they went, they never seemed to pass anything.' In the end the Queen explained to Alice: 'Now, *here,* you see, it takes all the running *you* can do, to keep the same place. If you want to get somewhere else, you must run at least twice as fast as that!' Lewis Carrol, *Through the Looking-Glass*, Warszawa: Lettrex, 1991, Chapter II.

recrudescence diminishes. In the succeeding phase of the Kuhnian 'normal research', efforts are focused on such promising innovations which are further improved by mutation and recombination. As a hypothesis it may be stated that the ratio of recrudescence is strongly correlated to the economic state of affairs – during periods of prosperity the recrudescence is almost invisible but emerges and gains vital status during relatively short periods of depression and stagnation. In reality all mechanisms of novelty generation act concurrently. It seems interesting to isolate each mechanism and study the impact of each separated mechanism on the modes of industrial development. The results of such a series of experiments are presented in Figure 7.1 and in Table 7.1 (for each mechanism, results of two simulation runs with relatively small and large probabilities of innovation emergence – labelled here as 'normal' and 'high' – are presented). Adaptive landscapes describing the performance index (technical competitiveness) are defined in the space of technical characteristics – $q(z)$ in equation (7.10). As may be expected real adaptive landscapes are dynamic entities with many local

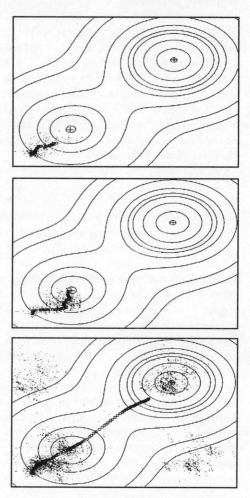

Figure 7.1. Trajectories of development for different modes of the search process

peaks. The adaptive landscape's surface depends on the evolution of the industry under consideration as well as on the co-evolution of other related industries, but also, in general, on the whole socio-economic evolution. In principle it is possible to model such a complicated landscape by relevant definition of function $q(z)$, but to control the results of experiments it is better to start the simulation with simple, stable adaptive landscapes. In the following experiment it is assumed that there are only two technical characteristics,[4] the adaptive landscape does not change its shape during the simulation and there are two local peaks with altitudes equal to 1.0 and 1.5. Values of $q(z)$ reflect relative preferences of different solutions, multiplication of $q(z)$ by any positive number does not change the shape of the landscape and the behaviour of the model. It means that solutions around the higher peak provide 50% better performance than the solutions around the lower peak. The map of this adaptive landscape is presented in Figure 7.1. The initial values of the product characteristics are much closer to the first lower peak so we may expect that the trajectory of evolution at the first stage of the industry development will evolve towards the lower peak and then that the firms will try to find better products with characteristics closer to the second, higher peak. It is important, and ought to be emphasized, that the firms do not know the shape of the adaptive landscape and the only way to gain knowledge about the local shape of the landscape is to make an experiment, that is, during the R&D process firms evaluate the performance index, that is, the technical competitiveness, of a specific product with assumed values of characteristics.[5] All such experiments made by all firms during the whole period of simulation are marked by dots (pixels) on the background of the adaptive landscape in Figure 7.1. The performance index (that is, technical competitiveness) of products defined by known values of their characteristics marked by dots is known for firms (and only this part of the adaptive landscape is known for individual firms, that is, those firms which make a specific 'experiment'). It may be said that dots mark all inventions found by the firms as the result of R&D process. The number and density of the dots in all three charts in Figure 7.1 also suggest differences in the vigorousness of the search process. Some of the inventions are adopted by firms and become innovations, that is, products offered for sale on the market. Average values of characteristics of products sold on the market at any time t are marked by squares.[6] We say that the average values of product characteristics sold on the market mark the trajectory of industry development in the adaptive landscape.

---

[4] The only reason to assume two characteristics is the convenience of graphical presentation of simulation results; there is no constraint to assume a greater number of characteristics. Findings for the two-dimensional landscape are valid for higher-dimensional ones.

[5] To enable proper evaluation of the simulation results, it is assumed that all firms are able to calculate exact values of the performance index (technical competitiveness). In real processes the accuracy of the performance index evaluation is firm specific and depends on a firm's routines and experience.

[6] The density of the squares also gives a hint on the dynamics of changes: the more distanced the successive squares are, the quicker the changes within the industry.

In the first experiment it was assumed that only mutation acts. The development of each firm is based only on its own knowledge and on autonomous research. The firms evolve almost directly through the shortest way towards the lower peak. The scope of search for invention is not very large (the top chart in Figure 7.1), and the research is focused around local firms' positions in the adaptive landscape. Progress is not very impressive, within the assumed period of simulation firms have not reached even the lower peak, the maximum average value of technical competitiveness is 0.82. If we add the possibility of interchanging knowledge (that is, imitation of innovation) the evolution is slightly quicker, and within the assumed period of simulation the firms reach the lower peak (Figure 7.1, the middle chart). The scope of search is also slightly wider than in the former experiment. Let us note that the trajectories of development in these two experiments significantly differ; the simulation conditions, besides the modes of research, in these experiments are exactly the same. The role of random factors in the development of industry will be investigated more closely in the next chapter; here it will be sufficient to say that even for the same simulation conditions and for such a simple adaptive landscape, the trajectories of development are frequently significantly different for different simulation runs.

Imitation may be based on the knowledge gained through private efforts (that is, by spending some private (individual firm) funds on imitation), and in this way increasing the probability of gaining the relevant knowledge (see equation (7.7)) or through public dissemination of knowledge (in our model parameter b_r in equation (7.7) is responsible for the dissemination of knowledge through public means). It turns out that the type of dissemination of knowledge does not influence significantly the speed of evolution (rates of change of technological competitiveness, productivity of capital or cost of production are very similar in experiments with public and private knowledge, as we call these two runs – see Table 7.1). But the type of dissemination of knowledge greatly influences the structure of industry. Many simulation runs of industrial development suggest that privacy of knowledge leads to much greater concentration of industry (see the relevant average values of Herfindahl firms' number equivalent n_H for imitation with private and public knowledge).[7] A similar tendency towards greater industry concentration is observed if there are some restrictions on imitation, which is clearly seen if we compare values of n_H in experiments with only mutation involved (that is, full privacy of knowledge) and both experiments with mutation and imitation as presented in Table 7.1.

Privacy of knowledge also leads to higher profit. In the absence of

---

[7] In all experiments there are 12 equal firms so the initial Herfindahl firms' number equivalent is 12. As it has been already mentioned, to make the results comparable the entry of new firms in all simulations in this section is prohibited.

imitation leaders of technological advancement 'feel' relatively safe, exploit their temporary monopoly position, and force the higher price of their products, which naturally leads to higher profit. Let us compare two simulation runs, the first with high innovation (mutation) ratio and the second with normal innovation and imitation ratio (see the results of these two runs in Table 7.1). In both cases the tempo of technological advancement is very similar, but the price and profit differ significantly. In the first case the average profit is about 7% and in the second one is slightly over zero. The high profit in the absence of imitation is due to the higher concentration of industry (applying only the results of autonomous research, some firms are not able to keep the pace of technological advancement and are superseded from the market) and is due to the higher products' price imposed by technological leaders to utilize their temporary monopoly positions. In the second case the concentration of industry is not so high; small firms are able to imitate the leaders, but to follow the leaders they are impelled to take credit (and repay it in future). The leaders feel less safe in this situation, and to keep the competitiveness of their products they offer them at a lower price. Therefore all firms, the leaders and followers, are satisfied with smaller profit to maintain their position on the market. In the next section it will be seen how different kinds of innovations – also with a different pace of change, focused on the improvement of technical performance, raising the productivity of capital, or the reduction of the unit costs – influence on the structure of industry; here we note only that rapid technological development leads to much greater industry concentration – compare the values of n_H in experiments with normal and high mutation, and in experiments with recrudescence in Table 7.1.

Greater values of probabilities of mutation and recombination accelerate evolution and lead to a relatively high ratio of technological development, that is, the higher productivity of capital A, the greater technical competitiveness q, and the smaller values of variable cost of production V (Table 7.1), but still do not allow a departure from the lower local peak (local optimum, as it is sometimes called) through finding products with characteristics very close to the higher peak (that is, of global optimum). We use the term 'evolutionary trap' to name the situation of confining the industry in the local, lower peak of the adaptive landscape. Many other simulation runs with different adaptive landscapes let us conclude that neither mutation nor recombination (imitation) allow us to escape from the majority of evolutionary traps. As our simulation experiments reveal, the mechanism of recrudescence makes this escape much easier. In the next simulation experiment this mechanism is added. In the first period (up to 50 years) mutation and imitation act on the normal levels, as in the former experiment, and recrudescence acts rarely ($u_1 = 0.02$). The industry development is similar to that in the previous runs. At $t = 50$ industry is very close to the first lower peak and at this moment we allow recrudescence to act on a much higher level ($u_1 = 0.3$); within 15 years products with characteristics very close to the higher peak are found. At $t = 70$ the probability of recrudescence is reduced to the lower value (0.02). The trajectory of development in this run is shown in the bottom chart of Figure 7.1. The scope of search in this run is much wider than in all previous runs. Far-distanced areas are sampled but most of these attempts are fruitless. Not all far-placed inventions are generated by recrudescence; most of them are the result of a recombination of solutions placed at these two peaks,[8] but what is crucial is that the first inventions placed at the higher peak are always generated by recrudescence and open the way for the recombination of products 'placed' at these two peaks.

It may be said that recrudescence acts as a trigger, initiating the phase of radical transformations. Not all inventions providing better products performance are accepted; frequently modifications of routines which generate technical inventions placed at the higher peak also cause reduction of productivity of capital or a rise in the unit costs, and therefore they are not accepted simply on the basis of economic judgements. The necessity of correlation of technical performance with economic factors (as productivity of capital and costs of production, but also other factors, for example, a firm's current investment capabilities) causes many promising inventions to be rejected by firms, and in practice the probability of the emergence of radical innovation is significantly smaller than the probability of finding radical invention.

The emergence of radical innovation is a kind of leap, a punctuated process, but the shift from the lower to the higher peak is not a sharp (punctuated) process; rather, it is a much more gradual process of shifting the position of the industry in the adaptive landscape. The main reason for this gradualism is that the overall competitiveness of products is the function of the technical competitiveness and the price – see equation (7.10). To keep the overall competitiveness on a relatively high level, firms lower the price of products characterized by smaller technical competitiveness (that is, placed at the lower peak) and vice versa products with higher competitiveness (that is, placed at the higher peak) are slightly more expensive (to gain greater profit), so the values of the overall competitiveness for the products of firms in the vanguard of technological development are only slightly greater than the competitiveness of the old-fashioned products. Therefore the elimination of the worst products from the market is not so sharp as may be expected on the basis of the values of

---

[8] In multi-peak adaptive landscapes, with many diversified industries included, when co-evolution of multi-industry economy is studied, recombination plays a much more important role. Concurrently with recrudescence, inter-industry recombination of routines applied by firms of different industries may cause the emergence of radical innovation within existing industries, or lead to the emergence of new industries not yet present in the economy.

technical competitiveness only. In some circumstances the substitution phase
may last quite a long time, but in all cases we observe the steady tendency
to reduce production of the old-fashioned products and to increase the
production of the modern ones.

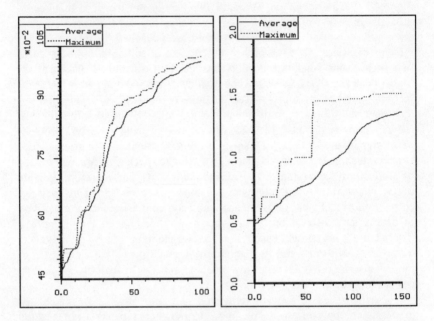

*Figure 7.2. Technical competitiveness in the two runs: mutation and
              imitation (left), and mutation, imitation and recrudescence
              (right)*

The substitution phase (that is, in our simulation passing from the lower
to the higher peak) is much shorter and the process of transformation is
much quicker if the entry of new firms is allowed – numerous runs with free
entry confirm this finding, and the results of some of them are presented in
following sections. The substitution process is also observed within a single
firm – in many cases, when the radical innovation is found the costs of
modernization are normally so huge that even the big firm is not able to
afford it. Stopping the production in the 'old' unit is not economically viable
so the only rational decision is to continue the 'old' production and to open
a new unit with the modern technology already incorporated. In the course
of time the old production is successively reduced and the new one grows.
Usually, in the first phase of substitution within a firm the 'old-fashioned'
production is still profitable and because of the larger volume of the 'old'
production the firm is able to finance the quicker development of the new,
small 'modern' unit from the profit worked out by 'the old-fashioned unit'.

Different modes of innovation search lead to a different evolution of the characteristics of development. In Figure 7.2 the development of technical competitiveness in two runs is presented, that is, (1) only mutation and imitations of routines act (the left-hand chart) and (2) with recrudescence involved (the right-hand chart). If we compare the development in the initial phases of these two runs, when the industry goes towards the first lower peak, it is difficult to detect significant differences in the mean characteristics of development, for example, in the changes of average technical competitiveness. But because of different modes of search for innovation the development of the frontiers of technological development differs significantly. In the case of a search for innovation by applying only mutation and imitation, the development of the technological frontier is more or less gradual (see, for example, the maximum technical competitiveness in the left-hand chart of Figure 7.2).

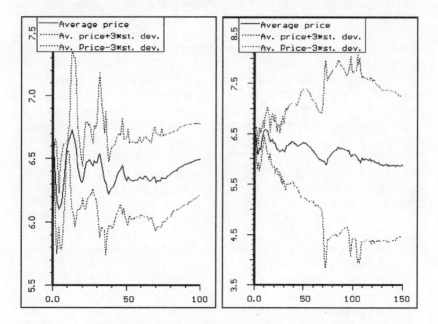

Figure 7.3. Price and its diversity in two runs: mutation and imitation (left), and mutation, imitation and recrudescence (right)

The discrepancy between the frontier and the mean industry development is not very high (the two curves are placed very close). It is not the case if a recrudescence mechanism is involved, where jumps in the development of the technological frontier are clearly visible – see the maximum technical competitiveness in the right-hand chart of Figure 7.2. The jumps are observed on the route towards the local peak (that is, for $t < 50$, which suggests that even if recrudescence acts on the low level it also generates innovations) and also in the transition phase, of passing from the lower to the higher peaks. The discrepancy between the frontier of development and the mean industry development is much more significant in the presence of the recrudescence mechanism.

In Figure 7.3 the changes of the average price and the price diversity for the same two runs as in Figure 7.2 are presented. The structure of the price of the product offered for sale on the market is also affected by technological development. When the rate of improvement is small the diversity of price within the industry is not very high. The standard deviation of price in the case of the modest ('normal') rate of development is about 2%, but the price diversity significantly increases in the case of the emergence of radical innovation: see the right-hand chart of Figure 7.3 for t greater than 50, and also the left-hand chart of the same figure in the periods of significant fluctuations of price and its standard deviation which are correlated with the emergence of significant improvements. Standard deviation of price in the case of the emergence of radical innovation (with recrudescence) is a few times greater than in the case of relatively smooth progress (compare the relevant values of standard deviation presented in Table 7.1). Such structure of price is naturally related to the earlier mentioned strategy of firms producing 'obsolete' products which attempt to keep the overall product competitiveness on a relatively high level, through lowering the price of obsolete products. But high diversity of price is not only the result of a high rate of technological development, it is also the result of privacy of knowledge and barriers to imitation. The standard deviation of price in the experiment with a relatively low rate of technological progress with mutation as the only source of innovation (that is, high privacy of knowledge) is even greater than in the case of quick progress but with a relatively high rate of dissemination ('publicity') of knowledge (compare the results for 'innovation' and 'innovation, imitation, and recrudescence' in Table 7.1).

INNOVATION REGIMES

Three basic kinds of innovation are captured by our model, namely innovations leading to: (1) reduction of the unit cost of production, (2) advancement of the product's technical performance, and (3) increase in the productivity of capital. In general, any real innovation causes changes of all three features of technological development. We are able to control the type of innovations and, for example, to allow the emergence of innovations which cause changes in only one separated feature of progress, and concurrently to keep the other two fixed. Therefore we may speak about three basic modes of technological development; these three modes of development are called 'regimes': the cost regime, the technical performance regime and the capital productivity regime. In this section the influence of these different types of innovation on the development of the industry will be investigated, particularly on the industry concentration and on the product price distribution. As in the preceding section, to make the results comparable it is assumed that there are no new entrants and the competition process is confined to the initial 12 firms. The initial conditions of the simulation are set in such a way that in all the experiments presented in this section the innovation process is a gradual one, without any jumps, that is, recrudescence is not present and no fulguration is observed.

Table 7.2. Price and industry structure in different innovation regimes

	n_H	Π/K %	Price	Price st.dev. %	A max	q max	V min
Variable cost							
normal	7.14	0.617	5.37	1.68	0.100	0.32	2.59
fast	2.33	−0.795	2.73	2.46	0.100	0.32	0.44
Technical performance							
normal	8.90	1.847	6.62	3.44	0.100	0.58	5.00
fast	2.39	10.610	7.42	27.45	0.100	8.49	5.00
fast with							
entrants	9.90	−0.544	6.38	12.91	0.100	14.34	5.00
Productivity of capital							
normal	12.00	1.672	6.10	2.10	0.177	0.32	5.00
fast	11.16	6.932	5.49	4.50	1.160	0.32	5.00
'Complex'							
normal (A)	2.04	3.232	4.12	7.28	0.112	0.64	1.46
normal (B)	9.04	5.883	6.17	4.05	0.175	0.44	4.25
fast (A)	3.10	11.756	4.04	9.15	0.384	0.82	2.60
fast (B)	4.35	0.833	3.30	4.95	0.153	0.92	0.58

Note: values of firms number equivalent n_H, the ratio of Profit/Capital Π/K, and Price are average values during the whole period of simulation from 0 to 100.

The results of this series of experiments are summed up in Table 7.2. In Figure 7.4 the development of the variable cost of production, the technical competitiveness and the productivity of capital in these three regimes for a 'normal' rate of innovation emergence are presented.

In the simulation runs with the reduction of unit cost of production as the only target of innovation activity (technical competitiveness and productivity of capital being constant) two modes of development are distinguished – the normal and the fast ones, related to the rate of cost reduction: in the first run, labelled 'normal', the average annual rate of the unit cost reduction is about 0.6% and in the second run, labelled 'fast', the cost reduction is about 3.5% annually.

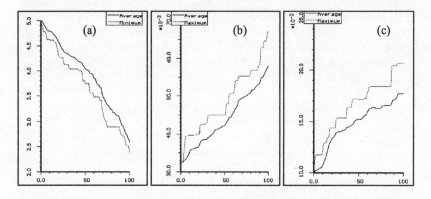

Figure 7.4. Innovation regimes: variable cost of production (a), technical competitiveness (b) and productivity of capital (c)

Reduction of the cost of production also leads to a reduction in price, but the rate of price reduction is much smaller than the rate of cost reduction.

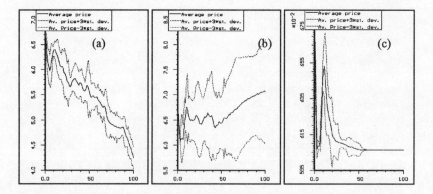

Figure 7.5. Price for different innovation regimes: cost (a), technical performance (b) and productivity (c)

In the case of the normal rate of the cost reduction the price decreases only 0.25% annually (see Figure 7.5(a)); so at the end of the simulation the price margin is significantly higher than at the beginning (the price/cost ratio is equal to 1.7 at the end of the simulation, compared to 1.3 at the beginning); and in the case of the fast rate of cost reduction (3.5% annually) the price is reduced only slightly more than 1.5% annually, and the price margin at the end of the simulation is 3.2. Such a pattern of price development is understandable in the light of the simulation results presented in Chapter 6 (page 124) related to the study of industry behaviour for different values of the cost ratio. If we reduce the unit cost of production, keeping the productivity of capital constant, we also reduce the cost ratio. As is seen in Figure 6.9, in the course of diminishing values of cost ratio the price margin rises, and this tendency is observed in the simulations with the cost regime – the price ratio is significantly higher at the end of the simulation than it is at the beginning.

A reduction of the cost of production narrows the possibilities for the 'obsolete' firms to apply relevant strategies to keep the pace forced by the leaders. The possibility of making the obsolete products more competitive through price reduction is very limited, so the non-innovators and firms which are not able to imitate the innovation and reduce the costs of production within a relatively short period are quickly eliminated from the market. The Herfindahl firms' number equivalent in this experiment is reduced from the initial 12 firms to four firms at the end of the simulation (average value of n_H is equal to 7.14 firms).

Heavy cost reduction rate, as in the fast mode, leads to much quicker elimination of 'obsolete' competitors from the market. At the end of the simulation run the Herfindahl firms' number equivalent is equal to 1.06 (there is one big firm and two very small competitors – the average n_H number equivalent is equal to 2.33 in this run).

Because of the strong tendency towards high industry concentration and the very limited possibility for the 'obsolete' firms to choose a relevant price strategy, the price diversity in the cost regime is not very high – the average standard deviation is equal to 1.68% in the first experiment and 2.46% in the second one (Table 7.2 and Figure 7.5(a)).

In contrast to the situation in the cost regime, the possibilities of choosing a relevant price policy to keep the position on the market are much wider in the case of innovations leading to an improvement of the product's technical performance. Reduction of the price compensates for the temporal technical backwardness of the product and allows the overall competitiveness of obsolete products to be kept almost at the same level as the advanced ones. This prolongs the period for followers to imitate the technology leader. In the technical regime, two modes of development are also tested: normal with the average annual rate of technical competitiveness about 0.7%, and the fast one, with the annual growth of the technical competitiveness equal to 3.2%. The price policy of technological leaders in the technical performance regime helps their followers to maintain the pace of technological progress. The leaders increase the price slightly to attain a higher profit – they choose the strategy of balanced price rising, to gain higher profit, and concurrently to keep the overall competitiveness of their products at a relatively high level. So in the technical regime two opposite tendencies concerning the price policy are observed – a reduction of the price by followers (to raise their product competitiveness and to keep their place on the market) and an increase in the price by the leaders (to gain higher profit from their temporary 'monopoly position'). This leads to a much higher diversity of price in these two innovation regimes – compare the two diagrams in Figure 7.5(a) and (b). The average standard deviation of price in the run with the normal rate of growth of technical competitiveness is 3.44%, that is, slightly more than twice the relevant value in the first experiment in the cost regime, and it is over 27% for the fast rate of technical competitiveness. Price fluctuations in the first phase of development (Figure 7.5(b)) are due to the above-mentioned interplay of the two different price policies. The steady growth of the average price in the second phase of development (after $t = 50$) is due to higher concentration of the industry.

If the conditions for pure competition are provided (for example, through allowing free entry of new firms) the price fluctuates around the equilibrium value, as it does in the initial phase (up to $t = 50$) of the simulation run presented in Figure 7.5(b). So it may be said that in contrast to the steady trend of price diminishing as observed in the cost regime no such mode of price development is observed in the technical regime – many simulation runs confirm the finding that fluctuations of price around the equilibrium value are a typical pattern of development in the technical regime. Rapid technical progress leads to much greater concentration of the industry – for 'normal' technical improvement the average value of the Herfindahl firms' number equivalent is 8.9 firms, but for rapid technical progress this number is 2.39. The price diversity in this run is almost eight times greater than for the normal rate of change of technical competitiveness (over 27%).

If we compare the modes of development in the cost regime and the technical regime, we then see that the cost reduction leads to relatively high concentration of the industry, high price reduction and a relatively small diversity of price, and almost opposite tendencies are observed in the technical regime – smaller concentration, almost no price reduction (in the long-term perspective) and high diversity of price.

In contrast to the two discussed regimes, the capital productivity regime may be called neutral. Even a high rate of productivity growth does not lead to large industry concentration. For 'a normal' rate of the productivity growth (0.6% annually) the concentration of industry is all the time almost the same (the Herfindahl number equivalent in the whole period of simulation is very close to 12 – see Table 7.2), and even a relatively high rate of the productivity change leads only to slightly greater concentration (for almost 4% annual growth of the productivity of capital the average Herfindahl number is 11.32, that is, very close to the initial 12 firms). The strategy of productivity improvement seems to be a rather ineffective weapon to eliminate competitors from the market although it provides comparably good economic effects, for example, the profit is almost the same as in the case of the technical regime and even slightly larger than in the case of the cost regime (see Table 7.2). But as was observed in numerous simulation runs, cost reduction (especially very rapid) leads to much higher concentration of the market and enables us to gain larger profit due to a (temporary) monopoly position on the market.

The results of simulation runs of the productivity regime seem to be fully consistent with the statistical analysis of economic growth made in the 1950s (see page 71). From this point of view our model and simulation results may hint of explanations for the results of this statistical study, particularly for the results which are in evident conflict with the neoclassical view of growth along the production function – that the ratio of capital engaged to the volume of production is constant during the analysed period. As Kaldor (1985, p. 64) writes about 'one of the best established "stylised facts" of capitalist development: that while the capital/labour ratio is rising more or less in proportion to productivity, and it is highest amongst the richest nations and lowest among the poorest, the capital/output ratio is much the same as between poor and rich countries – it is no higher in America ... than it is in India.' This view is also supported by the results of simulation runs with a so-called 'complex' innovation regime, that is, in which simulation conditions are created in such a way that routine modifications influence concurrently the unit cost of production, the product's technical performance and the productivity of capital.

A number of simulation runs for the 'complex' regime were done and a large spectrum of behaviour was observed; the results of four of them are presented in Table 7.2. Random factors play an essential role in this regime; frequently an innovation generated at the beginning of the simulation decides on the future path of development for the whole industry (that is, this innovation creates a chreod, in the terminology of Waddington). We rarely observe harmonious development leading to moderate rates of improvement of the productivity of capital (A), the technical competitiveness (q) and reduction of the unit cost of production (V). The main reason is that the probability of the emergence of innovation which enables simultaneous reduction of the cost of production, increase of the technical competitiveness and the productivity of capital is very small. The most typical situation is that firms find inventions enabling an advance of only one of these features (either q, V or A), and the two other features are improved in succeeding stages of development of the basic innovation as a result of future research efforts leading to improvements of that basic innovation. The most frequent mode of development is that firms accept much more eagerly inventions leading to cost reduction and/or to rising technical competitiveness. The productivity of capital is frequently kept almost at the same level. The results of such typical situations are presented in Table 7.2 (the 'complex' regime labelled normal (A)) and in Figure 7.6.

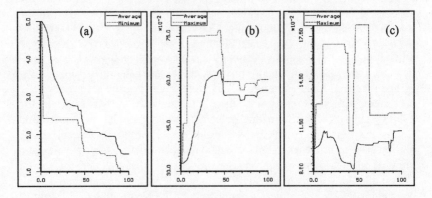

*Figure 7.6. Variable cost of production (a), technical competitiveness (b)
and productivity of capital (c) in the 'complex' regime*

An average productivity of capital (equal to 0.11) is only slightly greater than the initial value (0.10), but development of the productivity of capital is not static, and as we see in Figure 7.6(c) it fluctuates. The fluctuations of the productivity of capital, as well as the cost of production and technical competitiveness, are due to the intertwined (pleiotropic) character of the impact of innovation on industry development in the complex regime. In the initial phase of development cost reduction and improvement of technical performance are observed (Figure 7.6(a) and (b)). At the end of the fourth decade an invention reducing significantly the cost of production is found. But reduction of the unit cost of production in that invention is coupled with a decrease in technical competitiveness; nevertheless the invention is accepted purely for economic reasons. As it turned out it was very difficult to improve the technical performance starting from that formerly accepted innovation. In the second half of the simulation period the firms' innovative efforts are concentrated on the cost reduction and the technical competitiveness is kept almost constant. If we compare the results of the former ('pure') innovation regimes with the results of the 'complex' regime we see a much higher discrepancy between the frontier of technological development (as measured by the maximum of technical competitiveness, the maximum productivity of capital, and the minimum of the unit cost of production) and the average performance of the industry.

Analysis of the simulation results for the complex regime suggests that there is no stable pattern of behaviour, random factors play an essential role and the behaviour of industry (for example, such characteristics as profit/capital rate, industry concentration and price diversity), depends strongly on a prevailing innovation regime, for example, if, due to purely random factors, R&D efforts result in the emergence of innovation reducing the unit cost then we observe higher industry concentration, but if due to random factors the technical regime prevails, then we may observe greater diversity of price and a smaller tendency towards higher industry concentration. Random factors influence not only the modes of development of some industry characteristics, but as will be seen in the next chapter, they also play an essential role in the structural development of the whole industry.

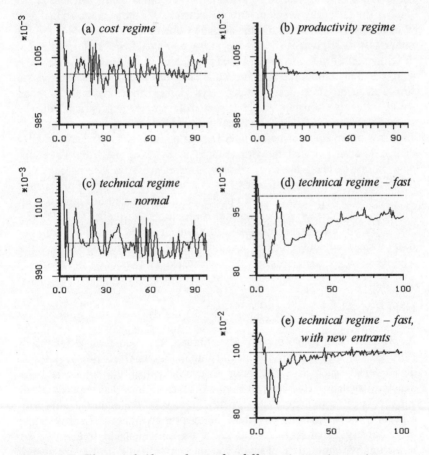

Figure 7.7. The supply/demand ratio for different innovation regimes

The simulation results for different innovative regimes have revealed an interesting property of the industry development related to the supply and demand balance. For the cost regime and for the productivity regime the supply to demand ratio fluctuates around the equilibrium value (see Figure 7.7(a) and (b)), and the mode of the S/D ratio development does not depend on the rate of change. From the qualitative point of view the picture is almost the same for low, moderate and high rates of innovation. An average value of the S/D ratio for these two regimes is always slightly above one (for example, for the cost regime (fast) it is equal to 1.0014). A very similar picture of development is seen for low and moderate (labelled normal) rates of growth of technical competitiveness (see Figure 7.7(c)), the average value of S/D in the whole period of simulation is equal to 1.0003. But, for some reason, for fast technical development instability of the supply and demand occurs. The value of the S/D ratio drops below one and is the smaller the faster the development, for example, for the average annual rate of development equal to 1.5% the average value of the S/D is 0.984, and for rather fast development (3.2%) the average value of S/D ratio is 0.927 – development of the ratio in this case is presented in Figure 7.7(d). To make supply and demand more balanced an attempt has been made to change the firm's decision strategies in many ways (for example, by making much stronger the relationship of the expected development of price with the current imbalance of supply and demand) and the results were always very similar – the average value of the S/D ratio is always significantly smaller than one. It seems that the firms act so as to leave the 'free place' for newcomers, to make the entry of new firms easier. And it turns out to be true – the situation is significantly better if we allow the entry of new firms. The development of the S/D ratio in this case is presented in Figure 7.7(e). The average value of S/D in this run is significantly smaller (0.983). The free entry of new competitors also causes much quicker recovery from the deep imbalance and quicker development of the industry towards the equilibrium.

ENTRY AND THE INDUSTRY STRUCTURE

As we have seen in the previous experiments, the acquiescence for firms' entry greatly influences the values of important characteristics of industry development, such as profit, price structure, and of the supply and the demand balance (Table 7.2 and Figure 7.7). It follows that opportunity of entry of new competitors also greatly influences the industry structure, especially in the periods of radical innovation emergence. To investigate how industry structure is formed under the conditions of free entry, the following two simulation runs with specific initial conditions were prepared. In both runs, in the first phase of simulation (that is, up to $t = 30$) only incremental innovations are introduced (that is, they cause only moderate: reduction in the cost of production, increase in technical competitiveness and rise in the productivity of capital). In the 30th year the recrudescence mechanism of innovation generation is activated. In effect, radical innovation emerges followed by a quick and significant reduction in the cost of production, a rise in the technical competitiveness and a rise in the productivity of capital within the whole industry. Conditions of simulation in the two runs were prepared in such a way that in both experiments the changes of the three characteristics of industry development are very similar, as presented in Figure 7.8.

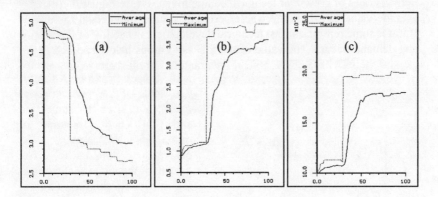

Figure 7.8. Cost of production (a), technical competitiveness (b) and productivity of capital (c) in the 'no entry–free entry' experiment

It is true that the emergence of such radical innovation in real industrial processes is a very improbable phenomenon, but to see more clearly the impact of innovation on the development of the industry, such extremely radical innovation emergence was intentionally forced. The only difference in the initial conditions created in these two runs is that in the first simulation run no entry of new firms is allowed, in contrast to the second run where the free entry of new competitors is enabled.

Naturally, the first difference in the industrial development of these two runs lies in the number of firms and firms' units, which is presented in Figure 7.9. If no entry is allowed (the upper chart) all 12 initial firms are present in the market up to $t = 65$, but from that year more and more firms are eliminated from the market, so at the end of the simulation only two of them are present. Diversification of the industry structure due to emergence of innovations is observed from the beginning of the simulation, but in the first phase of development, that is, when only incremental innovations emerge, the diversification is relatively small and the concentration grows only gradually (see n_H – the Herfindahl firms' number equivalent in the upper chart). With the four-years' delay, after the emergence of the radical innovation, a significant diversification of firms' size is observed, no firm is eliminated but some of them have significant shares of the market so the

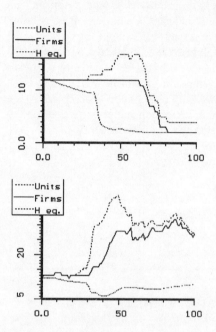

concentration grows very quickly. The radical innovation also causes the emergence of multi-unit firms – as can be seen in the upper chart from $t = 30$ more and more firms become multi-unit operations (there were up to 16 units present). Even at the end of the simulation, when only two firms compete on the market, each firm has two units. The bulk of the production is made in the modern units but still a small fraction of production is based on the obsolete technologies.[9] The growth of the number of firms in the free entry simulation run is presented in the bottom chart of Figure 7.9. In the first phase of development of the industry new firms enter the market only incidentally. But following the emergence of radical innovation, firms grow very quickly in number, up to the maximum of 32 firms. Concurrently with the growth of the number of firms a similar increase in the number of units is observed (there are a maximum of 41 units). At the end of the simulation 28 firms are present on the market. Some of the initial firms adopt the new technology, open new units, and are present on the market up

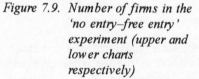

Figure 7.9. Number of firms in the 'no entry–free entry' experiment (upper and lower charts respectively)

---

[9] The exact values at the end of the simulation are as follows: for the largest firm (no. 10), the market share in the global production of the modern unit is 45.2% and the price of the product 5.67 (the overall competitiveness of the modern production is 0.1222), in the 'obsolete' unit 6.3% of the global production is made, and the price of the product is much lower – 3.25 (but because of the lower price the overall competitiveness is only slightly smaller than the modern production, 0.115), for the second largest firm (no. 1) the relevant values are very similar, the market share of the modern unit is 42.4% and the product price 5.7 (the overall competitiveness is 0.1218), in the 'obsolete' unit 6.1% of the global production is made, and the product price is 3.15 (the overall competitiveness is 0.114).

to the end of the simulation, but the majority of the original firms are eliminated from the market, so at the end of the simulation the number of units is very close to the number of firms. Diversification of the industry in the first phase of development is very similar to that in the run with no entry; since the emergence of the radical innovation a similar tendency towards higher concentration is also observed, but because of the increasing number of successful entrants the concentration is never as high as in the former run – the minimum Herfindahl index in this run is equal to six firms. At about $t = 40$ the process of concentration growth is stopped and since that moment a steady tendency towards pure competition is observed. At the end of the simulation the Herfindahl index of concentration is equal to ten firms, that is, five times greater than in the run with no entry.

Table 7.3.   The 'no entry–free entry' experiment

	n_H	Π/K	Price	Price st.dev.	A	q	V
		%		%	max	max	min
no entry							
0–100	3.08	14.30	5.67	11.64	0.18	3.60	2.99
95–100	2.00	26.48	5.37	15.21	0.18	3.60	2.90
free entry							
0–100	9.04	0.23	4.88	8.92	0.17	3.69	3.12
95–100	10.12	0.31	4.01	6.37	0.17	3.70	3.12

The shares of the eight largest firms in both simulation runs, which are presented in Figure 7.10, also give some view on the development of the structure of industry. As was mentioned before (Figure 7.9, Table 7.3, and footnote 9) at the end of simulation the Herfindahl firms' number equivalent in the run with no entry is equal to two, and these two firms which survived are labelled 1 and 10 (see the left-hand chart in Figure 7.10). What needs to be noted is that these two firms were not the biggest ones just at the moment of emergence of radical innovation, in fact both firms were steadily eliminated from the market (see the first phase of industry development in the left-hand chart of Figure 7.10). The innovation was discovered by firm 1 and applied at $t = 30$; the fact that the radical innovation was invented by small firms is partly due to our assumption that the probability of the emergence of radical innovation is greater for small firms. The reward for being the first innovator is greater profit and the largest share on the market. The only firm which successfully adopted new technology and followed the first innovator is firm 10; all other firms, in spite of their relative advantages at the moment of emergence of radical innovation, are eliminated from the market. So at the end of the simulation the industry represents the case of classical duopoly.

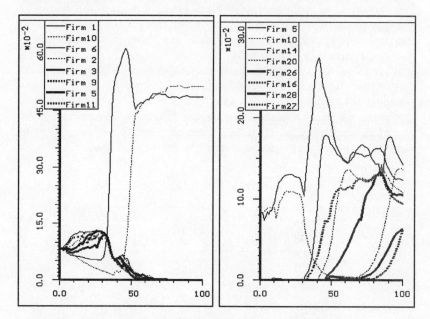

Figure 7.10. Market shares of the eight largest firms in the 'no entry–free entry' experiment

The picture is radically different in the case of free entry. The first firm which applied the radical innovation in this run is firm 5 (the right-hand chart in Figure 7.10), some other firms quickly adopted this innovation, but as it turned out all the 'old' firms are eliminated from the market and their places are captured by newcomers.[10]

As a result of stronger competition the old firms are quickly eliminated from the market, so within the eight largest firms operating on the market at the end of simulation there is only one old firm (that is, the founder of the advanced technology, firm 5). The distribution of firms' shares at the end of the simulation is almost balanced and the Herfindahl number equivalent is equal to 10.12 at the end of simulation – see Table 7.3; the share of the largest firm in the last year is about 15%, five other firms have only slightly smaller shares (from 9% to 14%), and late followers have

---

[10] The firm labelled 10 at the end of the simulation, in the right-hand chart, is in fact the new firm, the old firm with the same label 10 was eliminated from the market at $t = 59$, and its place is occupied by a new firm which entered the market at $t = 68$ – in fact this new firm becomes the second largest firm with a share only slightly smaller than that of the leader.

shares of about 7%, but, because of small improvements introduced by them, their shares grow significantly quicker than those of all other firms. Up to the moment of the emergence of radical innovation the supply and the demand are almost balanced in both simulation runs (see Figure 7.11). Emergence of the radical innovation also causes a rapid increase in technical competitiveness. As has been shown in the previous section with the simulation of the technical performance regime, the quick growth of technical competitiveness causes a large imbalance of the supply and the demand (see Figure 7.7(d) and (e)). This imbalance is also observed in the two discussed simulation runs after the emergence of the radical innovation. If no new competitors enter the market we observe a kind of stabilization of the supply-demand imbalance at the level of 3% (the S/D ratio is about 0.97 – see the upper chart of Figure 7.11) but if the entry of new firms is allowed we observe a tendency toward balancing the supply and demand (bottom chart of Figure 7.11 after $t = 40$). The average value of the S/D ratio after the emergence of radical innovation is 95.9% in the no-entry run and 99.1% in the free-entry run. The

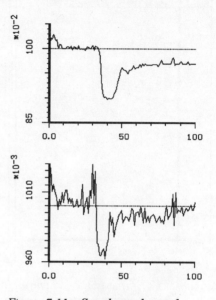

Figure 7.11. Supply to demand ratio in the 'no entry–free entry' experiment (upper and lower charts respectively)

possibility of free entry also causes much smaller maximal imbalance just after the emergence of radical innovation. The minimum value of the S/D ratio is equal to 90% if no competitors enter the market and is equal to 96% if free entry is allowed.

The free entry also causes a different development of price and its structure within the industry (Table 7.3). In both runs the price is only slightly reduced in the first phase of development, because of an incremental reduction of the unit cost of production (see both charts in Figure 7.12). The emergence of radical innovation causes significant reduction in the unit cost of production and as might be expected this ought to result in the parallel significant reduction of the price. The process of price reduction occurs in the first years after the emergence of radical innovation, but because of a higher concentration of the industry it is stopped in the run with no entry allowed.

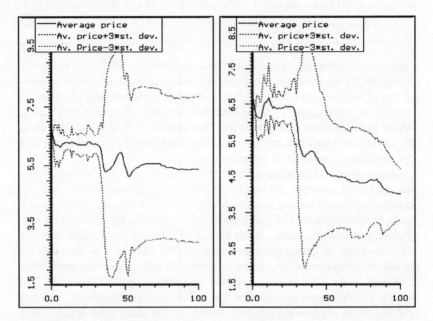

Figure 7.12.   Price in the 'no entry –free entry' experiment (left and right charts respectively)

The tendency towards price reduction caused by the cost reduction is neutralized by the reverse tendency towards greater industry concentration. It is not the case in the simulation with free entry allowed, where the price is quickly reduced in the first period after the emergence of radical innovation and continues to be reduced (although not so quickly) in the following decades because of incremental reduction in the unit cost of production and more competitive conditions on the market (smaller concentration of the industry). Emergence of the radical innovation also causes a significant increase in the diversity of price. In the simulation with no entry the high diversity occurs just after the emergence of the innovation and is kept almost on the same level during the following whole period up to the end of the simulation (see left-hand chart of Figure 7.12). In contrast to the conservation of the structure of prices within industry in the case of no entry the continuous tendency to reduce the diversity of price is observed if free entry is allowed (the right-hand chart in Figure 7.12; compare also the relevant values of the standard deviation of price in Table 7.3).

8. Chance and Necessity in Economic Development

Cumulative causation,[1] path-dependence and irreversibility are immanent properties of all evolutionary processes. These phenomena are frequently observed in the behaviour of models rooted in the evolutionary *episteme*, in contrast to 'mechanistic', general equilibrium models of neoclassical theory, which excludes these phenomena from the domain of its research. The ideas of cumulative causation and irreversibility have long been contrasted with the equilibrium analysis of orthodoxy.

The problem of path-dependence in economics was first recognized by the physicist Joseph Bertrand (in 1883), who discovered that, if out-of-equilibrium trading is incorporated into the Walrasian model, then it leads to indeterminate and path-dependent results that are inconsistent with Walras's general approach. In his essay (1934), Nicholas Kaldor also saw the possibility of path-dependence in economic models. The idea that the future development of an economic system is affected by the path it has followed in the past is now accepted by many economic theorists. This contrasts with the mechanical view that, within well-defined limits, from any starting point, a given system will develop to the same equilibrium – thus from the mechanistic-neoclassical viewpoint real time and history could be excluded from consideration. The development of modern mathematics, especially the study of non-linear dynamic models, has attracted the attention of many economists and put path-dependence back on the agenda of economic analysis, even for orthodox theorists.

One interesting case of path-dependence of current interest is the idea of 'lock-in' (for example, Arthur, 1988, 1989) which states that with increasing returns, for instance, the more a technology is adopted the more it will be improved and be productive. Arthur (1988) points out five particularly important sources of 'increasing return to adoption', namely learning by using, network externalities, scale economies in production, informational increasing returns and technological interrelatedness. As Arthur (1988, p. 597) states, to observe the lock-in phenomena two properties ought to be preserved: '(i) that choices between alternative technologies are affected by the number of each alternative present in the adoption market at the time of

---

[1] Cumulative causation was frequently mentioned by Thorstein Veblen (1899) and was developed later on by Gunnar Myrdal (1939, 1957), William Kapp (1976) and Nicholas Kaldor (1966, 1972, 1978, 1985).

choice; equivalently, that choices are affected by current market shares; (ii) that small events outside the model may influence the process'.

Irreversibility was recognized as an important feature of physical systems by Ludwig Boltzmann (in 1872), and later this idea was developed by the founders of quantum mechanics, and adopted by chemists (dissipative structures). Georgescu-Roegen (1971) points out that it is useless to model social or economic processes by means of mathematical models which entail reversible time. In his opinion, the social sciences could gain much profit in understanding socio-economic phenomena by making closer analogies between such phenomena and the irreversible processes of thermodynamics or biological evolution.

The phenomena of cumulative causation, path-dependence and irreversibility are observed in the behaviour of our model in the presence of innovation. They appear to be natural phenomena, being the result of the evolutionary and self-organizational mechanisms embedded in the model. An emergence (fulguration) of significant innovation gives rise to the specific course of future development and closes many other possible alternatives existing until then (see page 185). Frequently in the behaviour of our model we observe that the technology adopted, which by pure chance focuses, for example, on improving the technological performance, hampers the further emergence of innovations aimed at reducing the unit costs and/or improving the productivity; and vice versa, sometimes a specific set of routines allows for the technological performance index to be radically improved on one occasion and then blocks any further improvements of that technology, but paves the way to a change (chreod) in which the reduction of cost or increase of productivity of capital is the definitive effect of research (compare the results presented in the previous chapter of the simulation related to the modes of search and the innovation regimes). Basically, the course of events in our model depends primarily on the past evolution of the pool of routines within the whole industry, and the past evolution of the set of routines of an individual firm. A specific role in determining the course of evolution is played by the latent routines which are beyond the action of the selective forces. Therefore, the contents of the set of latent routines of each firm strongly depend on random factors and the past interaction of a firm with all other economic agents (competitors, cooperators, public institutions, university research units, and so on). The phenomena of path-dependence and irreversibility as observed in our model are an outcome of cooperation between the search mechanisms built into the model (mutation–innovation, recombination–imitation and recrudescence, see Chapter 7) and selection mechanisms (presented in Chapter 5).

As has been mentioned in the discussion on search mechanisms (innovation strategies – page 173), the path along which an industry develops strongly depends on the modes of search for innovation. All the results of model simulation support the general finding related to path-dependence that the path of development is always historical and unique. Even if we provide exactly the same simulation conditions and make numerous simulation runs for those conditions, the probability of developing along the same path is almost zero. In this sense uniqueness of development in our model represents a natural property observed in the real processes of socio-economic development.

We may consider the development of socio-economic processes on at least two levels: the level of routines (that is, hereditary information) and the level of aggregated characteristics of development (in our model – the productivity of capital, the unit cost of production and the technical characteristics of products). We have to deal with the problem of path-dependence and irreversibility on these two levels.

Our simulation runs reveal that the indeterminacy of the trajectory of development strongly depends on the dimensions of the adaptive landscape. Even for a very simple, stable adaptive landscape with only one peak, when the final target is predetermined, the path of reaching the peak is highly indeterminate for a relatively large number of technical characteristics. For two or three characteristics the path is almost always along the shortest way from the current position of an industry to the peak, only slightly deviating from it. But for more than five characteristics the scope of search for innovation is much larger; the set of inventions with the same adaptive value is so expanded that the probability of the same innovation emerging in different runs is very small. For a high-dimensional adaptive landscape, the development of industry along the path traced by the shortest way to the adaptive peak is very rare. In all our simulations the path looks rather like a zigzag or a winding road. Frequently the future path is predetermined just at the beginning of the simulation run. It is difficult to represent graphically, in our three-dimensional world, the industry trajectory traced in high-dimensional adaptive landscapes. To show how big the deviations of trajectories are in different simulation runs let us take, for example, the values of the characteristics in the middle of the route obtained in four runs (two for the two-dimensional adaptive landscape and two for the seven-dimensional landscape). Besides the dimensionality of the adaptive landscape, the conditions of simulation in all four runs are the same; in particular there is only one peak, the initial values of all technical characteristics are equal to zero and the target characteristics (that is, the coordinates of the peak) are all equal to one. For a two-dimensional adaptive landscape the deviations of the average values of characteristics in the middle of the route are not significant, they are equal to (0.48, 0.45) in the first run, and (0.47, 0.52) in the second one. In the seven-dimensional adaptive landscape the deviations are much more significant, and the relevant values are equal to (0.21, 0.57, 0.59, 0.32, 0.75, 0.64, 0.47) in the first run, and (0.49, 0.69, 0.53, 0.42, 0.52, 0.37, 0.43) in the second one.

At any time the whole population of products sold on the market may also be characterized by their distribution within the space of product characteristics. Besides the above-mentioned significant deviations of average values of relevant product characteristics for a high-dimensional adaptive landscape, we also observe a much greater dispersion of each characteristic within the population of products in each simulation run. The population of products may be represented at any time as a multidimensional cloud (or clouds) of different density; it may be said that the more dimensional the adaptive landscape is, the greater the relative size of the cloud.[2]

But even for small-dimensional adaptive landscapes we observe an immense indeterminacy of development on the routine level. In all evolutionary processes a dimension of the hereditary (in our case routines) space is much greater than the dimension of the phenotype space. This property implies that the same set of phenotypes (characteristics) may be fulfilled by different sets of routines.

This means that even for two- or three-dimensional adaptive landscapes, when the paths (trajectories) of development are more or less similar, the development on the routine level is highly heterogeneous. There is no space (or necessity) to write out all 50 values of routines (as we have done in our simulations) for different simulation runs, but we should say that for the same simulation conditions a large spectrum of the modes of development is observed on the routine level. In some experiments most of the routines are subject to evolution but in the majority of experiments the whole set of routines is divided into two subsets: the subset of highly conservative routines (that is, their values are not changed during the whole period of the simulation) and the subset of highly evolving routines. What is important is that the contents of the conservative and evolving subsets of routines significantly vary in different runs. One may get an impression that at some moment (or in a very short period) in the initial phase of industry development random factors control the process of choosing the sets of evolving and conservative routines, and from that moment the mode of development at the routine level seems to be highly predetermined. The predetermination of development and the heterogeneity of development also depend on the modes of search for innovation. The heterogeneity of development is much smaller if only mutation and low recombination are involved in the innovative process, and is much greater if transposition, transition and recrudescence act. If recrudescence is in action, then the predetermination of development occurs frequently in the phases of emergence of radical innovations. Random factors play an essential role during these crucial periods and in fact it is almost impossible to predict what kind of innovation will emerge, what values of technical characteristics or what combination of unit cost of production, productivity of capital and technical competitiveness there will be after the emergence of the radical

---

[2] Measured, for example, as an average value of the dispersions of all technical characteristics.

innovation. It seems possible to predict, albeit in some cases with considerable inaccuracy, the development of aggregate values of some characteristics of development (for example, average values of the technical characteristics, the average values of the price, the unit cost of production or the profit) but only if the industry develops along the slope towards the nearest, local adaptive peak. Prediction of development in the long perspective, in the multidimensional adaptive landscape with numerous peaks, is a futile task. As an example the results of development in a multi-peak, stable adaptive landscape will be given. For convenience of presentation the landscape is only two-dimensional.

It ought to be kept in mind that in real processes the conditions are much more complex – the landscape is multidimensional, with a very large number of peaks, and dynamic, that is, the surface of the landscape is changing all the time, some of the peaks disappear, some lose their importance and some new ones emerge. But it will be seen that even for this simple adaptive landscape the development of our artificial reality (as simulated by the computer) is much diversified, unpredictable and path-dependent. Over 50 simulation runs for the adaptive landscape, presented in Figure 8.1, were made. There are no two identical trajectories within all 50 simulation runs, but it is possible to distinguish a few types of trajectories (the eight representative trajectories are presented in Figure 8.1). As we see there are six peaks in the landscape: the three lowest are on the left and at the bottom of the map, the highest peak is on the right, and two middle peaks are placed in the centre of the map. In all eight runs the simulation conditions are exactly the same, particularly the starting point in the adaptive landscape (the initial location of the industry is on the left of the map, between the two low peaks). From the initial industry location three distinguishable varieties of trajectory development are recognized. The first two are towards the two nearest peaks (as in Figure 8.1(a) and (b)) and the third one is the route between the two lowest peaks towards the middle ones (as in Figure 8.1(c)). The route of future development is predetermined in the early stages of industry development. After 'choosing' the route towards the lowest peak (upper left), initiating the evolution in that direction, it is almost impossible to reverse the course of development, for example, towards the second lowest peak (that is, that in the lower left corner on the map). But even for very similar trajectories the differences and the deviations are clearly visible, for example, the trajectories in Figure 8.1(a), (f), (g) and (h) with the same tendency towards the lowest peak in the initial phase of development.

For the routes quite similar in the first phase of development the further development is still not predetermined – in four runs the firms reached the lowest peak, but from this position the future course of development is still open – it may reach one of the middle peaks and stay there for a long time (as in Figure 8.1(a) and (f)) or pass through one of the middle peaks and

next reach the highest adaptive peak (as in Figure 8.1(g) and (h)). But once
the way of development from the lowest peak is chosen, the future route is
said to be almost predetermined, with only relatively small deviations of
trajectories between different runs being detected (similar to those in the
initial phase of development towards the lowest peak, as in Figure 8.1(a),
(f), (g) and (h)).

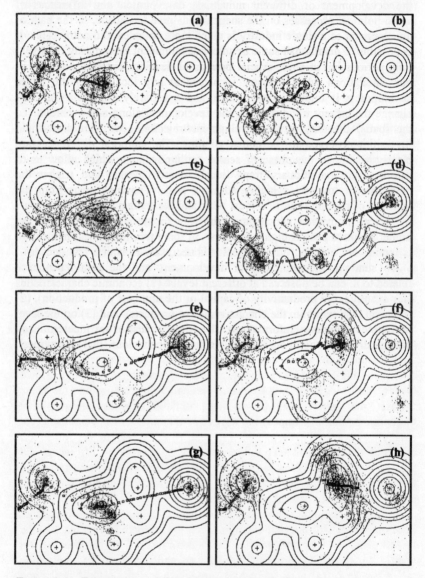

Figure 8.1. Trajectories of development and path-dependence

The same indeterminacy of future development, in spite of similarities in the first phase of development, is observed for two other initial modes of development – compare Figure 8.1(b) and (d), and Figure 8.1(c) and (e).

The results presented above are obtained for very simple and almost artificial conditions. In real socio-economic processes the conditions are much more complicated due, for example, to mutual dependencies between the development of different industries, co-evolution and influences of socio-political processes on the shape of adaptive landscape, so the path of development of a single industry is much more complex and untraceable. It is possible to distinguish some trends of development even during relatively long periods but at some crucial periods of development (for example, in our simulations when industry is placed at any local peak) the future development is highly indeterminate, and any purely random event may change the current trend, causing the development along a new chreod. To the spatial diversity of the development trajectories we should also add diversities observed in the course of time. The temporal differences are clearly visible in the phase of search for innovations which allow us to escape from evolutionary traps (local adaptive peaks) and trigger the development towards a higher adaptive peak. The time span from the moment of reaching the first local peak and the moment of the emergence of radical innovation which paves the way for development towards the higher adaptive peak is highly random – in some runs the radical innovation is found very quickly, but in others it is necessary to wait a few decades.

To sum up, indeterminacy of development, and the path-dependence related to it, can be observed at different levels: (1) economic characteristics (for example, the productivity of capital or the unit cost of production), (2) technical (for example, the characteristics of products), and (3) on the level of routines (hereditary information). The primary cause of any indeterminacy is naturally a change in our knowledge and our behaviour (that is, routines).

Appendix
Basic Values of the Model Parameters

The study of the model is based on computer simulation. In all experiments presented in the book, only one or two parameters are varied (that is, deviate from their basic values) in each series of experiments, all other parameter values being constant. Wherever possible the values of the model parameters were estimated on the basis of data of real industrial processes development. Because of the unavailability of real data, some of the values, especially the parameters relating to the search process, were chosen so as to get plausible results. The values of all parameters are typical of standard industry. The estimated values presented below form the so-called basic values of the model parameters.

It is assumed that at the initial moment ($t = 0$) there are 12 firms ($n = 12$) and the supply and demand are fully balanced. The parameters of the demand function are: the initial market size $N = 3,000$, no growth of the market size is assumed, so $\gamma = 0$, and the elasticity of the average price is $\beta = -0.30$.

The constant unit cost of production is equal to zero, $\eta = 0$.

No economies of scale are assumed, so $a = 0$, $b = 0$ in the function $v(Q)$.

The initial unit variable cost of production $V = 5.0$ and the initial product price is 6.80, so the initial margin of price is equal to 36%.

The elasticity of price in the competitiveness $\alpha = 2$.

The normal rate of return $\rho = 5\%$.

The credit rate is assumed to be lower than the interest rate, $\rho_1 = 3\%$.

The SV investment strategy for all firms with the average repay period $\mu_1 = 10$ years and the credit parameter $\mu_0 = 2.0$.

The fraction of firm's profit conveyed for saving, $ToSave = 1$.

The initial debt of all initial firms as well as all firms entering the market is equal to zero.[1]

---

[1] The positive initial debt has no essential influence on the behaviour of industry with a few big firms (monopoly, duopoly or oligopoly) because of a relatively large equilibrium price margin. For greatly concentrated industries the debt is quickly repaid from current firms' profits. For poorly concentrated industries (pure competition) positive profit means that at an initial phase of industry development firms are forced to set a higher price in order to repay their debt. In the succeeding phase industry develops as in the case of no initial debt, that is, firms reduce the price to its relatively small margin, and zero profit in equilibrium.

The equilibrium price for 12 firms (pure competition) for the base parameter values is equal to 6.5; if we assume the initial debt to equal 50% of the initial capital, the firms raise the price within the first five years of development up to 8.1 for $\mu_1 = 2$ years, (for a longer repayment period, for example, $\mu_1 = 5$ and $\mu_1 = 10$ years the maximum price is slightly lower – 7.4 and 7.0,

Besides the series of experiments related to price-setting procedures firms choose the O_1 objective with parameters $a_4 = 1$ and $a_5 = 5$.

The initial productivity of capital $A = 0.1$.

The physical capital depreciation rate $\delta = 0.1$.

Prediction of average price and average competitiveness in the next year is based on exponential extrapolations of the relevant values in the last five years.

Entrants to the industry have capital, *InitCapital*, equal to 0.5% of the total capital (or equal to 10 units if the value of 0.5% of total capital is lower than 10), that is, *InitCapital* = max {10, 0.005 K}.

SEARCH PROCESS

Research funds: $h_0 = 0.005$, $h_1 = 0$, $h_2 = 0$; the initial structure of research funds is: 50% for innovation, and 50% for imitation, so $g(0) = 0.5$. Parameter controlling the rate of change of the structure of research $G = 100$.

Number of explorations for innovation (no. of experiments): $e = 10$, $\psi = 0.25$, $E_0 = 0$.

The scope of exploration by mutation: $a^u = 5$, $b^u = 1$, $\vartheta = 0.5$.

Probability of mutation: $a^m = 0.01$, $b^m = 0.0$, $\zeta = 0.50$.

Probability of recombination: $a^r = 0.1$, $b^r = 0.0$, $\xi = 0.50$.

Probability of recrudescence: $u_1 = 0.0$, $u_2 = 0.005$.

Probability of a routine deletion: 0.0005.

Probability of a routine transition (from one firm to another): 0.005.

Normal probability of transposition (without recrudescence) is equal to zero. In the case of recrudescence the probability of transposition is equal to 0.3, and the probability of mutation is 0.01.

The number of technical characteristics $m = 2$.

The number of routines is 50, partitioned into 5 equal segments.

The range of routines is: $MinRut = 0$, $MaxRut = 255$.

The initial values of the routines are:

14	94	43	46	11	72	3	23	57	69
69	84	64	62	52	78	3	63	1	43
55	71	16	0	2	4	32	58	60	14
12	74	5	57	73	25	65	9	46	41
69	2	4	55	59	27	68	16	15	23

---

respectively). The maximum profit for these three runs is equal to 16.5%, 9% and 5.2%, respectively for μ_1 = 2, 5 and 10 years. If we assume the greater debt, for example, equal to 100% of the initial capital, the values of price and profit are greater, for example, the maximum price is 10.9, 8.5 and 7.5, and the maximum profit is 44%, 20% and 10.5%, respectively, for μ_1 = 2, 5 and 10 years.

The distance function in the modernization investment is

$$\|r - r^*\| = \left(\sum_i Abs(r_i - r_i^*) \right)^\kappa,$$

κ controls the value of modernization investment IM, and it is assumed that $\kappa = 1.0$, r and r^* are the currently applied and the alternative sets of routines, respectively.

The functions of routines transformation into the technical characteristics, productivity of capital $A(r)$, and variable cost of production $V(r)$ are assumed to be linear:

$$z_d(r) = c_{d0} + \sum_i c_{di} r_i, \qquad \text{for} \quad d = 1, 2, ..., m,$$

$$A(r) = a_0 + \sum_i a_i r_i,$$

$$V(r) = v_0 + \sum_i v_i r_i.$$

The values of c_{d0}, a_0 and v_0 control the initial value of z_d, A and V, the values of c_{di}, a_i and v_i control the sensitivity of z_d, A and V to modifications of routines.

It is not necessary to present all values of coefficients c_{di}, a_i and v_i. This would be a tedious task to produce matrices of fifty rows and up to seven columns; what is important is that the values were initially selected to yield plausible constants to the initial state of the industry and to provide numerous types of impact of routines on the values of A, V and q (that is, pleiotropic effects of routines mentioned on page 168).

The technical competitiveness function $q(z)$ is a sum of hills described by exponential functions:

$$q(z_1, z_2, ..., z_m) = \sum_{k=1}^{HN} A_k \exp\left(-s_k \sum_{i=1}^{m} (z_i - z_{ki})^2 \right).$$

Different adaptive landscapes (for example, as presented in Figure 7.1 and Figure 8.1) are shaped by assuming a number of hills HN in that landscape, and for each hill: its altitude A_k, the gradient s_k, and the peak's coordinates z_{ki}.

Bibliography

Abramovitz, M. (1956), 'Resources and Output Trends in the United States Since 1870', *American Economic Review*, 46, May.

Allen, P.M. (1989), 'Towards a new science of complex systems', *International Symposium on Evolutionary Dynamics and Non-Linear Economics*, Austin, Texas, USA, 16–19 April.

Amsterdamski, S. (1983), *Między historią a metodą. Spory o racjonalność nauki*, Warszawa: PIW.

Anderson, E.S. (1994), *Evolutionary Economics. Post-Schumpeterian Contributions*, London and New York: Pinter Publishers.

Arrow, K.J. (1962), 'Economic Welfare and the Allocation of Resources for Inventions', in R.R. Nelson (ed.), *The Rate and Direction of Invention Activity*, Princeton: Princeton University Press.

Arrow, K.J. (1986), 'Rationality of Self and Others in Economics System', *Journal of Business*, S385–S399. Reprinted in R.M. Hogarth and M.W. Reder (eds) (1987), *Rational Choice: The Contrast Between Economics and Psychology*, Chicago: University of Chicago Press.

Arthur, W.B. (1988), 'Competing Technologies: an Overview', in Dosi et al. (eds) (1988).

Arthur, W.B. (1989), 'Competing Technologies, Increasing Returns, and Lock-in by Historical Events', *The Economic Journal*, 99(1), March, 116–31.

Ayres, R.U. (1988), 'Technology: The Wealth of Nations', *Technological Forecasting and Social Change*, 33, 189–201.

Bateson, W. (1894), *Materials for the Study of Variation*, London: Macmillan.

Bell, D. (1976), *The Cultural Contradictions of Capitalism*, London: Heinemann.

Bell, D. (1985), *Powrót sacrum*, Poznań: Wyd. GŁOSY.

Bertrand, J. (1883), 'Théorie mathématique de la richese sociale, par L. Walras', *Journal des savants*, 499–508.

Beurlen, K. (1937), *Die Stammesgeschichtlichen Grundlangen der Abstammugslehre*, Jena: Gustav Fischer Verlag.

Binswanger, H.P., Ruttan, V.W. (1978), *Induced Innovation: Technology, Institutions and Development*, Baltimore, Md: John Hopkins University Press.

Boda, E. (1955), *Ludwig Boltzmann*, Wien.

Boulding, K.E. (1991), 'What is evolutionary economics?', *Journal of Evolutionary Economics*, 1(1), 9–17.

Brown, K.A. (1988), *Inventors at Work. Interviews with 16 notable American inventors*, Washington: Tempus.

Capra, F. (1985), 'Criteria of Systems Thinking', *FUTURES*, 17(5), 475–8.

Carson, H.L. (1975), 'The Genetics of Speciation at the Diploid Level', *The American Naturalist*, 109 (965), 83–92.

Cavalli-Sforza, L.L., Feldman, M.W. (1981), *Cultural Transmission and Evolution. A Quantitative Approach*, Princeton: Princeton University Press.

Chetvierikov, S.S. (1961), 'On certain aspects of the evolutionary process from the standpoint of modern genetics', *J. Explt. Biol.* (in Russian), A2: 3–54. (English translation – 1961, *Proc. Amer. Phil. Soc.* 105: 167–95.)

Coricelli, F., Dosi, G. (1988), 'Coordination and order in economic change and the interpretative power of economic theory', in Dosi et al. (eds) (1988).

208   *Bibliography*

Cyert, R., March, J. (1963), *A Behavioral Theory of the Firm*, Englewood Cliffs NJ: Prentice-Hall.

Dasgupta, P., Stiglitz, J. (1980), 'Industrial Structure and the Nature of Innovative Activity', *Economic Journal*, 90, 266–93.

Day, R.H., Eliasson, G. (eds) (1986), *The Dynamics of Market Economies*, Amsterdam: North-Holland.

Denbigh, G.K. (1979), *Świat i czas*, translated by J. Mietelski, Warszawa: PIW.

Denison, E.F. (1962), *The Sources of Economic Growth in the United States and the Alternatives Before Us*, Research Report (13), New York: Committeee for Economic Development.

Denison, E.F. (1967), *Why Growth Rates Differ*, Washington DC: Brookings Institution.

de Solla Price, D.J. (1965), *Węzłowe problemy historii nauki*, Warszawa.

de Vries, H. (1901–1903), *Die Mutationstheorie, Versuche und Beobachtungen über die Entstehung der Arten im Pflanzenreich*, Vols 1 and 2 (English translation, J.B. Farmer and A.D. Darbishere (1909–1910), Chicago: Open Court Publ. Co.).

Ditfurth, H. (1985), *Nie tylko z tego świata jesteśmy*, Warszawa: Inst. Wyd, PAX.

Dodson, Ch. (1938), *Progress and Religion – An Historical Enquiry*, London: Sheed & Ward (Polish edition: *Postęp i religia. Studia historyczne*. Warszawa: Inst. Wyd. PAX, (1958)).

Dosi, G. (1983), 'Technological Paradigms and Technological Trajectories. The determinants and directions of technical change and the transformation of the economy', in Ch. Freeman (ed.), *Long Waves in the World Economy*, London: Butterworths.

Dosi, G., Freeman, Ch., Nelson, R.R., Silverberg, G., Soete, L. (eds) (1988), *Technical Change and Economic Theory*, London: Pinter Publishers.

Dowkins, R. (1976), *The Selfish Gene*, Oxford: Oxford University Press.

Drucker, P.F. (1971), *The Age of Discontinuity. Guidelines to our Changing Society*, London: PAN Books Ltd.

Dubois, R. (1986), *Pochwała różnorodności*, Warszawa: PIW (Polish edition, originally published as *A God Within*).

Duhem, P. (1883), 'Physique et metaphysique', *Revue de Questions Scientifique*, serie 2, t.2.

Duhem, P. (1894), Quelques réflexions au sujet de la physique expérimentale, *Revue de Questions Scientifique*, serie 2, t. 3.

Duhem, P. (1914), *La théorie physique, son objet, sa structure*, Paris.

Eibl-Eibesfeldt, I. (1970), *Ethology: The Biology of Behaviour*, New York: Holt, Rinehart & Winston.

Eldredge, N., Gould, S.J. (1972), 'Punctuated equilibria: an alternative to phyletic gradualism', in T.J.M. Schopf (ed.), *Models in Paleobiology*, San Francisco: Freeman.

Eliasson, G. (1985), *The Firm and Financial Markets in the Swedish Micro-to-Macro Model*, Stockholm: Almquist & Wiksell International.

Etzioni, A. (1988), *The Moral Dimension: Toward a New Economics*, New York: Free Press.

Fabricant, S. (1954), 'Economic Progress and Economic Change', in *34th Annual Report*, New York: National Bureau of Economic Research.

Fiedor, B. (1986), *Neoklasyczna teoria postępu technicznego. Próba systematycznej i krytycznej analizy*, Wrocław: Wydawniatwo Uczelniane Akademii Ekonomicznej im. Oskara Langego, Prace Naukowe AE nr 345.

Fleck, L. (1980), *Entstehung und Entwicklung einer wissenschaftlichen Tatsache. Einführung in die Lehre vom Denkstil und Denkkollektiv*, Frankfurt am Main: Suhrkamp Verlag (Polish edition (1986), *Powstanie i rozwój faktu naukowego.*

Wprowadzenie do nauki o stylu myślowym i kolektywie myślowym, Lublin: Wydawnictwo Lubelskie; originally published in German in 1935).

Freeman, Ch. (1979), 'The determinants of innovation', *FUTURES* 11(3), 206–15.

Freeman, Ch. (ed.) (1983), *Long Waves in the World Economy*, London: Butterworths.

Freeman, Ch. (1986), 'The Diffusion of Technical Innovations and Change of Techno-economic Paradigm', *Conference on Innovation Diffusion*, Venice, Italy, 17–21 March.

Freeman, Ch., Clark, J., Soete, L. (1982), *Unemployment and Technical Innovation. A Study of Long Waves and Economic Development*, London: Frances Pinter.

Freeman, Ch., Perez, C. (1988), 'Structural crises of adjustment: business cycles and investment behaviour', in Dosi et al. (eds) (1988).

Freeman, Ch., Soete, L. (eds) (1990), *New Explorations in the Economics of Technical Change*, London and New York: Pinter Publishers.

Friedman, M. and Friedman, R. (1979), *Free to Choose. A Personal Statement*, New York: Avon Publishers.

Galar, R., Kwaśnicka, H., Kwaśnicki, W. (1980), 'Simulation of some Processes of Development', in L. Beker, G. Sevastano, G.C. Vansteenkiste (eds), *Simulation of Systems '79*, New York: North-Holland.

Georgescu-Roegen, N. (1971), *The Entropy Law and the Economic Process*, Cambridge, MA: Harvard University Press.

Gibbons, M., Metcalfe, J.S. (1989), 'Technology, Variety and Competition', *International Symposium on Evolutionary Dynamics and Non-Linear Economics*, Austin, Texas, USA, 16–19 April.

Goldschmidt, R. (1940), *The Material Basis of Evolution*, New Haven: Yale University Press.

Goodwin, R.M. (1987), 'The Economy as an Evolutionary Pulsator', in *The Long-Wave Debate. Selected Papers of IIASA International Meeting on Long-Term Fluctuations in Economic Growth*, Berlin: Springer-Verlag.

Goodwin, R.M. (1989), 'Economic Evolution and Evolution of Economics', *International Symposium on Evolutionary Dynamics and Non-Linear Economics*, Austin, Texas, USA, 16–19 April.

Goodwin, R.M. (1991a), 'Schumpeter, Keynes and the theory of economic evolution', *Journal of Evolutionary Economics*, 1, 29–47.

Goodwin, R.M. (1991b), 'Economic Evolution, Chaotic Dynamics and the Marx–Keynes–Schumpeter System', in G.M. Hodgson and E. Screpanti (eds), *Rethinking Economics. Market, Technology and Economic Evolution*, Aldershot: Edward Elgar Publishing Limited.

Goodwin, R.M., Kruger, M. Vorcelli, A. (1984), *Nonlinear Models of Fluctuating Growth*, Berlin: Springer-Verlag.

Gordon, R.A. (1951), *Business Fluctuations*, New York: Harper & Row.

Gordon, W., Adams, J. (1989), *Economics as a Social Science: An Evolutionary Approach*, Riverdale, Md.

Gould, S.J., Eldredge, N. (1977), 'Punctuated Equilibria: The Tempo and Mode of Evolution Reconsidered', *Paleobiology*, 3, 115–51.

Graham, A.K. (1980), 'Lessons from the 1920s for the Computer Industry', Report D-3196-1, Cambridge: Sloan School of Management MIT.

Halal, E.L. (1985), 'Beyond Left versus Right. Evolution of Political Economy in an Information Age', *FUTURES*, June, 202–13.

Hall, A.R. (1966), *Rewolucja naukowa 1500–1800. Kształtowanie się nowożytnej postawy naukowej*, Inst. Warszawa: Wyd. PAX (originally published in 1954 (second edition 1962) as *The Scientific Revolution 1500–1800, The Formation of the Modern*

Scientific Attitude, London: Longman).

Hansson, I., Stuart, Ch. (1990), 'Malthusian selection of preferences', *American Economic Review*, 80(2), June, 529–44.

Hanusch, H. (ed.) (1988), *Evolutionary Economics: Application of Schumpeter's Ideas*, Cambridge: Cambridge University Press.

Hayek, F.A. (1945), 'The Use of Knowledge in Society', *American Economic Review*, September.

Hayek, F.A. (1948), *Individualism and Economic Order*, Chicago: University of Chicago Press.

Hayek, F.A. (1979), *The Counter-Revolution of Science. Studies on the Abuse of Reason*, Indianapolis: Liberty Press (the first edition published in 1952 by The Free Press, Glencoe, Illinois).

Hayek, F.A. (1982), *Law, Legislation and Liberty*, 3-volume combined edn, London: Routledge & Kegan Paul.

Heertje, A. (1988), 'Schumpeter and technical change', in Hanusch (ed.) (1988).

Heisenberg, W. (1979), *Ponad granicami*, translated by Krzysztof Wolicki, PIW, Warszawa (originally published in 1971 as *Schritte über Grenzen*, München: R. Pipe & Co. Verlag).

Heisenberg, W. (1987), *Część i całość*, translated by K. Napiórkowski, Warszawa: PIW. (originally edited as *Der Teil und das Ganze. Gespräche im umkreis der Atomphysik*, München: R. Piper & Co. Verlag (1969)).

Heller, M., Życiński, J. (1986), *Wszechświat i filozofia. Szkice z filozofii i historii nauki*, Kraków: Druk. Wyd. im. W.L. Anczyca.

Hicks, J.R. (1932), *The Theory of Wages*, New York: Macmillan.

Hodgson, G.M. (1988), *Economics and Institutions: A Manifesto for a Modern Institutional Economics*, Cambridge: Polity Press.

Hodgson G.M. (1993), *Economics and Evolution. Bringing Life Back into Economics*, Cambridge: Polity Press.

Hodgson, G.M., Samuels, W.J., Tools, M.R. (eds) (1994), *The Elgar Companion to Institutional and Evolutionary Economics*, Aldershot: Edward Elgar Publishing.

Hodgson, G.M., Screpanti, E. (eds) (1991), *Rethinking Economics: Markets, Technology and Economic Evolution*, Aldershot: Edward Elgar Publishing.

Huber, J. (1985), 'Conceptions of the Dual Economy', *Technological Forecasting and Social Change*, 27, 63–7.

Ingrao, B., Israel, G. (1985), 'General economic equilibrium: A history of ineffectual paradigmatic shifts', *Fundamenta Scientiae*, 6, 1–45, 89–125.

Iwai, K. (1984a), 'Schumpeterian dynamics: an evolutionary model of innovation and imitation', *Journal of Economic Behavior and Organization*, 5, 159–90.

Iwai, K. (1984b), 'Schumpeterian dynamics, part II: Technological progress, firm growth and "economic selection"', *Journal of Economic Behavior and Organization*, 5, 321–51.

Iwai, K. (1991), 'Towards a disequilibrium theory of long-run profits', *Journal of Evolutionary Economics*, 1(1), 19–21.

Jacob, F. (1987), *Gra możliwości. Esej o różnorodności życia*, Warszawa: PIW, translated by M. Kunicki-Goldfinger, French original *Le jeu des possibles. Essay sur la diversité du vivant* (1982).

Jelinek, M., Goldhar, J.P. (1984), 'The Strategic Implications of the Factory of the Future', *Sloan Management Review*, Summer.

Jewkes, J., Sawers, D., Stillerman R. (1969, first edn 1958), *The sources of inventions*, London: Macmillan.

Kaldor, N. (1934), 'A classificatory note on the determinateness of equilibrium', *Review of Economic Studies*, 1(1), February, 122–36.

Kaldor, N. (1961), 'Capital Accumulation and Economic Growth', in Lutz F. (ed.) *The Theory of Capital*, London, Macmillan.

Kaldor, N. (1966), *Causes of the Slow Rate of Growth in the United Kingdom*, Cambridge: Cambridge University Press.

Kaldor, N. (1972), 'The Irrelevance of Equilibrium Economics', *The Economic Journal*, 82(4), December, 1237–55.

Kaldor, N. (1978), *Further Essays on Economic Theory*, London: Duckworth.

Kaldor, N. (1985), *Economics without Equilibrium*, Cardiff: University College Cardiff Press.

Kamien, M., Schwartz, N. (1982), *Market Structure and Innovation*, Cambridge: Cambridge University Press.

Kapp, W.K. (1976), 'The Nature and Significance of Institutional Economics', *Kyklos*, 29, 209–32.

Kendrick, J.W. (1956), 'Productivity Trends: Capital and Labor', *Review of Economics and Statistics*, August.

Kendrick, J.W. (1961), *Productivity Trends in the United States*, National Bureau of Economic Research, Research Report, Princeton, NJ: Princeton University Press.

Keynes, J.M. (1965), *General Theory of Employment, Interest and Money*, New York: Harcourt Brace Jovanovich (first edition in 1936).

Kirman, A. (1989), 'The Intrinsic Limits of Modern Economic Theory: The Emperor Has No Clothes', *The Economic Journal*, 99, 126–39.

Klein, B.H. (1988), 'Luck, necessity, and dynamics flexibility', in Hanusch (ed.) (1988).

Koestler, A. (1967), *The Act of Creation*, New York.

Kondratieff, N.D. (1935), 'The Long Waves in Economic Life', *Review of Economic Statistics*, 17, 105–15.

Krasnodębski, Z. (1986), *Rozumienie ludzkiego zachowania. Rozważania o filozoficznych podstawach nauk humanistycznych i społecznych*, Warszawa: PIW.

Kuhn, Th.S. (1957), *The Copernican Revolution*, Cambridge: Harvard University Press (Polish edition *Przewrót kopernikański. Astronomia planetarna w dziejach myśli*, Warszawa: PWN (1966)).

Kuhn Th.S. (1962), *The Structure of Scientific Revolutions*, Chicago.

Kuhn, Th.S. (1985), *Dwa bieguny – tradycja i nowatorstwo w badaniach naukowych*, Warszawa: PIW (English edition 1977, *The Essential Tension*, Chicago: The University of Chicago Press).

Kuznets, S. (1966), (6th edition 1973), *Modern Economic Growth*, New Haven: Yale University Press.

Kuznets, S. (1973), 'Modern Economic Growth: Findings and Reflections', *American Economic Review*, 63, 247–258.

Kwaśnicka, H., Galar, R., Kwaśnicki, W. (1983), 'Technological substitution forecasting with a model based on biological analogy', *Technological Forecasting and Social Change*, 23, 41–58.

Kwaśnicka, H., Kwaśnicki, W. (1984), 'MISS–E: A Method of Modeling and Simulation of Dynamic Systems', *Technological Forecasting and Social Change*, 26, 353–88.

Kwaśnicka, H., Kwaśnicki, W. (1986a), 'Diversity and Development: tempo and mode of evolutionary processes', *Technological Forecasting and Social Change*, 30, 223–43.

Kwaśnicka, H., Kwaśnicki, W. (1986b), 'Ewolucja wyższych taksonów – propozycja ogólnego mechanizmu' (Higher Taxa Evolution – Proposition of a General Mechanism of Development), Report PRE 168, Ośrodek Badań Prognostycznych, Politechnika Wrocławska.

Kwaśnicki, W. (1979), 'Symulacja pewnej klasy ewolucyjnych procesów rozwoju' (Simulation of some class of evolutionary processes of development), Report 105, Inst.

Cybern. Techn., Politechnika Wrocławska.

Kwaśnicki, W. (1987), 'Fulguracje w rozwoju wiedzy' (Fulguration and knowledge development), Report SPR 168, Ośrodek Badań Prognostycznych, Politechnika Wrocławska.

Kwaśnicki, W. (1988), 'Ewolucyjne spojrzenie na proces powstawania nowości w nauce i technice' (An evolutionary approach to novelty formation in science and technology), *Prace Naukoznawcze i Prognostyczne*, 3–4(60–61).

Kwaśnicki, W. (1989), 'Fulguracje w rozwoju wiedzy' (Fulgurations in knowledge development), *Prace Naukoznawcze i Prognostyczne*, 1(62).

Kwaśnicki, W., Kwaśnicka, H. (1987), 'Struktura informacji dziedzicznej a optymalność procesów ewolucyjnych' (Structure of the hereditary information and the optimality of evolutionary processes), *Kosmos*, 36(3), 315–336.

Kwaśnicki, W., Kwaśnicka, H. (1989a), 'Taksonomia wiedzy – próba periodyzacji' (Taxonomy of Knowledge. A Tentative Periodization), *Zagadnienia Naukoznawstwa*, 3–4(99–100), 415–47.

Kwaśnicki, W., Kwaśnicka, H. (1989b), 'Multi-Unit Firms in an Evolutionary Model of a Single Industry Development', *International Symposium on Evolutionary Dynamics and Nonlinear Economics*, Austin, Texas, USA: 16–19 April.

Kwaśnicki, W., Kwaśnicka, H. (1992), Market, Innovation, Competition. An evolutionary model of industrial dynamics, *Journal of Economic Behavior and Organization*, 19, 343–68.

Kwaśnicki W., Wróblewska I. (1986), 'Propozycja taksonomii w rozwoju wiedzy' (Taxonomy of knowledge development), Raport SPR 151, Osrodek Badań Prognostycznych, Politechnika Wrocławska.

Langlois, R.N. (1986), 'The new institutional economics', in R.N. Langlois, *Economics as a Process: Essays in the New Institutional Economics*, Cambridge: Cambridge University Press.

Larousse (1990), *Ziemia, Rośliny, Zwierzęta*, Warszawa: BGW (translated by J. Wernerowa and J. Żabiński, French original *Pur Connaître vol. II 'La Nature'*).

Lehmann-Waffenschmidt, M. (1990), *Economic Evolution: A General Equilibrium Analysis*, Heidelberg: Springer.

Lendaris, G.G. (1980), 'Structural modeling – A tutorial guide', *IEEE Transaction on Systems, Man, and Cybernetics*, SMC–10, 807–40.

Lerner, I.M. (1954), *Genetic Homeostasis*, Edinburgh: Oliver & Boyd.

Levin, R.C. (1978), 'Technical Change, Barriers to Entry and Market Structure', *Economica*, 45, 347–61.

Lorenz, K. (1977), *Odwrotna strona zwierciadła. Próba historii naturalnej ludzkiego poznania*, Warszawa, PIW (Polish edition, originally published as *Die Ruckseite des Spiegels. Versuch einer Naturgeschichte menschlichen Erkennens*).

Lucas, R.E. (1988), 'On the mechanics of economic development', *Journal of Monetary Economics*, 22, 3-42.

McConnell, C.R. (1984), *Economics: Principles, Problems, and Policies*, 9th edition, McGraw-Hill Book Company,.

Marien, M. (1977), 'The Two Visions of Post-Industrial Society', *FUTURES*, October, 414–31.

Marshall, A. (1920), (1890), *The Principles of Economics*, 8th edition, London: Macmillan.

Mather, R.C. (1943), 'Poligenetic inheritance and natural selection', *Biological Review*, 18: 32–64.

Maynard Smith, J. (1982), *Evolutionary Game Theory*, Cambridge: Cambridge University Press.

Mayr, E. (1963), *Animal Species and Evolution*, Cambridge, MA: Harvard University Press.

Mayr, E. (1982a), 'Speciation and Macroevolution', *Evolution*, 36(6), 1119–32.

Mayr, E. (1982b), *The Growth of Biological Thought, Diversity, Evolution, and Inheritance*, Cambridge, MA: Harvard University Press

Means, G.C., et al. (1975), *The Roots of Inflation*, New York: Burt Franklin.

Mensch, G., Schopp, R. (1977), 'Stalemate in Technology (1925–1935); the interplay of stagnation and innovation', Annual Meeting of Economic History Association, New Orleans, La., 15–17 September.

Mill, J.S. (1950), *Philosophy of Scientific Method*, New York: Hafner Publishing Co..

Miller, A.S. (1983), 'The End of a 400-years Boom', *Technological Forecasting and Social Change*, 24(3), 255–68.

Miller, A.S. (1984), 'Taking Needs Seriously. Observations on the Necessity of Constitutional Change', *Washington and Lee Law Review*, 41(4), 1243–306.

Mirowski, P. (ed.) (1986), *The Reconstruction of Economic Theory*, Boston: Kluwer-Nijhoff.

Mirowski, P. (1989), *More Heat than Light: Economics as Social Physics, Physics as Nature's Economics*, Cambridge: Cambridge University Press.

Mises, L. von (1957), *Theory and History. An Interpretation of Social and Economic Evolution*, New Haven: Yale University Press.

Mitchell, H.G. (1927), *Business Cycles: The Problem and Its Setting*, New York: National Bureau of Economic Research.

Motycka, A. (1990), *Główny problem epistemologiczny filozofii nauki*, Wrocław: Ossolineum.

Murphy, J.F. (1973), *Psychological Dimensions of Leisure*, 'Society and Leisure'.

Myrdal, G. (1939), *Monetary Equilibrium*, London: Hodge.

Myrdal, G. (1944), *An American Dilemma: The Negro Problem and Modern Democracy*, New York: Harper & Row.

Myrdal, G. (1957), *Economic Theory and Underdeveloped Regions*, London: Duckworth.

Nelson, R.R. (1987), *Understanding Technical Change as an Evolutionary Process*, Amsterdam: North-Holland.

Nelson, R.R., Winter, S.G. (1977), 'In Search of Useful Theory of Innovation,' *Research Policy*, 6(1).

Nelson, R.R., Winter, S.G. (1982), *An Evolutionary Theory of Economic Change*, Cambridge, MA: Harvard University Press.

Neumann, J.V., Morgenstern, O. (1947), *The Theory of Games and Economic Behavior*, Princeton: Princeton University Press.

North, D.C. (1981), *Structure and Change in Economic History*, New York: Norton.

Ortega y Gasset, J. (1967), *The Origin of Philosophy*, New York: Norton.

Peirce, C.S. (1934), *Collected Papers of Charles Sanders Peirce*, vol. 5 *Pragmatism and Pragmaticism*, C. Hartshorne, P. Weiss (eds), Cambridge, MA: Harvard University Press.

Piaget, J. (1977), *Psychologia i epistemologia*, translated by Z. Zakrzewska, Warszawa: PWN.

Plott, C.R. (1986), 'Laboratory Experiments in Economics: the Implications of Posted Price Institutions', *Science*, 232, 9 May, 732–8.

Poincaré, H. (1891), Les géometries non-euclidiennes, *Revue Générale des Sciences*, t. II.

Poincaré, H. (1925), *La science et l'hypothese*, Paris.

Poincaré, H. (1935), *La valeur de la science*, Paris.

Polanyi, M. (1962), *Personal Knowledge: Towards a Post-Critical Philosophy*, New York: Harper Torchbooks.

Polanyi, M. (1967), *The Tacit Dimension*, Garden City, N.Y.: Doubleday Anchor.

Popper, K.R. (1979), *Objective Knowledge*, Oxford: Clarendon Press.

Popper, K.R., Eccles, J.C. (1977), *The Self and Its Brain*, Springer International.

Prigogine, I. (1989), 'Bounded Rationality: From Dynamical Systems to Socio-Economic Models', *International Symposium on Evolutionary Dynamics and Non-Linear Economics*, Austin, Texas, USA, 16–19, April.

Quine, W.V.O. (1969) (1953), *Z punktu widzenia logiki*, translated by B. Stanosz, Warszawa: PIW.

Rahmeyer, F. (1989), 'The evolutionary approach to innovation activity', *Journal of Institutional and Theoretical Economics*, 145(2), June, 275–97.

Ramsey, F.P. (1928), 'A Mathematical Theory of Saving', *Economic Journal* 38(152), 543–559.

Rhodes, F.H.T. (1983), 'Gradualism, Punctuated Equilibrium and the Origin of Species', *Nature*, 305, 269–72.

Riggleman, J.R. (1933), 'Building Cycles in the United States (1897–1932)', *Journal of the American Statistical Association*, XXVIII.

Romer, P.M. (1989), 'Capital accumulation in the theory of long-run growth', in R.J. Barro (ed.), *Modern Business Cycle Theory*, Oxford: Clarendon Press.

Rostow, W.W. (1989), 'Non-Linear Dynamics: Implications for Economics in Historical Perspective', *International Symposium on Evolutionary Dynamics and Non-Linear Economics*, Austin, Texas, USA, 16–19 April.

Sachs, M. (1978), 'Pojęcie czasu w fizyce i kosmologii', *Problemy*, 6.

Sahal, D. (1981), *Patterns of Technological Innovation*, Addison-Wesley Publishing Company, Inc.

Samuelson, P. (1980), *Economics*, 11th edition., New York: McGraw-Hill.

Saviotti, P.P., Metcalfe, J.D. (1990), 'Present development and trends in evolutionary economics', Mimeo.

Scheler, M. (1986), 'O sensie cierpienia', *ZNAK*, 384–385 (11–12), 3–44.

Schindewolf, O.H. (1950), *Grundfragen der Paläontologie*, Stuttgart: Schweizerbatsche Verlägsbuchhandlung.

Schrödinger, E. (1952), 'Are there Quantum Jumps?', *The British Journal for the Philosophy of Science*, Vol. II, pp. 109–10.

Schumpeter, J.A. (1939), *Business Cycles*, New York: McGraw-Hill.

Schumpeter, J.A. (1942), *Capitalism, Socialism and Democracy*, Harper & Row (1950, Oxford University Press, Oxford, reprinted Harper Colophon, 1975).

Schumpeter, J.A. (1954), *History of Economic Analysis*, New York: Oxford University Press.

Schumpeter, J.A. (1960) (1912), *Teoria wzrostu gospodarczego*, Warszawa: PWN (Polish edition; originally published in German, 1912, *Theorie der wirtschaftlichen Entwicklung*, Leipzig: Duncker & Humbolt.).

Shackle, G.L.S. (1972), *Epistemics and Economics: A Critique of Economic Doctrines*, Cambridge: Cambridge University Press.

Siciński, A. (1974), *Młodzi roku 2000*, Warszawa: Inst. Wyd. CRZZ.

Siemianowski, A. (1989), *Zasady konwencjonalistycznej filozofii nauki*, Warszawa: PWN.

Silverberg, G. (1987), 'Technical Progress, Capital Accumulation and Effective Demand: A Self-Organizational Model', in D. Batten (ed.), *Economic Evolution and Structural Change*, Berlin–Heidelberg–New York: Springer-Verlag.

Simon, H.A. (1955), 'A Behavioral Model of Rational Choice', *Quarterly Journal of Economics*, 69, 99–118 (reprinted in Simon (1957)).

Simon, H.A. (1957), *Models of Men*, New York: Wiley.

Simon, H.A. (1959a), 'Rational Decision-Making in Business Organization', *American*

Political Science Reviews, September.

Simon, H.A. (1959b), 'Theories of Decision-Making in Economics', *American Economic Review*, 49, 253–83.

Simon, H.A. (1965), *Administrative Behavior*, 2nd edition, New York: Free Press.

Simon, H.A. (1979), 'Rational Decision-Making in Business Organizations', *American Economic Review*, 69, 493–513.

Simon, H.A. (1984), 'The Behavioral and Rational Foundations of Economic Dynamics', *Journal of Economic Behavior and Organization*, 5, 35–55.

Simon, H.A. (1986), 'On behavioral and rational foundations of economic dynamics', in Day, Eliasson (eds) (1986).

Simon, H.A. (1988), 'Human Nature in Politics: The Dialogue of Psychology with Political Science', in M. Campanella (ed.), *Between Rationality and Cognition*: *Policy-making under Conditions of Uncertainty, Complexity and Turbulence*, Torino: Albert Meynier (first published in *American Political Science Review*).

Smith, A. (1776), *The Wealth of Nations* (all references are to the 5th edition of Edwin Cannan, London: Methuen & Co., Ltd (1930)).

Smith, V.L. (1986), 'Experimental Methods in Political Economy of Exchange', *Science* 234, 10 October, 167–73.

Solow, R.M. (1957), 'Technical Change and the Aggregate Production Function', *Review of Economics and Statistics*, 39, August, 312–320.

Stanley, S.M. (1982), 'Macroevolution and the Fossil Record', *Evolution*, 36(3), 460–73.

Sterman, J.D. (1987), 'Testing Behavioral Simulation Models by Direct Experiment', *Management Science*, 33, 1572–92.

Sterman, J.D. (1988), 'Deterministic chaos in models of human behavior: methodological issues and experimental results', *System Dynamic Review,* 4(1–2), 148–78.

Stolper, W.F. (1988), 'Development: theory and empirical evidence', in Hanusch (ed.) (1988).

Tannehill, M., Tannehill, L. (1984), *The Market for Liberty*, New York: Libertatian Review Foundation.

Teece, D.J. (1981), 'The market for know how and the efficient international transfer of technology', *The Annals of the Academy of Political Social Science*, November.

Toffler, A. (1985), *Previews and Premises*, New York: Bantam Books, Inc.

Tool, M.R. (1991), 'Contributions to an Institutional Theory of Price Determination', in Hodgson, Screpanti (eds) (1991).

Tuan, Yi-Fu (1987), *Przestrzeń i miejsce*, translated by A. Morawinska, Warszawa: PIW (English edition: *Space and Place. The Perspective of Experience* (1977), Minneapolis, Minnesota: University of Minnesota Press).

Turgot, A.R.J. (1946), 'Reflection on the Formation and Distribution of Wealth', in D.A. Leonard (ed.), *Masterworks of Economics*: *Digest of 10 Classics*, New York: Doubleday.

Tversky, A., Kahneman, D. (1974), 'Judgment under Uncertainty: Heuristics and Biases', *Science* 185, 27 September, 1124–31.

Tversky, A., Kahneman, D. (1981), 'The Framing of Decision and the Psychology of Choice', *Science*, 211, 30 January, 453–8.

Tversky, A., Kahneman, D. (1987), 'Rational Choice and the Framing of Decisions', in B. Hogart and D. Reder (eds), *Rational Choice*: *The Contrast Between Economics and Psychology*, Chicago: University of Chicago Press.

Tylecote, A. (1992), *The Long Waves in the World Economy*, London, New York: Routledge.

Urbanek, A. (1984), 'Powstawanie "Powstawania ..." – darwinowska koncepcja doboru naturalnego jako odkrycie naukowe', *Nauka Polska,* 1, 3–29.

Ursprung, H.W. (1988), 'Evolution and the economic approach to human behaviour', *Journal of Social and Biological Structure*, 11, 257–79.

van Duijn, J.J. (1983), *The Long Wave in Economic Life*, London: George Allen & Unwin.

Veblen, T.B. (1899), *The Theory of the Leisure Class: An Economic Study of Institutions*, New York: Macmillan.

Veblen, T.B. (1919), *The Place of Science in Modern Civilisation and Other Essays*, New York: Huebsch; reprint 1990 with a new introduction by Warren J. Samuels, New Brunswick, NJ: Transaction Publishers.

Verdoorn, P.J. (1951), 'On an Empirical Law Governing the Productivity of Labor', *Econometrica*, 19, 209–10.

Verspagen, B. (1993), *Uneven Growth Between Interdependent Economies. An evolutionary view on technology gaps, trade and growth*, Aldershot: Avebury.

Waddington, C.H. (1974), 'A Catastrophe Theory of Evolution', *Annals of the New York Academy of Sciences*, 231, 32–42.

Waddington, C.H. (1977), 'Stabilization of Systems, Chreods and Epigenetic Landscapes', *FUTURES*, 9(2), 139–46.

Wallace, A.R. (1859), 'On the tendency of varieties to depart indefinitely from the original type', *Journal of the Proceedings of the Linnean Society (Zoology)*, 3 (read 1 July 1858).

Wallace, A.R. (1898), *The Wonderful Century. Its Successes and Failures*, New York.

Walras, L. (1874), *Elements D'Economique Politique Pure* (1954), *Elements of Pure Economics, or the Theory of Social Wealth*, translated by W. Jaffé, New York Augustus Kelley.

Waszkiewicz, J. (1982), 'Specyfika wielkich przedsięwzięć', *Prace Naukoznawcze i Prognostyczne*, 3–4(36–37), 101–112.

Waszkiewicz, J. (1987), 'Przemiany apriorycznych struktur poznawczych. Część I. Geneza abstrakcyjnego pojęcia przestrzeni', *Prace Nauoznawcze i Prognostyczne*, 3–4(56–57), 95–115.

Weisskopf, W.A. (1983), 'Reflections on Uncertainty in Economics', *Geneva Papers on Risk and Insurance*, 335–60.

Winter, S. (1971), 'Satisfying, selection, and the innovating remnant', *Quarterly Journal of Economics*, 85(2), May, 237–61.

Winter, S. (1984), 'Schumpeterian competition in alternative technological regimes', *Journal of Economic Behavior and Organization*, 5, 287–320.

Witt, U. (1991), 'Reflections on the Present State of Evolutionary Economic Theory', in Hodgson, Screpanti (eds) (1991).

Wright, S. (1932), 'The Roles of Mutation, Inbreeding, Cross-breeding and Selection in Evolution', *Proc. VI Internat. Genet. Cong.*, 1, 356–66.

Wright, S. (1982), 'Character Change, Speciation and the Higher Taxa', *Evolution*, 36(3), 427–43.

Wright T.P. (1936), 'Factors Affecting the Cost of Airplanes', *Journal of Aeronautical Sciences*, 3, 122–28.

Znaniecki, F. (1921), *Upadek cywilizacji zachodniej. Szkic z pogranicza filozofii kultury i socjologii*, Poznań.

Index

abstract journals 62
active routines 165
Adams, J. 75
Alberti, Leon Battista 37
Amsterdamski, Stefan 30
archetypal paragons 23
archetype 24, 25, 28
Aristotle 37, 39, 64

Bacon, Francis 40, 42, 53, 54
Baconian *episteme* 54, 56, 58, 61, 65
Baer, Karl Ernst von 31
Bakunin, Mikail 45
Bateson, William 28
beauty 7, 36, 37, 74
Bell, Daniel 36, 45, 51
Bennet, Abraham 58
Bentham, Jeremy 46
Bernard, Claude 60
Bernoulli, Daniel 58
Beurlen, K. 28
Binswanger, H.P. 74
Bismarck, Otto von 47
Blair, John M. 103
Bloch, F. 63
Boda, E. 16
Bohr, Niels H. 62
Boltzmann, Ludwig E. 16, 42, 59, 60, 196
Bonnet, Charles de 58
Born, Max 34, 62
Boulding, Kenneth E. 5
bounded rationality 76, 78, 102, 145, 147, 149, 152
Brillouin, L.N. 63
Brown, Kenneth A. 18
Burnett, Edward 64

Capra, Fritjof 63
Cassegrain, N. 55
Cauchy, Augustin L. 58
Chomsky, Noam 34, 35
chreod 25, 185, 196, 201
Clapeyron, Benoit P. 58
Clausius, Rudolf E. 59

cognitariat 50
comparative *episteme* 64
competitiveness 85, 87–89, 94–96, 103, 104, 121, 146, 156, 163, 164, 169, 173, 174, 175–186, 188–190, 193, 198, 203, 204, 205
complex *techne* 64, 65
Constantine the Great 39
Copernicus, Nicolaus 40
Coricelli, F. 77
cosmetic 23–25, 29
Coulomb, Charles de 57, 58
Crick, Francis 43
Cuvier, Georges 58, 64, 68
Cyert, R. 110

d'Alembert, Jean Le Rond 58
Dalton, John 58
Dante, Alighieri 37
Darwin, Charles 16, 27, 42, 59, 68
Darwin, Horace 61
Davisson, C.J. 62
Dawson, Christopher 64
Day, Richard 75
de Vries, H. 28
Democrytus 38
Denison, E.F. 72
Descartes, René 11, 27, 37, 40–42, 53, 54, 55, 68
Dirac, Paul A. 37, 62
diversity 20, 23–25, 32, 78, 79, 80, 138, 154, 157, 159, 162, 179, 180, 183, 184, 187, 194, 201
Dodson, Ch. 40
Domar, Evsey 71
Dosi, Giovanni 24, 67, 75, 77
Drucker, Peter F. 45, 46, 50
Dubois, R. 27
Duhem, Pierre 7–12
Durkheim, Emile 36

Eccles, J.C. 21, 27
École Politechnique 58
economies of scale 48, 49, 90, 121, 125, 127–135, 203

economies of scope 49
Edison, Thomas A. 60, 61, 65
educational environment 23
Eibl–Eibesfeldt, Irenäus 34, 35
Einstein, Albert 5, 39, 60, 62, 68
Eldredge, Niles 28
Eliasson, Gunnar 14, 75
epigenetic environment 21
episteme 51–59, 61–65, 73, 75, 79, 195
epistemological 12, 16, 32, 33, 44, 73
equilibrium 3, 24, 31, 32, 52, 73, 76,
    77, 79–82, 101, 102, 108, 117–124,
    126–132, 134, 136, 138, 139,
    140–147, 154, 155, 159, 160, 184,
    188, 195, 203
Erasmus from Rotterdam 40
Euler, Leonhard 58
evolution 1, 13, 16, 17, 20–22, 25, 26,
    28, 29, 31–33, 36, 39, 42, 58, 59, 64,
    68, 69, 71, 74, 78, 81, 114, 115, 121,
    129, 130, 131, 159, 162, 163, 165,
    169, 173–177, 179, 196, 198, 199,
    201
evolutionary 3, 12–17, 19, 20, 24, 26,
    29, 30, 33, 43, 71, 73, 74, 75, 76,
    79–85, 88, 89, 110, 149, 162, 163,
    171, 172, 176, 195, 196, 198, 201
Evolutionary Stable Strategy 110
experimentum crucis 8

factors of production 49, 71, 72
Fiedor, Bogusław, 71
Fleck, Ludwik 12
fluctuations 83, 87, 113, 114, 119, 137,
    138, 140, 144, 145, 146–148,
    152–154, 156–160, 180, 184, 186
Ford, Henry 48
Freeman, Christopher 24, 49, 52, 160
Fresnel, Augustin J. 58
Friedman, Milton 49
fulguration 17, 19, 21, 24–28, 42, 82,
    181, 196

Galerius 39
Galileo Galilei 4, 11, 37, 53, 68
Gauss, Carl F. 58
genotype 16, 17, 19, 21
Georgescu–Roegen, Nicholas 3, 74, 81,
    196
Germer, L.H. 62
GOELRO PLAN 65

Goethe, Johann Wolfgang von 37
Goldschmidt, R. 28
Gordon, Wendell 75
Gordon, R.A. 160
Gould, Stephen J. 28
Gresham College 54

Haeckel, Ernst 31
Halal, E.L. 50
Hall, A.R. 56, 57
Hanusch, Horst 75
Harley, R.W.L. 63
Harrod, Roy F. 71
Harvard University 61
Harvey, William 53
Hayek, Friedrich A. von 77, 148
Heaviside, Oliver 62
Heisenberg, Werner 5, 11, 30, 37, 62,
    63
Heller, Michał 37
hereditary information 18, 23, 24, 28,
    29, 30, 83, 162, 197, 201
Herfindahl 112, 113, 118, 120, 129,
    130, 175, 183–185, 189, 191, 192
Herschel, William 55, 58, 59
Hertz, Heinrich Rudolf 11, 59
Hesiod 39
Hirschman 113
Hodgson, Geoffrey 3, 75
Hubble, Edwin P. 62
Huber, J. 50
Hume, David 46

idealization 9–12, 14, 52, 111
individuality 18, 19, 23
Ingrao, Bruno 74
innovation 26, 28, 61, 66, 71, 74, 75,
    81, 83–87, 89, 90, 102, 122, 142,
    146–148, 159, 160, 162, 164–166,
    169, 170, 171–173, 175–194,
    196–199, 201, 204
intellectual selective environment 23
invention 18, 27, 28, 41, 44, 55, 58,
    61, 62, 84, 86, 175, 177, 186
invention factory 61
irreversibility 76, 81, 82, 195–197
Israel, Giorgio 74
Iwai, K. 144, 145

Jacob, François 34
Jansky, Karl Guthe 62

Jelinek, M. 49
Jevons, William Stanley 74
Jewkes, J. 18
Jordanm, Pascual 62
Juglar 160, 161

Kaldor, Nicolas 103, 185, 195
Kant, Immanuel 33, 34, 44
Keller, Helen 34, 35
Kepler, Johannes 4, 11
Keynes, John Maynard 47
Kirchhoff, Gustav R. 9, 60
Kitchin 160
knowledge 1, 10, 13, 16–32, 34–36, 42,
    43, 44, 49–52, 55, 62, 64, 66, 67, 68,
    72, 73, 76–78, 82–86, 88, 102, 149,
    150, 155, 160, 165, 167, 168, 172,
    174, 175, 180, 201
Koestler, Arthur 27, 37, 172
Krasnodębski, Zdzisław 38
Kropotkin, Peter 45
Kuhn, Thomas S. 12, 19, 24, 28, 40,
    56, 67
Kuznets, S. 28, 160

Lamarck Jean Baptiste de 58, 68
Langlois, Richard L. 75
Laplace, Pierre S. 58
latent routines 165, 196
Lavoisier, Antioine Laurent 57
Lawrence, Ernest O. 62
Lehmann–Waffenschmidt, M. 74
Leibniz, Gottfried D. 39, 41, 56, 57
Lendaris, G.G. 4
Leukippos 38
Linnaeus, Carolus 41, 56
Livingstone, M. Stanley 62
Locke, John 45
Lorenz, Konrad 16, 17, 20, 34, 44, 64
Lotka, A.J. 63
Lucas, R.E. 74
Lucretius 41

Machiavelli, Niccolló 40
macro–economics 83
Maimonides 39
Malthus, Thomas R. 27
March, James G. 110
marginalist theory 103
Marien, M. 50
markup 91, 103, 105–111, 116

Marshall, Alfred 73, 75
Marx, Karl 36, 45, 47
Maxwell, James C. 42, 59
Maynard Smith 110
Mayzel, Wacław 60
McConnell, Campbell R. 89, 101, 116,
    138
Meade 71
Means, Gardiner C. 103
Mediterranean Culture 32
Mendeleyev, Dmitrij I. 59
Mensch, G. 24, 28
meso–economics 83
Michelson, Albert A. 60
Miescher, Johann Friedrich 59, 61
Mill, John Stuart 5, 6, 25
Miller, A.S. 45
Mirowski, Philip 3, 74
Mises, Ludwig von 148
Mitchell, H.G. 160
monopolistic competition 115
Montaigne, Michel Eyguem de 40
Montesquieu, Charles Louis de
    Secondat 45
Morley, Edward W. 60
Mott, N.F. 63
Motycka, Alina 16
Müller, Max 64
Murphy, J.F. 38
mutation 19, 26, 28, 29, 165, 166, 167,
    168, 171–173, 175, 176, 178–180,
    196, 198, 204

Nelson, Richard R. 14, 17, 24, 75, 77,
    80, 91, 92, 162, 163
neoclassical 3, 4, 13, 14, 71, 73–79,
    81, 82, 101–103, 110, 117, 119, 126,
    135, 141, 145–147, 185, 195
Newton, Isaac 6, 9, 11, 12, 38, 54–57,
    68
North, Douglas C. 74

objective 38, 43, 54, 61, 90, 91, 93,
    102–105, 107, 110–115, 117, 140,
    141, 149, 150, 155, 156, 169, 204
oligopoly 115, 116, 122, 129, 130, 131,
    132, 136, 141, 154, 155, 159, 203
Olszewski, Karol 60
optimization 73, 76, 81, 82, 91, 104,
    149–152
Ortega y Gasset, J. 27

220 *Index*

orthodox 14, 74, 76, 78, 80–82, 195
Otto, Rudolph 36

Paracelsus 54
paradigm 3, 13, 17, 24, 25, 30, 31, 33, 67, 68, 73
paragon 18–26, 28–33, 35, 36, 38, 40, 43, 44, 46, 48, 51, 67, 78, 162, 163
Pasteur, Louis 37, 60
path–dependence 195–197, 200, 201
Pauli, Wolfgang 62
Peirce, Charles Sanders 27
perception of time 43, 73, 80
Perez, Carlota 52
personality 18, 19, 21, 23, 24
phenotype 19, 24, 198
Philosophical Transactions 57
Piaget, Jean 31
Piazzi, Giuseppe 58
Planck, Max 5, 44, 60
Plato 11, 39, 40, 44
Plotyn 37
Poincaré, Henri 8–10, 12
Poisson, Siméon 58
Polanyi, Michael 20, 77
Popper, Karl 12, 16, 21, 27, 34, 37, 172
price determination 102, 103
price elasticities 89, 138
price elasticity 136, 138, 139, 141
price makers 88, 103
price takers 88, 103
price–setting 91, 103–105, 110, 204
Prigogine, Ilya 5
production function 71, 185
profit maximization 49, 80, 110, 111, 116, 117
Proust, Louis 58
public household 51
pure competition 115, 118–120, 122–126, 136, 137, 139, 141, 154, 155, 158, 159, 184, 191, 203
pure monopoly 115, 118, 130
Pythagoras 37

quantum mechanics 43, 62, 63, 68, 196
quasi–equilibrium phase 24
Quine, Willard V. 7, 12

random factors 26, 73, 80, 81, 83, 89, 96, 159, 168, 175, 185, 186, 187,

196, 198
Ray, John 56
Reber, Grote 62
recombination 19, 21, 26, 28, 29, 163, 165, 167, 168, 171, 173, 176, 177, 196, 198, 204
recrudescence 26–28, 168, 171, 172, 173, 176–181, 189, 196, 198, 204
Renaissance 40–42, 55, 59, 73
Richter, Jeremias Beniamin 58
Riggleman, J.R. 160
Rivers, William H. 64
Romer, Ole 55
Romer, P.M. 74
Rousseau, Jean Jacques 45
routine 77, 80, 83, 88, 91, 105, 109, 110, 115, 158, 159, 162, 163–171, 174, 177, 179, 185, 196–198, 201, 204, 205
Ruska, Ernst 62
Ruttan, V.W. 74

St. Augustus 39, 40
Sachs, M. 38
Sahal, D. 24, 67
Scheler, Max 36, 37
Schindewolf, O.H. 28
Schleiermacher, Friedrich 36
Schrödinger, Erwin 31, 62
Schumpeter, Joseph Alois 20, 24, 71, 75, 79, 146, 147, 161, 162
selective environment 22
self–organization 83
Shackle, George L.S. 103
Siciński A. 38
Silverberg, Gerald 75, 103, 104
Simon, Herbert A. 3, 78, 86, 87, 149, 150, 152
Smith, Adam 46, 47, 50, 82
Smith, William 58
Solow, Robert M. 71, 72
Spencer, Herbert 42
Spengler, Oswald 64
Stanley, G.J. 60
stepwise concretization 12, 14, 88, 111, 162, 170
Sterman, J.D. 160
substitution phase 24
Sullivan, Anne M. 34, 35

tacit knowledge 20, 77

Taylor, Frederick W. 48
techne 51, 52, 54, 56, 61, 64–66
technical advance 71, 72
technical change 71, 74, 144
technical progress 74, 75, 184
technological change 71, 74, 75, 80, 83, 145
Teece, David 77
Tennessee Valley Authority 65
Theodosius 40
Thomson, Joseph J. 60
Tinbergen, Nikolaas 64
Toffler, Alvin 50
Tool, Marc R. 103
transition 13, 20, 24, 26, 29, 59, 61, 76, 81, 82, 165, 168, 180, 198, 204
transposition 26, 29, 165, 168, 198, 204
Tuan, Yi-Fu 38

van Duijn, J.J. 160
van Leeuwenhoek, Antoni 55
Veblen, Thorstein Bunde 73, 75, 195
Verspagen, Bart 71

Vesalius, Andreas 40, 53
Volta, Allesandro 58
Volterra, Vito 63

Waddington, C.H. 21, 25, 185
Wallace, Alfred R. 27, 42, 59, 68
Walras, Léon 73, 147, 195
Waszkiewicz, Jan 64
Watson, James 43
Weisskopf, W.A. 3
Western Hemisphere 33, 38, 39, 45
Whitehead, Alfred N. 63
Wicksell, John Gustav 148
Wien, Wilhelm 60
Wilson, A.H. 63
Winter, Sidney G. 14, 17, 24, 75, 77, 80, 91, 92, 162, 163
Witt, Ulrich 75
Wright, Sewall 28, 42, 62, 63
Wróblewski, Zygmunt F. 60

Young, Thomas 58

Życiński, Józef 37